Gender, Equality and Difference During and After State Socialism

Studies in Central and Eastern Europe

Edited for the International Council for Central and East European Studies by **Roger E. Kanet**, University of Miami, USA

Titles include:

Graeme Gill (*editor*)
POLITICS IN THE RUSSIAN REGIONS

Roger E. Kanet (*editor*)
RUSSIA
Re-Emerging Great Power

Rebecca Kay (*editor*)
GENDER, EQUALITY AND DIFFERENCE DURING AND AFTER STATE SOCIALISM

Katlijn Malfliet, Lien Verpoest and Evgeny Vinokurov (*editors*)
THE CIS, THE EU AND RUSSIA
Challenges of Integration

Stephen Velychenko (*editor*)
UKRAINE, THE EU AND RUSSIA
History, Culture and International Relations

Forthcoming titles include:

John Pickles (*editor*)
GLOBALIZATION AND REGIONALIZATION IN POST-SOCIALIST ECONOMIES
Common Economic Spaces of Europe

John Pickles (*editor*)
STATE AND SOCIETY IN POST-SOCIALIST ECONOMIES

Stephen White (*editor*)
MEDIA, CULTURE AND SOCIETY IN PUTIN'S RUSSIA

Stephen White (*editor*)
POLITICS AND THE RULING GROUP IN PUTIN'S RUSSIA

Thomas Bremer (*editor*)
RELIGION AND THE CONCEPTUAL BOUNDARY IN CENTRAL AND EASTERN EUROPE

Stephen Hutchings (*editor*)
RUSSIA AND ITS OTHER(S) ON FILM
Screening Intercultural Dialogue

Joan DeBardeleben (*editor*)
THE BOUNDARIES OF EU ENLARGEMENT
Finding a Place for Neighbours

Stanislav J. Kirschbaum (*editor*)
THE MEANING OF EUROPE, CENTRAL EUROPE AND THE EU

Studies in Central and Eastern Europe
Series Standing Order ISBN 0–230–51682–3 hardcover
(*outside North America only*)

Gender, Equality and Difference During and After State Socialism

Edited by

Rebecca Kay
Department of Central and East European Studies
University of Glasgow, UK

palgrave
macmillan

First published 2007 by
PALGRAVE MACMILLAN
Houndmills, Basingstoke, Hampshire RG21 6XS and
175 Fifth Avenue, New York, N.Y. 10010
Companies and representatives throughout the world

PALGRAVE MACMILLAN is the global academic imprint of the Palgrave Macmillan division of St. Martin's Press, LLC and of Palgrave Macmillan Ltd. Macmillan® is a registered trademark in the United States, United Kingdom and other countries. Palgrave is a registered trademark in the European Union and other countries.

ISBN-13: 978-0-230-52484-2 hardback
ISBN-10: 0-230-52484-2 hardback

This book is printed on paper suitable for recycling and made from fully managed and sustained forest sources. Logging, pulping and manufacturing processes are expected to conform to the environmental regulations of the country of origin.

A catalogue record for this book is available from the British Library.

A catalog record for this book is available from the Library of Congress.

10 9 8 7 6 5 4 3 2 1
16 15 14 13 12 11 10 09 08 07

Printed and bound in Great Britain by
Antony Rowe Ltd, Chippenham and Eastbourne

Contents

List of Tables and Figures

Tables

Figures

Preface by General Editor

When the International Council for Central and East European Studies (ICCEES) was founded at the first international and multidisciplinary conference of scholars working in this field, held in Banff, Alberta, Canada, on 4–7 September 1974, it was given the name International Committee for Soviet and East European Studies (ICSEES). Its major purpose was to provide for greater exchange between research centres and scholars around the world who were devoted to the study of the USSR and the communist states and societies of Eastern Europe. These developments were the main motivation for bringing together the very different national organisations in the field and for forming a permanent committee of their representatives, which would serve as an umbrella organisation, as well as a promoter of closer co-operation. Four national scholarly associations launched ICSEES at the Banff conference: the American Association for the Advancement of Slavic Studies (AAASS), the National Association for Soviet and East European Studies in Great Britain (NASEES), the British Universities Association of Slavists (BUAS), and the Canadian Association of Slavists (CAS).

Over the past three decades six additional Congresses have been held: in Garmisch-Partenkirchen, Germany, 1980; Washington, USA, 1985; Harrogate, UK, 1990; Warsaw, Poland, 1995; Tampere, Finland, 2000; and Berlin, Germany, 2005. The next Congress is scheduled for 2010 in Stockholm, Sweden. The original four national associations that sponsored the first Congress have been joined by an additional seventeen full and six associate member associations, with significantly more than a thousand scholars participating at each of the recent Congresses.

It is now a little over three decades since scholars felt the need to co-ordinate the efforts in the 'free world' to describe and analyse the communist political systems, their societies and economies, and East–West relations in particular. Halfway through this period, the communist system collapsed, the region that was the object of study was reorganised, and many of the new states that emerged set out on a path of democratic development, economic growth and, in many cases, inclusion in Western institutions. The process turned out to be complex, and there were setbacks. Yet, by 2004, the European Union as well as the North Atlantic Treaty Organisation had welcomed those post-communist states that had met all of the requirements for membership. Not all of the applicant states achieved this objective; but the process is ongoing.

For this reason, perhaps even more than before, the region that encompassed the former communist world demands study, explanation and analysis, as both centripetal and centrifugal forces are at work in each state and across the region. We are most fortunate that the community of scholars addressing these issues now includes many astute analysts from the region itself.

Acknowledgements

I would like to thank Roger Kanet, for his work as editor of the series in Central and East European Studies of which this volume forms a part. His good advice, cheerful reminders and always positive and encouraging responses have been extremely helpful in getting this work completed.

I would also like to thank Moya Flynn and Jon Oldfield at the Department of Central and East European Studies, University of Glasgow for reading and commenting on parts of the manuscript and for their support as friends and colleagues. Maggie Baister and Sarah Lennon have also been a huge support providing last-minute technical support and keeping things running in the department whilst I was otherwise engaged.

Finally, thanks go to all the contributors to this volume, for their goodwill, hard work and patience. It has been a pleasure working with you all.

Notes on the Contributors

Ildikó Asztalos Morrell is Lecturer in Sociology at Mälardalen University College, Sweden. She is currently on research leave at Uppsala University and at the University College of Southern Stockholm. Her research focuses on gender relations, economic transformation and labour in Hungary, both historically and in the contemporary context. She is a member of the Baltic Sea Foundation-funded research project 'Parenthood vs. wage labour. Emancipation rhetoric and gender practices in Hungary and Soviet Russia 1955–1985'. Her most important publications are *Emancipation's Dead-End Roads: Studies in the Formation and Development of the Hungarian Model for Agriculture and Gender 1956–1989* (Uppsala, 1999) and *Gender Regimes, Citizen Participation and Rural Restructuring* (Elsevier, 2007), co-edited with Bettina Bock.

Sue Bridger has published numerous articles on women in Russia. She is the author of *Women in the Soviet Countryside* (CUP, 1987), and co-author, with R. Kay and K. Pinnick, of *No More Heroines? Russia, Women and the Market* (Routledge, 1996). She is the editor of *Women and Political Change: Perspectives from East-Central Europe* (Palgrave Macmillan, 1999) and co-editor, with F. Pine, of *Surviving Post-Socialism: Local Strategies and Regional Responses in Eastern Europe* (Routledge, 1998). She is currently writing a book on Soviet women cosmonauts.

Mary Buckley is Fellow and Director of Studies in Social and Political Sciences at Hughes Hall, Cambridge. She has published on Soviet ideology, gender politics, society and the state under Gorbachev, Stalinism, rural Stakhanovism, Russian domestic and foreign policy, terrorism and human trafficking. Her most recent books are *Mobilizing Soviet Peasants* (Rowman and Littlefield, 2006) and *The Bush Doctrine and the War on Terrorism*, co-edited (Routledge, 2006).

Helene Carlbäck is Senior Lecturer in History at the Centre for Baltic and East European Studies (CBEES) at Södertörn University College, Stockholm, Sweden. Her current research focuses on gender and family in Soviet history and she is a member of the Baltic Sea Foundation-funded research project 'Parenthood vs. wage labour. Emancipation rhetoric and gender practices in Hungary and Soviet Russia 1955–1985'. She is author of a number of books and articles on various aspects of Soviet history.

Yulia Gradskova graduated from the History Department of Moscow State University in 1990 and worked as a researcher of gender problems at Moscow State University in 1997–2002. Currently she is completing her thesis dealing with practices of maternity and beauty in Soviet Russia 1930–1960s at Södertörn University College, Sweden. Her research explores the ways in which femininities were enacted through Soviet everyday practices based on discourse analysis of women's publications and oral histories.

Rebecca Kay is Professor of Russian Gender Studies at the Department of Central and East European Studies, University of Glasgow. Her research explores the gendered impacts of social, economic, political and cultural transformations in contemporary Russia. Her major publications include: *Men in Contemporary Russia: the Fallen Heroes of Post-Soviet Change?* (Ashgate, 2006), *Russian Women and their Organizations: Gender, Discrimination and Grassroots Women's Organizations 1991–96* (Palgrave Macmillan, 2000) and *No More Heroines? Russia, Women and the Market*, with Sue Bridger and Kathryn Pinnick (Routledge, 1996).

Larisa Kosygina is a PhD student at the Centre for Russian and East European Studies, University of Birmingham and a Ford Foundation International Fellow. She is currently completing her thesis: 'Migrants without Russian Citizenship from former Soviet-Republics in Russia: Experience of Adaptation'. Previously she was a lecturer at Novosibirsk State Academy of Economics and Management. Her research experience includes work on the projects: 'The effectiveness of programmes for the integration of forced migrants: a gender perspective' supported by INTAS (2001–3) and 'Cultural stereotypes and their influence on professional orientation of youth', supported by the Heinrich Böll Foundation (1998–9).

Francesca Stella is a PhD student at the Department of Central and East European Studies, University of Glasgow. She is currently completing her thesis on lesbian identities and spaces in post-Soviet urban Russia. This research, funded by a University of Glasgow scholarship, looks at the role of lesbian spaces and networks in shaping collective and individual identities; it also examines how broader cultural understandings of gender/sexual roles and private/public spaces are implicated in the construction of non-heterosexual identities.

Vikki Turbine is an ESRC sponsored doctoral researcher in the Department of Central and East European Studies at the University of Glasgow. She is currently completing her thesis, which explores Russian women's perceptions of human rights and the use of rights-based approaches in everyday life.

Natalia Vinokurova is Senior Researcher at the Central Economics & Mathematics Institute (CEMI), Russian Academy of Sciences. She has researched and published on a wide range of gender issues in Russia and the Soviet Union including family, marriage and divorce, labour market activities and experiences of economic transformation. Her principal publications include: *Zhenshchiny v nauke i obrazovanii* (Moscow, forthcoming), *Brauchen Frauen Helden? Russische Frauen zwischen Tradition und Moderne*, co-authored with H. K. Herold (Bremen, 2001) and 'Gendernye aspekty menedzhmenta', *Narodonaselenie*, 1 (2006).

Introduction: Gender, Equality and the State from 'Socialism' to 'Democracy'?

Rebecca Kay

Gender has long been recognised by sociologists, anthropologists, political scientists and historians (amongst others) as a crucial structure influencing the organisation of societies and the positioning of women and men in relation to both public and private divisions of power and authority. The socially constructed and culturally defined understandings of femininity and masculinity upon which the gender order[1] of any society is founded, affect the roles and responsibilities attributed to women and men, both in the private sphere of home and family and in the public domains of economic, political and social interaction, and, indeed, in intersections between the two. Dominant discourses and understandings of gender, propagated through media and cultural representations of women and men, public rhetoric and popular debate, prioritise equality and difference to varying degrees, both drawing on and feeding into state-led ideologies and policies. These in turn play an important role in determining the extent to which gender impacts upon the opportunities, rights, entitlements and duties of male and female citizens. Indeed, as Connell has pointed out, the state is 'not just a regulatory agency, it is a creative force in the dynamic of gender', one which 'creates new categories and new historical possibilities'.[2]

For many years, scholars from a range of disciplines have been concerned with the study of gender and its implications for the lives and experiences of women and men in the countries of the former Soviet bloc. It is clear that whatever the state-led pronouncements in support of egalitarianism and women's emancipation, gender had a profound impact on the organisation of these societies during state socialism. Men and women were not equal, either in public or in private, and indeed the contract between the state and its citizens was frequently specifically gendered – whilst men were expected to contribute to the national economy through wage labour and to be ready and able to defend the nation in times of war, women were expected to combine their duties as workers and mothers, contributing both to the national economy and to the physical reproduction of the nation.[3] Since the fall of the state-socialist regimes, studies of gender have found that existing inequalities have frequently been exacerbated and that new forms of discrimination and marginalisation have emerged in the context of political and economic transformations. Yet, contemporary research has also revealed an increasingly pluralistic society, incorporating various new forms of gendered agency as well as some specific challenges to rigid understandings of 'masculine' and 'feminine' behaviours, roles and relationships.[4]

The revolutions of 1989/91 were clearly a turning point for the people, societies and states of the former communist bloc and this historic moment can also be viewed as pivotal in relation to gender and its study. It is pivotal, not because attitudes towards and experiences of gender changed overnight – indeed many clear lines of continuity can be traced between the periods of state socialism and post-socialism – but because the economic, political and ideological contexts of men's and women's lives were transformed. The opportunities and challenges which women and men are faced with, as well as the strategies, practices and identities they develop in response, have been shaped both by deeply entrenched attitudes towards gender and by new developments and negotiations in understandings of what is 'masculine' and what is 'feminine'. The latter have included shifts brought about by the end of Cold War isolationism and the exposure of post-socialist societies to global markets and socio-cultural interactions.[5] This book explores both sides of that pivotal moment, examining a number of defining features and issues from each side, and showing how these relate to broader ideological, economic, political and social contexts.

From 'state socialism' to 'democracy': the role of the state

A central aspect of these shifting contexts has been the changing nature of the state and its role in shaping the 'dynamic of gender'. Prior to the demise of state socialism, the states of the Soviet bloc overtly claimed a dominant role in controlling economic and political systems and processes and shaping the societies which they governed. Gender was an important element in these processes and state-led ideology and policy was deliberately invasive, seeking to reshape gendered identities and manipulate male and female roles and behaviours in both public and private. Yet, debates on the nature of and means to achieving sexual equality were generally reduced to the 'woman question'. The goal of women's 'emancipation' was proclaimed as an ideological imperative with little if any deeper analysis of the complex ways in which gender structures and informs human interaction and contributes to unequal distributions of power, resources, opportunities and obligations, impacting on the lives and practices of both women and men. The relatively closed nature of these societies and censored flows of information between policy-making bodies; professional, intellectual and managerial elites; and grassroots level insight and experience, stifled opportunities for a more nuanced and complex public debate.

As a result, approaches to gender equality were largely instrumental and focused primarily on altering women's roles, practices and identities in order to suit economic, demographic and political priorities. These priorities varied over time and place such that, whilst there were common strands to state policy and ideology across the history of state socialism and throughout the region, there were also significant differences between countries and distinct periods of time. Moreover, economic, demographic and political priorities were frequently competing: states which had proclaimed an ideological commitment to gender equality, demonstrated first and foremost through women's active involvement in paid employment and political representation, were also concerned with negative demographic trends, aspects of social cohesion and the demands of an increasingly sophisticated, educated and urbanised population. Solutions to these problems were often sought in attempts to strengthen the family, largely through the reassertion of women's domestic roles and responsibilities as mothers, wives and housewives.[6] Thus, women became the objects of state policies, which, even whilst they claimed to be furthering women's 'emancipation', were, in fact, constantly influenced by pervasive gendered assumptions about innate differences in male and female abilities, interests and skills. These assumptions influenced the thinking and behaviour of policy-makers, economic managers, male and female workers, husbands, wives, mothers and fathers, regardless of state-led proclamations of equality. As a result, many women's experiences of 'emancipation' were anything but liberating.

Following the collapse of the state-socialist regimes, considerable emphasis was placed on the need to redefine the relationship between states and societies in the region. International advisers, local policy-makers and intellectual elites called for a contraction of the state and its withdrawal from interference in the private lives of citizens. Neo-liberal economic and political agendas underpinning these proposals suggested that free markets and liberal democracies were the best guarantors of individual freedoms, equality of opportunities and a self-perpetuating upward spiral of prosperity.[7] Yet, studies focused at the micro level of day-to-day life have repeatedly found that people's interpretations of their shifting relationship with the state are characterised by a sense of abandonment and withdrawal of support, which has thrown families and communities back on their own resources.[8] It has been noted that the impacts of these processes are implicitly and explicitly gendered. Women are often left plugging the gaps left by the withdrawal of welfare support, both through their caring activities in the private sphere of home and family and through their engagement in the 'third sector' activities of non-governmental organisations and voluntary associations.[9] Men's less direct involvement in many of these activities has freed them to pursue higher status and more highly paid forms of employment in the public sphere. And yet, their relative exclusion from the close, caring relationships which frequently sustain these more informal activities, has left many men vulnerable to what Ashwin and Lytkina have described as a process of 'domestic marginalisation',[10] as well as trivialising or obscuring their needs in relation to the development of state-led policies and mechanisms of welfare and social security.[11]

Formally, the majority of post-socialist states continue to claim a commitment to equality between the sexes in their constitutions and have signed up to international agreements and declarations and included equality clauses in major pieces of legislation. Yet these states no longer claim so direct or pervasive a role in shaping the behaviour, defining the roles and influencing the relationships of women and men as their predecessors. The majority of post-socialist states have relinquished their formerly overt mechanisms of control over political and social processes, leading to a diversification of social movements and organisations, a wider range of discourses and debate in academic, media and political arenas, and new opportunities for a variety of lifestyle choices and forms of cultural self-expression. Many of these new freedoms have offered opportunities for further exploration and renegotiation of gendered practices and relations. Academic centres and associations for women's studies and gender studies have been established across the region,[12] for example, as well as a multitude of women's organisations and groups, some or which work more formally on projects and issues ranging from trafficking and gendered violence to women's enterprise and cultural initiatives, whilst others act much more informally, offering collective security and mutual support to their members.[13] Particularly in the larger cities and amongst the younger generations a diversification of styles of dress and relaxed codes of informal interaction between the sexes can be observed.

And yet, the public statements of policy-makers and state representatives, as well as dominant media discourses and widespread social trends, have tended to reinforce rather than question rigid normative assumptions about gender. Discussions of how gender relations might be renegotiated in the post-socialist era have often focused on the mistakes and 'distortions' of the past, and in particular what has frequently been termed the 'over-emancipation' of women.[14] Rather than analysing the various factors contributing to the many shortcomings of previous gender policies and practices, dominant discourses reflected in the media and in the statements of high-profile public figures, have often resorted instead to assertions of 'natural' differences between the sexes and 'common sense' arguments about the separate roles and responsibilities of men and women. Such assumptions are reflected in the statements and behaviours of policy-makers and of those empowered to implement policy and to enforce the legislation that claims to protect gender equality. During a Presidential address to the Council of the Federation in May 2006, for example, President Putin spoke at length about his concerns in relation to Russia's low birth rate, the difficulties faced by women attempting to combine motherhood and employment outside the home and the need for a range of measures of state support for mothers and children. Men, their needs, roles and potential contribution to family life did not warrant a single mention in this part of the speech.[15] Gendered divisions of carework and their implications for men's and women's activities in both public and private and for their access to both formal and informal forms of social security and support are framed by the perpetuation of such assumptions and their reflection in policy-making and implementation. Thus, gendered experiences of and responses to socio-economic and political change bear witness to the complex interactions between and mutual influence of the ways in which gender is perceived, understood and performed at personal, interpersonal, family, social, institutional and state levels – the agency of individual men and women both shapes and is shaped by the structures which define their social, economic and political environments.

Researching gender before and after the fall of communism

From a scholarly perspective, the transformations of the 1990s have also represented something of a watershed in methodological and theoretical terms. Before the fall of communism, studies of gender tended to focus primarily on the 'big picture', analysing state-led ideologies and policies and scouring official statistics in an attempt to piece together the realities of women's and men's lives and their experiences of 'equality'.[16] In-depth studies at the micro level were for the most part impossible until the final years of the state-socialist regime. From the early 1990s onwards, however, detailed ethnographic studies became both much more feasible and increasingly popular and have shed light on the intricacies and contradictions of gender relations as they take place at the micro level of day-to-day life.[17] As the ever changing and increasingly complex nature of post-socialist states and societies has made the 'big picture' ever harder to pin down, these snapshots have provided invaluable insight into the gendered impacts of economic, political and social transformations on individuals and communities. Simultaneously, new perspectives on the past have been revealed as methodologies such as oral history and new access to archival sources and previously censored writings has become possible.[18] The micro-level pictures revealed in these ways complement ongoing macro-level studies of state-led developments, both contemporary and historical, and of the impacts of dominant discourses, many of which are revealed by analysis of media representations of a specific issue.

The contributions to this volume demonstrate the complexity of research currently available. The authors draw on a wide variety of, mainly qualitative, research methods ranging from ethnographic interviews, participant observation and oral history to detailed analyses of media discourses and the writings of policy-makers and their expert advisers. The result is a multifaceted portrait of the ways in which gender as a social construct incorporating complex dynamics of power and identity has influenced and continues to influence the organisation of society. This takes place at multiple, yet intricately interconnected levels including: policy-making and implementation; the negotiation of gendered roles and practices within a range of social contexts: the workplace, the family, the street; and personal experiences, identities and attitudes to the self and others as gendered beings.

As is often the case, methodological innovations in the study of post-socialist societies, not only in the field of gender, have also led to theoretical developments. The focus on state-led ideologies and systems of governance which dominated academic study prior to the fall of communism, resulted in a view of those societies and their populations as fundamentally different from those of the 'capitalist', 'democratic' west. Yet, in terms of sexual politics, as earlier theorists of gender and the state posited, and as the chapters in Part I of this book make clear, the differences between 'communist' states and their 'liberal' 'capitalist' rivals were frequently nowhere near as great in practice as ideological rhetoric on both sides of the 'iron curtain' implied.[19]

The more detailed insight into the lived realities of women's and men's experience made possible by recent empirical studies has revealed a multitude of issues and variety of responses which transcend geographical, political and cultural boundaries. Theoretical models which were once thought of as relevant to only one or other 'type' of society have been shown to have 'transnational' explanatory power.[20] Yet, attempts to explain developments in the post-socialist world on the basis of theoretical and conceptual approaches emanating from the west have also been critiqued.[21] It has become clear that existing theories must expand and adapt to explain the complexities of transnational similarities and local differences revealed in this way.

Multifaceted and often multidisciplinary studies of gender, such as those represented in this volume, contribute to these wider debates about the nature of both socialist and post-socialist societies, the relationship between states and citizens and the significance of gender to social, economic and political developments. These debates resonate well beyond the confines of a region which was once behind the 'iron curtain'. The majority of contributions to this volume focus on one specific country or region and often also on a specific moment in time. Nonetheless, their findings point to overarching dilemmas in the struggle for gender equality such as: women's struggle to combine paid labour with family roles; the discomfort both men and women frequently experience when they transgress gender norms of behaviour and identity; and the gaps between policy development, implementation and practice. Each of these dilemmas is complicated by the pervasiveness of normative assumptions relating to gender which affect the thinking and behaviour of women and men, policy-makers, managers and practitioners across a wide range of contexts.

Implicitly or explicitly these norms are held in place by the inequalities of power and access to resources which underpin the status quo. In many instances these inequalities appear to favour men. In this volume, Asztalos Morell, for example, reviews Hungarian debates regarding women's incorporation into production during the 1960s and notes resistance by both male workers and male managers to policies which they perceived as a threat to male privilege in the realm of employment. Kosygina discusses the difficulties faced by forced migrants in the post-Soviet Russian labour market and finds that as well as sharing the constraints and challenges experienced by male migrants, female migrants are doubly disadvantaged due to their sex. However, particularly in the more diverse societies and complex economic and political contexts of the contemporary period, inequalities too are complex and fractured. In some instances, particularly in the private sphere of home and family, men may find the status quo working against them, for example in relation to their position as fathers and their rights and opportunities to care for their children.[22] Many groups, for example lesbian women, economic migrants and trafficked women, are confronted by intersecting normative expectations and inequalities of power, which are expressed and experienced in terms of economic status, ethnicity, generation and sexuality as well as gender.[23] The contributions brought together in this volume explore these complexities and the combinations of agency, structure and identity which shape women's and men's experiences of and responses to social, economic and political inequalities and challenges.

Structure of the book and its chapters

Reflecting the emphasis placed above on the fall of communism as a pivotal moment in the lives of women and men living in the post-socialist region and in terms of researching gender in that region, this book is structured in a loosely chronological fashion and divided into two parts. The first part focuses on the era of state socialism, the second on the period since its demise. More specifically, the first part explores definitions and negotiations of women's roles in both the public and private spheres following the Second World War.

Part I: Equal but different: state socialism and women's roles in public and private life

Women's full and equal participation in paid labour outside the home played a central role in the socialist states' ideological commitment to gender equality and female emancipation. Moreover, extensive expansion of the post-war economies in many countries of the region demanded additional labour power. Thus, economic and ideological priorities appeared to converge, making it logical that previously unemployed women be drawn into waged labour as quickly as possible. Indeed in most countries of the region this was a central plank in state policy. In the Soviet Union women made up 51 per cent of the labour force by the early 1970s, a higher proportion than in any other industrialised nation and one which, in the context of full employment meant that virtually all women of working age were in either full-time employment or education.

Yet, the question of how best to combine women's dual roles as worker and mother remained a thorny issue. Through the 1960s and 1970s, as the societies in question modernised and became increasingly pluralistic, changing demographic, economic and social priorities were pushing in a different direction: towards the prioritisation of motherhood and family-oriented roles for women. Simultaneously, the state renounced some of the most restrictive and authoritarian elements of control and demands for strict ideological conformity. As a result theoreticians, demographers, economists, educational specialists and sociologists entered into frequently tortuous, contradictory and increasingly diverse debates about the correct balance to be struck between women's dual roles.[24]

These debates drew heavily on, and simultaneously reinforced, deep-seated cultural understandings of femininity and the close association between femaleness and motherhood which had survived in both popular practices and state-led rhetoric despite the regimes' earlier claims to strict egalitarianism. Moreover, while the potential consequences for men of women's increased participation in the labour force were discussed both in terms of threats to men's relative power and secure position in the workplace and in terms of more private issues of identity and authority within the family, the question of a need to redefine or renegotiate the balance of men's activities between work and home was approached with much more caution.[25] The contributors to this first part of the book explore these issues and the broader questions which they raise in relation to perceptions of femininity, attitudes towards gender and state-led attempts to control and (re)shape women's behaviour both at home and at work. Several chapters specifically draw the reader's attention to points of comparison and even mutual influence between the sexual politics of states and societies on 'opposite' sides of the 'iron curtain'.

Yulia Gradskova begins this part with an exploration of women's beauty practices in post-war Soviet Russia, from the late 1940s until the early 1960s. Based on oral history interviews with women in three cities – Moscow, Saratov and Ufa – as well as an analysis of women's magazines and popular advice literature, Gradskova challenges 'common sense' understandings of 'beauty' in the Soviet Union. These, she argues, have stemmed from attempts to classify Soviet practices either in terms of a unique 'Soviet' experience, or with reference to 'western' and/or 'traditional' values. This has led to a number of false dichotomies and assumptions: that Soviet women were 'liberated' from the kinds of oppressive concern with beauty and appearance imposed on women in capitalist societies; that Soviet women were too poor to take care of their appearance or to consider such frivolities as 'beauty'; or that Soviet women struggled against the socialist state with its modernising and work-oriented priorities to preserve traditional ideals of femininity and beauty. Instead, Gradskova argues that women drew on a range of ideologies, norms and ideals in their beauty practices and that the state was, perhaps typically, inconsistent in its attempts to control women's access to western fashions and beauty ideals. Consumption, normative notions of 'femininity', economic practicalities and wider social and cultural expectations shaped and constrained Soviet women's beauty practices in ways which were at once peculiar to the Soviet context but also strikingly similar to the experiences of women in capitalist societies. 'Doing femininity' in post-war Soviet Russia, Gradskova concludes, required knowledge of multiple norms, codes and techniques of beauty. Women's practices embodied a complex combination of Soviet, traditional and western values.

The following three chapters by Ildikó Asztalos Morell, Natalia Vinokurova and Helene Carlbäck draw on an ongoing research collaboration between Swedish, Hungarian and Russian scholars, in a project 'Parenthood versus wage labour. Emancipation rhetorics and gender practices in Soviet Russia and Hungary 1955–1985'. Asztalos Morell begins with an examination of the writings of Hungarian labour market experts during the 1960s and their perspectives on women's dual roles as mothers and workers. During this period, ideological rhetoric was increasingly open to question and debate and the technocratic elites with whom the experts allied themselves were rapidly gaining power. Labour market experts were tasked with resolving the challenges brought about by a growing number of women in a labour force organised on the assumption of the male worker, free from family duties and roles, as the norm. Asztalos Morell points out that the overwhelming majority of the experts in question were men and that they tended rather to respond to and appease the concerns of male managers and workers than to represent women's views and concerns. Their recommendations focused strongly on organising labour such that women would be able to combine their dual functions and men's status and earning power would not be challenged by competition from women workers. Although they distanced themselves from blatantly essentialist discourses and supported an ideological rhetoric of equality, the experts overwhelmingly called for a 'realistic' response to the issues in question. They failed to problematise the underlying gender contract, accepting instead a view of women's reproductive responsibilities as natural. Thus, despite the claims of state-socialist regimes to privilege women's interests and ensure equality in the public spheres of employment and political representation, women's issues continued to be defined from a male perspective, based on the interests of men as workers, managers, experts or party executives.

Natalia Vinokurova's chapter returns to the Soviet Union and examines the gender implications of social and economic transformations occurring in that country in the 1960s and 1970s. Importantly, she argues that the preoccupation with and prioritisation of the private sphere, which came to characterise the Brezhnev era of the 1970s, would have been impossible without the economic, social and cultural shifts which took place a decade earlier, during the Khrushchev era. Ironically, in the very era that women achieved full employment and benefited from significant increases in levels of education and training, social and cultural trends including growing consumption and separate housing for nuclear families were re-emphasising and adding to the burdens of women's family responsibilities and roles. Drawing on oral histories and ethnographic interviews, analysis of media and cultural discourses, as well as analysis of statistical data, Vinokurova argues that women coped with their growing double burden by a combination of state support structures and informal arrangements based in particular on female networks of reciprocal favours and support. Although she also finds some increase in men's unpaid contributions to family life in this period, Vinokurova suggests that, in spite of widespread rhetorical support, from both women and men, for a principle of gender equality, the division of labour in most families was based on a model of gender complementarity rather than equality. Both in public and private, despite claims of egalitarianism, male and female activities, aptitudes and responsibilities remained rather strictly separated.

Helene Carlbäck's chapter is the most explicitly comparative in the book. Carlbäck investigates women's position in the labour force and domestic life in Sweden and Soviet Russia by means of a comparison of public discourses and gender practices relating to women's domestic roles, their employment outside the home and the provision of public childcare in both countries. Focusing on the 1960s, Carlbäck analyses gender discourses from women's magazines and other media and compares statistical data from both countries. She finds much to compare despite the clearly different socio-economic and political systems of the two countries. A blend of liberal, romantic and Marxist gender ideologies formed the basis of policies and discourses in both countries, and in both countries rhetoric and practice are shown to shift over time, interestingly, in rather opposite directions. Carlbäck's comparisons are made all the more interesting by the fact that both Sweden and the Soviet Union have at various junctures been perceived, and indeed presented themselves, as models of gender equality and state support for women. Nonetheless, essentialist assumptions regarding women's gender-specific caring skills were influential in both countries. These held in place a division of labour in the family which overburdened women and which, during the period under study, both the Soviet and the Swedish state sought to resolve through providing public childcare, rather than challenging gender norms in parenting and carework.

Sue Bridger's chapter brings this part of the book to a close both chronologically and thematically through a discussion of the pronatalist campaign of the late Soviet era and, in particular, its revival of the image of the 'heroine-mother' as a model for Russian women. Bridger examines the campaign from a range of perspectives including: its promotion through the press in national women's magazines and national rural magazines; the research and comment of Soviet sociologists and demographers; and the experiences and responses of Russian women as reflected in the upsurge of readers' letters to the press during the Gorbachev era. This multifaceted analysis demonstrates the instrumental nature of Soviet policies with regard to women. Gender ideologies, educational theories and socialist morality were called upon in media attempts to persuade women to bear more children in a period when demographic concerns held sway. Whilst sociologists and demographers took a more measured approach, they too prioritised the demographic interests of the state, seeking the most effective and efficient ways to raise the birth rate and maintain the desired ethnic balance within the population. Yet, Bridger's analysis of women's letters to the press in the late 1980s demonstrates that their responses to and evaluations of the campaign and the state-led policies it represented were shaped by a range of factors: economic, social and personal, as well as political and ideological. Not surprisingly then, women proved less malleable in terms of their reproductive behaviour than the state might have wished. The question of how to increase the birth rate and resolve Russia's, by now long-standing, 'demographic crisis' continues to exercise policy-makers to this day. Yet, as Bridger concludes, the increased economic uncertainty and socio-cultural transformations of the post-Soviet era have further reduced perceptions of what constitutes the 'ideal' family size.

Part II: (Re-)negotiating gender, equality and difference in the post-socialist era: rights, participation and marginalisation

The end of state socialism heralded the start of a new era of paradoxes in the realm of gender. In virtually every country of the region, the state has renounced its previous ideological insistence on women's 'emancipation' as a central facet of policy-making and public discourse, apparently unleashing the full force of widely supported assumptions about the innate and immutable differences between women and men. Such deterministic understandings of gender have encouraged support for rigid divisions between male and female roles and responsibilities with de facto consequences for women's and men's opportunities and rights. Some observers have termed this process a post-socialist patriarchal renaissance.[26]

Yet, simultaneously, the post-socialist states have continued to uphold ideals of equality, at least in their legal commitments to international conventions and in the inclusion of equality clauses in most key areas of national legislation. Post-socialist societies meanwhile have embraced notions of personal liberty, freedom of choice and expressions of identity and have become increasingly open to global cultural, economic and political influences. As a consequence they have become as complex and diverse as any postmodern society. Thus, it has become increasingly difficult to pin down a singular set of discourses, experiences or understandings of gender in the post-socialist era. The five chapters of Part II of this book focus on post-Soviet Russia and reflect some of the plurality of experiences and discourses which have developed within that society. They also demonstrate the tensions between the uniqueness of each microlevel study with its own historical, cultural and socio-economic specificities, and the similarities which transcend not only local or issue-based boundaries but also national and regional borders. Each chapter draws on extensive qualitative research to reveal the complex gendered realities of particular groups or communities of individuals: fathers, lesbians, forced migrants. Gendered perceptions and representations of rights and their infringement are also discussed, through enquiry into provincial women's understandings of human rights and via an analysis of media discourses on the issue of human trafficking, as well as in relation to the groups mentioned above.

Rebecca Kay's chapter, which starts this part of the book, focuses specifically on the interactions between multiple structures and individual agency in determining men's experiences, practices and rights as fathers. Picking up where Bridger left off, Kay argues that the pronatalism of the late Soviet period supported and revitalised a long-standing 'cult of motherhood' in Russian culture, which codes parenting and childcare as female. As a result fathers and fatherhood are marginalised in much public and popular discourse and in social policy-making and implementation. Deep-rooted convictions about the gender of care and the centrality of motherhood to women's identities, and suspicions about men's capabilities and reliability as parents, influence the practices and attitudes of social service providers, courts, teachers, mothers and fathers themselves, presenting multiple barriers to those men who might seek to challenge the status quo. Kay's qualitative research with men living in provincial Russia has suggested that many men view fatherhood as a key life-experience and a central part of their identity. Yet even those who have become sole carers for their children find it hard to override stereotypes of masculinity and femininity which are not flexible enough to incorporate the realities of their lives. Drawing on wider theories of the power and complexity of gender as a social construct, Kay concludes that in Russia, as elsewhere, men's experiences of fatherhood, their behaviour as fathers, and the relationships they develop with their children, are framed by a range of intersecting factors, including: legal definitions of fathers' rights, broader societal attitudes towards parenting, culturally embedded expectations and understandings of gender and the practical realities of fathers' relationships and interactions within families, communities and institutions.

Francesca Stella further interrogates the interaction between formal rights and exclusionary social and cultural practices in her exploration of perceptions of civic and cultural rights among lesbian and bisexual women. Based on the findings of her qualitative study of the lives and experiences of lesbian women in Moscow and Ul'ianovsk, Stella argues that 'western' debates about sexual citizenship which prioritise formal equality through legal and civil rights are perceived as only partially relevant by her respondents. For many of these women, involvement in community projects and carving out shared spaces of belonging was seen as a more effective and realistic, if more gradual, approach to overcoming experiences of discrimination, civic exclusion and public invisibility. As Stella points out, women's views and practices were shaped by a range of factors including, but not limited to, their sexual orientation: age, location and relationship status were also significant. Framing her empirical data in a careful analysis of the political, social and cultural context of contemporary Russia, Stella demonstrates that perceptions of the most effective ways to challenge exclusion and promote social change are influenced by specific models of citizenship, historical and contemporary developments in the relationship between states and societies and culturally rooted attitudes towards gender and sexuality.

Questions about the usefulness of rights discourses and practices, developed primarily on the basis of western institutional frameworks and experiences, are also raised in the following chapter by Vikki Turbine. Her study of provincial Russian women's perceptions of human rights highlights the necessity of considering wider frameworks and practices in order to understand perceptions of entitlement, discrimination and rights violations. Turbine explores the ways in which Soviet legacies and post-Soviet experience converge, leading women to prioritise socio-economic entitlements and to seek to resolve 'problems' through informal means. She argues that human rights are variously understood as a moral norm, a package of rights, or a particular form of 'crisis' intervention, but are commonly viewed as abstract in comparison with the real problems of women's daily lives and therefore as largely irrelevant as a tool for resolving these issues. Turbine finds that women generally prefer to use familiar informal networks and turn to trusted interlocutors for information and advice. Yet she cautions that whilst such approaches may be temporarily empowering and relatively efficient in solving immediate problems, they may also ultimately entrench negative perceptions of rights-based approaches and exclude women from this aspect of national and global citizenship.

Infringements of women's rights, their perceptions of discrimination and their strategies for overcoming such difficulties are also highlighted by Larisa Kosygina's study of the experiences of forced migrants in the Russian labour market. Kosygina argues that female forced migrants are doubly disadvantaged, on the one hand by the gender inequalities which are embedded in the structure of the Russian labour market and which shape the practices and attitudes of both employers and employees, and on the other hand by the loss of symbolic, material and social capital as a result of migration. Kosygina draws attention to the importance of continuities and discontinuities, both over time and between identities, practices and external structures, in shaping people's perceptions of discrimination and entitlement. She notes that gender discrimination in the labour market is passed over as unremarkable in many respondents' stories, whilst discrimination on the grounds of age is more readily identified as problematic. Kosygina argues that this discrepancy results from considerable continuities between the past and present in terms of gendered segregation of occupation, inequalities in pay and generalised perceptions of gender-appropriate roles for women and men. The latter are shared by employees and employers alike, further reducing a sense of conflict or unjust treatment where discrimination arises on the grounds of gender.

The book draws to a close with Mary Buckley's chapter on representations and interpretations of human trafficking in the contemporary Russian press. Buckley returns to a more macro-level analysis of media discourses and their interaction with state policy-making and wider sociocultural perceptions and attitudes, as employed by some of the authors in Part I, Carlbäck and Bridger in particular. Focusing on a selection of articles from eight national newspapers, Buckley identifies three main strands in press reporting on the issue of human trafficking: those seeking to apportion blame; informative reporting; and sensationalist interpretations and accounts. Gendered, ethnicised and geopolitical configurations of power and representation inform these strands in a variety of ways, apportioning blame to the 'west', the 'market', and 'non-Russian' men, for example, or representing women as passive victims and/or sexualised objects, used and abused for male consumption. Buckley concludes by calling for a more nuanced analysis of the different dimensions of human trafficking in order to more fully understand the workings of and put an end to illegitimate mechanisms of influence and power which underpin and sustain this phenomenon.

Conclusion

The ten contributors to this volume share a fascination with and a strong commitment to unpacking, analysing and offering insight into the workings of gender and its impacts on women's and men's lives. Each chapter draws on detailed and original research and together they contribute to a multifaceted and historically grounded picture of the ways in which gendered structures, identities and practices have developed and continue to develop in Russia, Central and Eastern Europe during state socialism and after its demise. Taken together these chapters confirm the importance of the ideologically driven configuration of social, economic and political structures and priorities which shaped gender relations during the period of state socialism and the ongoing influence of that legacy for the countries of the region. And yet they also clearly demonstrate the importance of wider international contexts and the parallels and intersections between experiences, understandings and negotiations of gender in that region and beyond. In this sense the studies presented here, both individually and collectively, make an important contribution to wider understandings of gender and of its relevance to contemporary concerns of transnational significance including: the relationship between states and citizens, the nature of citizenship and the nuanced ways in which 'equality' and 'rights' are perceived and experienced in practice, the power of discourse and the intersections between representations of gender and the lived experiences of women and men.

Notes

1. Robert Connell developed the concept of the gender order to signify the independent power of gender as a coherent system of social organisation defining the power relations between and definitions of masculinities and femininities. R. Connell, *Gender and Power: Society, the Person and Sexual Politics* (Cambridge: Polity Press, 1987), pp. 98–9.
2. R. Connell, 'The State, Gender and Sexual Politics', *Theory and Society*, 19, 5 (1990): 507–44, p. 530.
3. M. Buckley, *Women and Ideology in the Soviet Union* (Cambridge: Cambridge University Press, 1989); B. Evans Clements, R. Friedman and D. Healey (eds), *Russian Masculinities in History and Culture* (Basingstoke: Palgrave Macmillan,

2002); S. Gal and G. Kligman, *The Politics of Gender after Socialism: a Comparative-Historical Essay* (Princeton: Princeton University Press, 2000).

4. See for example, S. Bridger, R. Kay and K. Pinnick, *No More Heroines? Russia, Women and the Market* (London: Routledge, 1996); S. Gal and G. Kligman (eds), *Reproducing Gender: Politics, Publics and Everyday Life after Socialism* (Princeton: Princeton University Press, 2000); S. Ushakin, *Muzhe(N)stvennosti. Sbornik Statei* (Moscow: Novoe literaturnoe obozrenie, 2002); R. Kay, *Men in Contemporary Russia: the Fallen Heroes of Post-Soviet Change?* (Aldershot: Ashgate, 2006).
5. H. Pilkington, E. Omel'chenko, M. Flynn, U. Bliudina and E. Starkova, *Looking West? Cultural Globalization and Russian Youth Cultures* (Pennsylvania: Pennsylvania State University Press, 2004), pp. 84–9, 160–3.
6. Romania offered perhaps the most extreme example with Ceaucescu's draconian measures to promote childbearing and restrict women's access to contraception and abortion. See G. Kligman, *The Politics of Duplicity: Controlling Reproduction in Ceausescu's Romania* (Berkeley: University of California Press, 1998). See also S. Bridger in this volume, for a discussion of pronatalist campaigns in the late Soviet period.
7. D. Kalb, 'Afterword: Globalism and Postsocialist Prospects', in C. Hann (ed.), *Postsocialism: Ideals Ideologies and Practices in Eurasia* (London: Routledge, 2002), pp. 318–22.
8. See for example, S. Bridger and F. Pine (eds), *Surviving Post-Socialism: Local Strategies and Regional Responses in Eastern Europe and the Former Soviet Union* (London: Routledge, 1998); M. Burawoy and K. Verdery (eds), *Uncertain Transition: Ehtnographies of Change in the Postsocialist World* (Oxford: Rowman and Littlefield, 1999); H. Haukanes and F. Pine (eds), *Generations, Kinship and Care: Gendered Provisions of Social Security in Central Eastern Europe* (Bergen: Centre for Women's and Gender Research, University of Bergen, 2005).
9. Haukanes and Pine (2005); F. Pine, 'Retreat to the Household? Gendered Domains in Postsocialist Poland', in C. Hann (ed.), *Postsocialism: Ideals, Ideologies and Practices in Eurasia* (London: Routledge, 2002); S. Salmenniemi, 'Civic Activity – Feminine Activity? Gender, Civil Society and Citizenship in Post-Soviet Russia', *Sociology*, 39, 4 (2005): 735–53; R. Kay, 'Grassroots Women's Activism in Russia, 1992–96: Surviving Social Change Together?' in M. Mikula (ed.), *Women, Activism and Social Change* (London: Routledge, 2005).
10. S. Ashwin and T. Lytkina, 'Men in Crisis in Russia – the Role of Domestic Marginalization', *Gender and Society*, 18, 2 (2004): 189–206.
11. R. Kay, 'Caring for Men in Contemporary Russia: Gendered Constructions of Need and Hybrid Forms of Social Security', *Focaal, European Journal of Anthropology* (forthcoming, 2007).
12. N. Rimashevskaia, 'The New Women's Studies', in M. Buckley (ed.), *Perestroika and Soviet Women* (Cambridge: Cambridge University Press, 1992); A. Posadskaya, *Women in Russia: a New Era in Russian Feminism* (London: Verso, 1994); S. Pavlychko, 'Feminism in Post-Communist Ukrainian Society', in R. Marsh (ed.), *Women in Russia and Ukraine* (Cambridge: Cambridge University Press, 1996), p. 310; N. White, 'Women in Changing Societies: Latvia and Lithuania', in M. Buckley (ed.), *Post-Soviet Women: From the Baltic to Central Asia* (Cambridge: Cambridge University Press, 1997), pp. 212–14.
13. R. Kay, *Russian Women and their Organizations: Gender, Discrimination and Grassroots Women's Organizations 1991–96* (Basingstoke: Palgrave Macmillan,

2000); V. Sperling, *Organizing Women in Contemporary Russia* (Cambridge: Cambridge University Press, 1999); K. Kuehnast and C. Nechemias (eds), *Post-Soviet Women Encountering Transition: Nation Building, Economic Survival, and Civic Activism* (Washington, DC and Baltimore: Woodrow Wilson Center Press and Johns Hopkins University Press, 2004).
14. Kay (2000), pp. 33, 210.
15. V. Putin, *Poslanie Federal'nomu Sobraniu Rossiiskoi Federatsii,* http://www.Kremlin.ru/mainpage.shtml (10 May 2006).
16. Buckley (1989); S. Bridger, *Women in the Soviet Countryside: Women's Roles in Rural Development in the Soviet Union* (Cambridge: Cambridge University Press, 1987); G. W. Lapidus, *Women in Soviet Society: Equality, Development and Social Change* (Berkeley and London: University of California Press, 1978); C. Corrin, *Magyar Women: Hungarian Women's Lives, 1960s–1990s* (Basingstoke: Palgrave Macmillan, 1994).
17. See for example, Kuehnast and Nechemias (2004); Gal and Kligman (eds) (2000); Bridger and Pine (1998).
18. See for example, D. Bertaux, P. Thompson and A. Rotkirch (eds), *On Living Through Soviet Russia* (London: Routledge, 2004).
19. Connell (1990), p. 510.
20. The concept of 'transnationalism' was reflected on and developed during an ESRC-funded seminar series: 'Transnational issues, local concerns: insights from Russia, Central and Eastern Europe and the UK' (2003–4). Many of the issues discussed during that series were seen as transcending national boundaries and artificial 'east–west' divisions. The term 'transnational' is employed here as a means to capture this wider shared experience and thus to avoid essentialist explanations which reduce such issues to specifically 'post-socialist' phenomena. Yet, the importance of avoiding homogenising tendencies is also recognised. The term 'transnational' is therefore intended to allow an exploration of the tension between, on the one hand, an understanding that many social, economic and environmental issues are not unique to any one region, nation or locality and, on the other hand, an awareness of the importance of locally specific historical, cultural and socio-economic characteristics which shape people's understandings and experiences of, as well as their responses to, such issues. For further discussion see M. Flynn, R. Kay and J. Oldfield (eds), *Journal of Communist Studies and Transition Politics, Special Issue: Transnational Issues, Local Concerns, Insights from Russia, Central and Eastern Europe and the UK,* 22, 1 (2006).
21. See for example, C. Hann and E. Dunn (eds), *Civil Society: Challenging Western Models* (London: Routledge, 1996).
22. See for example Kay's chapter in this volume; Ashwin and Lytkina (2004); Kay (2006).
23. Stella, Kosygina and Buckley explore some of the experiences and representations of these groups in their contributions to this volume.
24. L. Attwood, *The New Soviet Man and Woman: Sex-Role Socialization in the USSR* (Bloomington and Indianapolis: Indiana University Press, 1990). See also chapters by Asztalos Morell and Bridger in this volume.
25. Attwood (1990), p. 180; Buckley (1989), p. 188.
26. N. Azhgikhina 'Russian Journalism after 2000: New Censorship, New Markets and New Communities', *Keynote Speech, BASEES Annual Conference* (Cambridge, 1–3 April 2006).

Part I

Equal but Different: State Socialism and Women's Roles in Public and Private Life

1

'We were very upset if we didn't look fashionable': Women's Beauty Practices in Post-war Russia

Yulia Gradskova

'Beauty' has attracted considerably less academic attention amongst scholars concerned with the Soviet gender order, than questions of gender ideology and gendered divisions of public and private sphere roles.[1] Where beauty has been discussed, it is usually treated as something of 'secondary importance', an aspect of broader studies of private life, intimacy, sexuality and consumption.[2] However, feminist researchers have noted that concepts of 'beauty' are extremely important to the production of femininity in any society, and can shed light on less overt mechanisms of domination which, due to their invisibility, may easily survive and/or adjust to transformations of the 'visible' political and social order.[3] From this perspective the Soviet case is particularly interesting. Although the majority of women were employed outside of the home and in spite of constant shortages of fashionable clothes and other beauty products, Soviet women continued to show an interest in 'looking nice' throughout the Soviet period. Indeed, during the perestroika years western visitors were often impressed by Soviet women's attempts to look 'as feminine as possible'.

This chapter explores the norms of female appearance and understandings of 'beauty' which informed women's practices in Soviet Russia from the late 1940s to the early 1960s. The arguments presented here draw on my wider PhD study: a historical anthropology of everyday norms with respect to practices and representations of beauty and maternity in Soviet Russia, 1930–1960s. This research is concerned with both normative discourses and everyday tactics and strategies of 'demonstrating beauty' and 'becoming beautiful'.[4] The concept of 'normativity' is central to the theoretical underpinning of this research. I understand 'normativity' as a set of regulations including external demands, 'routine practices'[5] and internalised codes and meanings in a Foucauldian sense of disciplinary practices. Thus, normativity is not only based on written prescriptions or direct force, but is also a collection of everyday practices which appropriate, mix and resist competing discourses on appearance, beauty and fashion. Therefore, my research methods include discourse analysis of Soviet magazines[6] and advice literature, as well as twenty-one oral history interviews conducted with women in 2003–4 in Moscow, Saratov and Ufa.[7] My interviewees were born between 1919 and 1947 and were mainly ethnic Russian and Bashkir. During interviews women's experiences of and attitudes towards personal appearance, attractiveness/unattractiveness, clothing practices, fashion, professional dress codes, use of make-up and jewellery were discussed. In most cases, respondents spoke very readily about the period of their lives when they were 'young and beautiful' and showed me many pictures from their younger years.

When I started this research I was repeatedly confronted by a number of common assumptions made by both western and Russian colleagues. These 'common sense' understandings of 'beauty' in the Soviet Union stem primarily from attempts to classify Soviet practices in terms of either a unique 'Soviet' experience, or with reference to 'western' and/or 'traditional' values. Issues of gender, equality, consumption and morality are central to and conceptualised differently in relation to each category. The practices and discourses of village culture, ethnic and religious customs, which the new regime struggled to transform following the revolution, are classified as 'traditional'. 'Traditional' practices are assumed to form part of wider authoritarian forms of social organisation including gender inequality and patriarchal control over female sexuality. The 'Soviet' category encompasses those practices and discourses associated with communist (Bolshevik) ideology, including politics of forced social, gender and ethnic equality. By contrast, discourses and practices associated with urban consumer culture, as well as with rationalised morality (civility) and fashion, are classified as 'western'.[8] 'Western' discourses and practices are also deemed to imply a certain liberalisation of sexual mores alongside a preservation of gender-specific divisions between public and private spheres.[9] Thus it is commonly assumed that:

- Soviet women were 'emancipated' from a need to care overly about their appearance and their femininity. Communist ideology prohibited luxury, and clothes, as well as other consumer goods and beauty products, were in short supply. Therefore, women escaped the powerful consumption discourses of the capitalist west and were not forced to 'dress up' as western women are.

- Soviet people were poor and it was impossible for women to take 'proper' care of themselves and their appearance. Western fashions were a vague but inaccessible ideal.
- Women wanted to preserve a traditionally feminine appearance, but the communist state prioritised people's 'work' qualities and strove to replace traditional 'femininity' with a population of gender non-specific workers.

This chapter questions such assumptions and explores discourses and everyday practices in order to reveal the ways in which women shaped, supported and/or challenged norms of female appearance and beauty in post-war Soviet Russia. While the assumptions outlined above separate and juxtapose 'Soviet', 'western' and 'traditional' practices, the argument which follows will demonstrate that everyday beauty practices are better explained through an analysis of their interdiscoursivity which acknowledges the mixture of practices and discourses which constitute and maintain everyday norms of beauty.

Changes in the 'beauty context'

The beauty discourses and practices which women described to me during interviews were framed by the social, political and economic context as it related to issues of personal hygiene, clothing and fashion. Towards the end of the 1930s women constituted about 40 per cent of the labour force, yet they were also required to be 'feminine' in their looks and behaviour. In contrast to the early 1920s, when women revolutionaries had focused almost solely on questions of functionality, paying little attention to the fit or condition of their clothes, the *kulturnost'* campaign of the 1930s resulted in important changes in beauty discourses. Films, fashion pages and photographs showed women in neat and pretty city clothes and urban women at least were expected to follow suit.[10] As early as 1928, in an article entitled, 'Is it time for workers to start thinking about the art of clothing?', Soviet Minister for Education, Anatolii Lunacharskii, argued: 'We have just overcome a time when ragged clothes were a kind of proletarian uniform . . . nature moves young people to play around a bit with their outfits and to try to accentuate their attractiveness, force and grace.'[11] *Kulturnost'* allowed for significant variations in appearance depending on income and taste. Women of the party and cultural elite (many of them wives of the elite) were expected to have higher incomes and more developed tastes in clothing and accessories.[12] Luxury items like fur coats and cosmetics were advertised on posters and in magazines,[13] yet Soviet interpretations of 'good taste' continued to frown upon 'showing off', luxury and flirtatiousness, maintaining norms of 'modesty' and 'not standing out' for the masses.

Consumer goods and services, from textiles and ready-to-wear clothes to bath houses, were subject to constant shortages. The living standards of the majority of the urban population – overcrowded communal flats and barracks, often lacking running water – made looking after one's body, clothes and shoes particularly difficult. Yet, discourses on hygiene insisted that regular care for skin, hair and clothes was the key to good, healthy looks. Nikolai Semashko, Minister for Health and author of many booklets and brochures about culture and health, insisted: 'Proletarian clothing should be hygienic above all else. Thus, we must fight mercilessly against those bourgeois "fashions" that damage the human organism.'[14] In the 1930s, a range of public services was established, including dressmakers, beauty counters in hairdressing salons and bath houses, and the Moscow house of fashion, opened in 1934.[15] Yet, official discourses on hygiene and natural beauty continued to insist that artificial 'additions' and 'decorations' were extraneous to true beauty. For example, the introduction to a 1950s brochure for beauty counter staff stresses that whilst various forms of cosmetics have been used in the past to mask imperfections, Soviet cosmetics are used to heal the skin.[16]

The Second World War led to a dramatic fall in living standards; however, it also resulted in a certain exposure to external influences. After the war, Soviet officers and soldiers returned home with so-called 'trophies' – clothes, shoes and fashion magazines. One of my respondents explained that in Ufa women used dressmaking patterns taken from German fashion magazines right into the 1960s. Meanwhile, new fashions and notions of beauty arrived as 'friendly imports' from the Baltic republics and the 'socialist countries' of Eastern Europe. Fashions from Riga began appearing in *Zhurnal mod* as early as 1945.[17] International technological advances such as artificial dyes, man-made textiles, hairstyling and cleansing products also impacted significantly on Soviet women's beauty practices. Ideals of beauty began to be equated with these new technologies: several interviewees described perming their hair for the first time during the war as a way of 'becoming beautiful'.

Yet other ideals and aspects of beauty discourses were preserved from the pre-war period. Women were still expected to be neat and modest in their appearance. The word 'fashion' (*moda*) was not used much in women's magazines and was reserved instead for professional publications such as *Zhurnal mod*, which was first published in 1945. Even here, an article about fashion attempted to differentiate between 'bourgeois' and Soviet fashion, claiming that the latter was 'for the people': 'The spirit and character of bourgeois fashion that was and is disfiguring of the human body is alien to us. We have always and will continue to fight unreasonable excess, cheap chic and loud clothes that are so frequent in bourgeois fashion.'[18] Soviet women were not meant to be 'too interested in clothes' and even less so in make-up. Instead they were expected to dress with care, to be able to sew well and to take care of their skin and hair. With this aim, advice on natural skin care and various methods for cleaning and washing clothes were published in women's magazines, books on household management and personal hygiene.[19]

More significant changes came in the late 1950s and early 1960s when 'fashion' was rehabilitated and questions of taste and manners became paramount.[20] In 1958, *Rabotnitsa* published an article by the well-known Soviet writer Lev Kassil who insisted that 'fashions change because wearing the same styles for a long time produces a certain weariness and dulls the faculties of the masses.' Thus, fashion was explained in functional language and could no longer be ignored. Simultaneously, production of ready-to-wear clothes and mass production of new man-made textiles and accessories were rising rapidly.[21] In 1956, sales indexes comparing current sales with 1940 levels, showed a 219 per cent increase in sales of clothing, a 205 per cent increase in sales of shoes, and a massive 939 per cent increase in sales of sewing machines.[22] Unfortunately, this growth in the number of Soviet women owning a sewing machine occurred just as international (western) fashion started to rely heavily on technological advances requiring mass production.

Natural versus artificial beauty

Soviet beauty discourses consistently emphasised the importance of women's bodies looking 'natural'. However, as in contemporary consumer culture, normative definitions of a 'natural look' prized youthful bodies with 'feminine' proportions rather than accepting a true diversity of female forms.[23] Some Soviet magazines and advice books explicitly linked looking 'nice' to looking 'feminine', based on an ideal body type. For example, in 1945 *Zhurnal mod* published an article with pictures illustrating the 'normal body' which suited all styles of dress and two bodies which were named 'problematic'. It is easy to see from the pictures that the ideal was a woman with a slim and defined waist, relatively narrow shoulders and long legs. My interviewees all agreed that this kind of body was 'nice'.

Whereas during the 1940s ideals of female beauty were mainly represented through pictures and films about young sportswomen, in the

1950s this ideal was propagated in more descriptive ways which made a clear link between 'female beauty' and 'femininity'. Kassil's article on fashion, cited above, states: 'The question of feminine behaviour and attire is in no way secondary. Not everything which is fitting for a fine young man [*dobryi molodets*] is equally fitting for a pretty young girl [*krasnaia devitsa*]! Woman's dress should correspond to the forms and lines of the female figure, accentuating her grace, soft lines and movements.'[24] The Russian terms used here conjure up folk images, demonstrating the 'traditional' roots of this discourse.

Advice literature and magazine articles giving beauty advice insisted that women should respect the 'natural' composition of their faces and figures: 'A woman should pay attention to her appearance and wear her hair in a style which suits her face. When choosing a hairstyle pay attention to your features, hair colour, neck.'[25] Ideals of 'natural beauty' also had sexual connotations. The moral health of the 'young natural look' was held up in opposition to the look of the sexually experienced woman. M., who was born in Minsk in 1933, but lived in Moscow at the time of fieldwork for this study, told a story about damaging her 'natural, youthful' beauty:

> When I left school and went to the institute, the girls around me started saying . . . that I should get a perm. All of them had one. So, I decided to do it as well. I went to the first hairdresser but she was very wise and told me: 'You have such nice hair; I'm not going to give you [a perm]. Your hair will lose its curl.' Then I went to another place. They didn't care what they did there. So, she gave me a perm and something very strange replaced the head of a pretty young girl.

Thus, the pressure to look 'natural' can be seen as a hegemonic concept linking Soviet beauty practices with western and traditional (village) practices and playing an important role in women's subordination.

Culture, 'good taste' and fashion

The idea of 'good taste', as mentioned above, was part of the *kulturnost'* campaign. Although this campaign belonged primarily to the pre-war period its rhetoric and goals persisted into the post-war era. This was particularly so in predominantly agricultural and peripheral regions, as well as in those regions where local, ethnic or religious forms of dress prevailed. Yet, the 'cultured' look – neat city dress – was particularly difficult to achieve in the post-war period, when the Soviet economy of shortages was exacerbated by wartime devastation. According to my respondents from agricultural regions, city clothes – skirts, blouses, even school uniforms – were seen as 'luxury clothing', sent by urban relatives or bought in cities on rare shopping excursions. H., who was born in 1927 in a Bashkir village, spoke of a trip to Samara:

> When I was a young girl I so wanted to wear a blouse and skirt, but they were difficult to get . . . Once I went with my grandmothers to Samara and there I immediately bought a blouse and a skirt! I wanted them so much!

On the other hand, Bashkir informants, especially those with higher education, also noted the disappearance of traditional rural beauty norms. While O., who was born in 1935, described the process as a conversion to modernity: 'All of us Bashkirs gradually became more modern', her younger sister, P., who was born four years later, in 1939, alluded to authoritarian pressures: 'National traditions were fast becoming more Russian . . . It seems like they were somehow suppressed by our parents. I may be wrong.'

This may imply that for Bashkir women acquiring a 'modern' look implied the destruction of traditional 'Bashkir' beauty practices. That new styles of clothing are described as 'Russian' rather than 'European', 'western' or 'modern' suggests that changing beauty practices were part of multidimensional and complex processes of modernisation and urbanisation which could also be understood and remembered in ethnic terms. This 'subaltern' interpretation[26] of Soviet beauty practices indicates that women's beauty practices in post-war Soviet Russia cannot simply be categorised as 'Soviet', 'traditional' or 'western'. Other categories for understanding these practices emerge depending, for example, on the socio-economic, cultural or geographical situation of a respondent. Thus, definitions of 'cultured' appearance and dress shifted in the aftermath of the Second World War. The central press reiterated Stalin's theory of Soviet culture as 'socialist in form, national in content' by claiming to include some 'ethnic elements' in modernised (western? Russian? Soviet?) styles of clothing and appearance.[27] This was particularly important in view of critiques of fashion as 'cosmopolitan', which the values of 'national traditions' were deemed to offset. On the other hand, national traditions were not to be overemphasised due to a 'threat of ethnographism, the mechanical repetition of archaic forms, and the mistaken pursuit of pseudo-populism'.[28]

While peripheral areas struggled to introduce 'cultured appearance' to everyday practices, central publications on beauty and appearance focused increasingly on developing aesthetic notions of 'good taste'. The ideal of the 'naturally beautiful female body' was fundamental to this process as were aesthetic arguments regarding matching and complementary styles. Thus, aesthetic, rather than overtly political, arguments were employed to explain the importance of 'avoiding luxury' and 'loud' styles as part of a discourse on 'good taste'. Aesthetic grounds were also used in critiques of 'fashion', in spite of its partial rehabilitation. It was argued that popular styles were not necessarily beautiful.[29]

In the late 1950s and early 1960s, Soviet designers began to copy international fashion trends to produce 'Soviet models' using 'friendly import' publications as a guide. Models in *Rabotnitsa*, for example, sported curly hairstyles and nylon dresses,[30] while advice literature included sections with knitting patterns from the 'countries of popular democracy' and advice on the purchase and care of synthetic garments, alongside the usual sections on dressmaking, laundering, skin and hair care.[31] Thus, Soviet fashion was not in fact separate from international trends. The stories of my informants and family photographs, which they showed me during interviews, support an understanding of fashion as 'global' (or western). Many of them described copying film stars' dresses, particularly those worn by Brigitte Bardot in the film *Babette goes to war*.[32] The competition between 'fashion' and 'good taste' was easily won by the former in the early 1960s. T., who was born in 1946 and was a student at Moscow University in the early 1960s, explained her friends' attitude to clothing: 'We were very upset if we didn't look fashionable.'

Looking 'fashionable' required that women keep abreast of changing styles, spend money and/or time acquiring them and alter their bodies to meet the requirements of each new look. Thus, curly hair required the use of curling irons heated over the open fire, or sleeping on hard rollers. Clothes and accessories defined as 'tasteful' were not always appropriate to women's living and working environments and were frequently introduced as a result of everyday norms, which incorporated various elements of patriarchal (traditional? Soviet? western?) femininity. Understandings of 'good taste' which were internalised by women often made their lives particularly difficult, requiring them to wear nylon stockings in temperatures of minus 20° for example. B., a Communist Party member and headmistress of the village school, born in 1919 into 'a quite cultured family', explained that she always had to have two pairs of shoes with her, one with high heels, so that she could comply with both 'school norms' and 'kolkhoz norms'.

Thus, discourses on 'cultured appearance', 'good taste' and 'fashion' do not support simplistic categorisations of beauty practices as 'Soviet', 'traditional' or 'western'. Western and consumption-oriented ideals were widely disseminated as a result of Soviet authoritarianism and colonial practices of 'teaching culture to the masses'. Meanwhile, practices of 'doing femininity through beauty' maintained 'traditional' patriarchal structures of domination.

Consumption, 'beauty qualifications' and the beauty shift

Naomi Wolf introduced the term 'beauty qualifications', claiming that in contemporary American society women require both professional and 'beauty' qualifications in order to work outside of the home. These qualifications include the special skills required to become 'attractive'.[33] Soviet normative attitudes to beauty in the post-war era also required women to possess certain skills and access particular resources. Throughout this era women had to cope with an 'economy of shortage' and 'making themselves beautiful' demanded a complex combination of scarce state resources and various forms of quasi-private entrepreneurship.[34] Soviet 'beauty qualifications' demanded special skills to navigate complex systems for 'acquiring' goods and services. Managing one's own resources was also important: as in a 'market economy' access to beauty services and products depended greatly on income. C., an engineer and wife of the chief engineer at her factory, had no difficulty accessing dressmaking services in Moscow during the late 1950s: 'When we were working, we could get dresses made at the atelier. It wasn't that expensive and not that many people used it.' However, J., who worked as an accountant in Saratov during this period, said that buying clothes and shoes raised serious financial problems:

> In the fifties shoes and clothes appeared again. That was in 1954, 1955. You could buy things. There was lots in the shops. It was expensive of course. Everything was expensive for us. With old money you could buy sandals for 160 roubles, that was expensive for us. [My salary was] 300 roubles. So we had to pay half a month's wages for a pair of shoes.

Besides income, privileges were another important aspect of social differentiation affecting women's ability to achieve normative beauty. Two respondents with privileged access to goods via workplace distribution explained how important this was for their beauty practices. D., a communication specialist for the Interior Ministry, explained that she had access to cheap, high quality dressmaking services, not available to the general public. V., who worked in a closed military plant in Moscow, explained that many beauty services were offered free of charge at the beauty salon there.

In a situation where goods were scarce, buying and selling privately was a common means both of obtaining beauty products and clothing and of making money through their sale, despite the criminalisation of such activities as 'speculation'. A., from Ufa, explained that in the post-war years she and the women she knew, 'wore whatever we could get. Clothes were partly sewn, partly bought on the black market [*tolchok*].' Such 'speculation' was viewed as necessary for survival, but also as a source of fear and shame. Even now, many women who were young in the 1940s–1950s are reluctant to talk about their 'speculation experience'. E., from Ufa, who was born in a village in Bashkortostan in 1932, began by presenting her knitting as a hobby, and only at the end of the interview admitted that she knitted because she 'needed the money'. Thus, she was able to use her 'beauty skills' in order to gain additional income. In other cases the reverse was true: respondents presented the 'need to be beautiful' as a main reason for seeking new sources of income. M., who was a student in Perm in the 1950s, explained that whilst most of her clothes were handmade, she did not sew them herself, but bought cloth and took it to a dressmaker: 'I gave private lessons from my first year at university. So I was able to have a new dress for every holiday and I was a very fashionable girl.'

Yet, in spite of the importance of money and privileges, women's greatest resource was time. Unlike men, women were considered naturally both able and interested in making their homes beautiful as well as trying to make themselves, their children and even their husbands look nice. One of the most important beauty assets for a woman was to own a sewing machine. Women sewed clothes for themselves and their children, and, sometimes, for their husbands and grandchildren. Girls were taught to sew at the age of 8–10. Exceptions were rare and respondents who had not made their own clothes described this as abnormal. Sometimes in addition to sewing, but rarely as a substitute, women knitted, embroidered and made lace. Friends at work, school or university exchanged tips and shared their expertise. Dressmaking patterns were taken from magazines, copied from friends and relatives and frequently simply made up, based on dresses women had seen in the streets or in films. However, women's sewing and knitting skills were most importantly employed for 'remaking' old clothes. The ability to transform unfashionable, worn-out or hand-me-down clothes into a new piece of clothing for yourself or your children was a source of pride for every woman in the 1930s–1950s, a kind of master's exam for her 'beauty qualification'.

K., from Saratov, who was born in 1932, proudly told of how she remade clothes:

> I made new from old as they say. I remade clothes for the children. I remember one time my neighbour gave me her silk dress. I took it and made a dress for my daughter. She was running around and clamouring, 'look, Aunty, what a nice thing my mother made from trash.' [The neighbour] answered, 'Oh, yes, I know, your mother can do it!' I remade everything. I took an old coat and made a coat for my older daughter, and then, from that, I made one for my younger daughter.

While prolonging the life of clothes was important for family survival, remaking skills were also important to female subjectivity. K. was proud not only because her talents helped her to save on family expenditure, but also because her dressmaking abilities brought her respect. The ability to make nice clothes, seen historically as the most appropriate female craft, demonstrated her 'female virtues' and confirmed her 'normative' femininity. Even in the 1950s–1960s when ready-to-wear clothes started to appear in the shops, knowing how to sew or knit continued to be an important signifier of 'correct' femininity, as many respondents eagerly explained. For example, P. from Ufa, who was born in 1939, said:

> In 1963 when we got married, my husband bought me coffee coloured shoes. They were very nice shoes and they were not expensive. He also bought me a brown velvet dress, but it was too big for me. I altered it completely so it fit me.

Yet, Soviet women, particularly in the post-war period, had to develop very different beauty practices and skills from those which were needed in a traditional society. Rural women migrating to the city found that traditional practices were disrupted and new standards of appearance and means of beauty production developed. They had to adapt to new ways of doing laundry and drying clothes, not in the open air, but in overcrowded communal apartments, as well as adopting city styles of dress and appearance. In the 1940s this usually meant cutting their braids, an experience described by many respondents as the starting point in women's adaptation to city life. However, even in the cities most Soviet women could not count on a developed public service sector, nor on the production of consumer goods such as washing machines or curling tongs. Thus, women paid a high price in terms of their 'beauty shift', something which became a central normative practice in Soviet constructions of femininity.

Respondents called on various discourses and beliefs to explain the 'necessity' of caring for their appearance: 'family and ethnic traditions' of woman's 'need to be beautiful' at least at certain stages in her life; Soviet discourses from the 1930s–1950s on 'cultured appearance'; or the influence of global patterns of consumption from which Soviet women could not be fully separated even by the iron curtain. The 'beauty shift', however, was a common feature of women's stories, running through these various discursive positions and frameworks and one which clearly contradicts some of the assumptions about Soviet women's 'emancipation' from a need to care too much about their appearance.

Beauty and identity – rites of passage to adulthood

In this final section of my chapter I have selected three of my younger respondents whose stories are illustrative of the changes and variations experienced by young women in relation to norms of beauty. Two of these respondents were born in the 1930s and one in the mid-1940s, two are Bashkir and one Russian. However, it is not my intention to argue that their narratives explain the impacts of generation or ethnicity on post-war Soviet beauty norms. Rather, I shall explore the ways in which their narratives concerning norms of 'beauty' illustrate the intersections between 'femininity' and 'tradition', 'modern consumption' and 'Soviet consciousness'.[35]

G. was born in 1935 in a small settlement in West Bashkortostan. Her father was killed in combat during the Second World War. G.'s mother, who had no formal education, raised her four children alone. G. went to the settlement's Bashkir school until the 7th grade, when, as a good pupil and the daughter of a fallen soldier, she was awarded a place at a boarding school in Ufa, officially the best school in Bashkortostan. On finishing school G. went on to study at Ufa Pedagogical Institute. Arriving in the city aged just 14 and as a pupil of an elite city school, she was eager to reproduce dominant discourses on modesty and achievement.

When talking about her clothing and appearance as an adolescent she constantly stressed aspects of 'similarity' and the 'unimportance' of ethnic or social differences. These statements were supported by several other respondents, particularly those born in the 1920s–1930s. G. interprets 'similarity' as a result of poverty, yet still gives it rather positive connotations: 'similarity' encouraged moral behaviour and allowed young people to concern themselves first and foremost with their studies and not with appearance or flirtation: 'There was no immodesty. It was that kind of social environment and that kind of a time . . . If you asked the nationality of people around me, I couldn't tell you. We were all as one.' And yet, she mixes traditional (village patriarchal) and Soviet (communist) definitions of the line between 'normal' and 'deviant' behaviour, offsetting studies (internal beauty) against flirtation (inappropriate sexual behaviour): 'We did not kiss in public. We studied hard. We stood out for achievements in our studies [not for our clothes].' G. clearly opposes the idea that being 'attractive' should be a primary goal for women. Yet, at the same time, she explicitly supports a heteronormative stance, insisting that marriage and children are very important for every woman: 'Women have their duties, men have theirs.'

G. reported that she was most commonly dressed in her school uniform, which she remembered fondly, and that she and the other girls in her class sewed their own dresses during 'vocational' classes, from a single roll of cloth bought by the school. Traditional ethnic styles were viewed positively, but only as a costume for folk dancing classes or as a small 'addition' such as an embroidered pattern. According to G., styles of dress changed in a kind of natural progression – only the 'old generation' (people older than her mother) really continued to wear traditional (ethnic Bashkir) dress, while young people 'automatically' preferred 'modern' ('non-ethnic', western) styles.

Thus, G.'s story can be read as an account of her transition from the village with its traditional rural culture to the urban culture of the city. In many ways her account appears to confirm some of the 'common sense' assumptions about Soviet beauty practices. Yet, these assumptions are also called into question by G., particularly the assumption that 'traditional femininity' was replaced by an androgynous Soviet worker style. G.'s interpretations of 'modesty' show how persistent connotations of patriarchal domination over female sexuality were and that they remained prominent even in the Soviet urban context alongside idealised notions of ethnic and social equality.

P. was born in a Bashkir village in 1939 and came to Ufa aged 18 to study at the Pedagogical Institute. S., whose parents came from Moscow, was born in 1945 just after the end of the war, in a small military settlement in the Far East. Her family moved back to Moscow when she was 6 years old. Like G., P. and S. completed secondary schooling and went on to higher education, at Ufa Pedagogical Institute and Moscow University respectively. All three married and had children soon after graduation. All three women lost their fathers at an early age and both S.'s and P.'s mothers were school teachers. It is not surprising, therefore, that they share similar memories of discovering beauty: a lack of clothes, shoes and textiles dominates their stories.

All three women stressed the importance of education and were good students at school and in higher education. However, unlike G., S. and P. present their experiences in ways which clearly question assumptions that Soviet women were either 'liberated' from a need to pay attention to their appearance, or that they were too impoverished to do so. Both women made it clear that 'beauty' was important to them and to their contemporaries and offered various examples of the efforts 'girls' went to in order to look nice. P., for example, demonstrated what might be viewed as a 'western' attitude to consumption when she explained how important it was for her to buy new clothes: she and her friend always tried to eat lunch at home in order to save their student grants for clothes. She changed her hair colour so frequently as a student that in any one year it ranged from blonde to black, and recalled how young women tried to wear stylish clothes, for example very tight skirts, in the fashion of the styliagi.[36]

When S. had to choose which secondary school to attend, she deliberately chose one that offered a special course on sewing and she was very proud of the pretty dresses she made. In this her narrative mixed the village tradition of homemade clothes with the 'modern', urban demands for consumption and 'fashionable' appearances. She stressed that 'girls always tried hard to look nice', making time, for example, to check their looks, apply powder or lipstick, and fix their hair in the toilets between lessons.

Unlike G., S. and P. did not subscribe to a norm of 'sameness', choosing to 'stand out' and emphasise their unique look instead. However, they presented this as consistent with dominant Soviet discourses on 'modesty' and 'egalitarianism'. For example, during S.'s interview she said the following about school parties:

> When I was at another school, in the 7th grade, you were allowed to wear your holiday dress for school parties. The girls tried to look pretty. They tried not to wear the same dress to the next party. It was nothing very special, some had clothes, others didn't. But at the new school I went to after 7th grade, we were only allowed to wear a white apron. Right up until 11th grade. And, I would say, maybe, maybe it was a good thing. Not everybody has the same opportunities. It's true. But, the girls tried hard. They tried in spite of everything . . . They tried to make their skirts fluff out more. Or they changed their collars. You were supposed to have an ordinary collar in school. But, I made mine from poplin. So, first you wore one collar, then, the other one.

The women's descriptions of their personal circumstances and clothing habits reveal other differences in experience, particularly between P. and S. P. described her childhood in a Bashkir kolkhoz as characterised by equality of hardship. In fact, she pointed out that she had enjoyed certain advantages because her mother was educated. She was the only child in the whole village who wore a 'real school uniform' which had been sent to her by distant relatives in Kazan. Both P. and G. felt that moving to Ufa, a 'big' city, capital of the republic, to study meant they became someone with a future, distinguished by their education.

By comparison, S. experienced far less dramatic upward social mobility. She too presented her life as 'difficult' where the pursuit of 'beauty' was concerned. The room her family lived in was so small that for several years it was impossible for them to own a sewing machine, it was difficult to buy clothes and, frequently, even cloth. However, she mentioned a number of dresses and even a coat, which her family had been able to buy for her when she was 9 years old, at a state-owned dressmakers. In order to dress nicely and fashionably, S. used her beauty skills and paid careful attention to her appearance. Her beauty shift included dressmaking, queuing to buy clothes and cloth, and hunting for both goods and fashion magazines, in particularly the Estonian *Siluett*: 'To buy one you had to run from one kiosk to another.' Nonetheless, S. claimed that her look was 'modest' when compared to others, especially female students from the much more 'fashionable' department of philology. These girls were considered particularly fashionable, not least because they were able to buy cast-offs from foreign students in their department.

S. and P. also had rather different attitudes to the 'beauty practices' of their youth, as well as to beauty as a source of identity. P. tended to enjoy her achievements, framing experimentation with personal appearance in terms of culture, education and urban lifestyles. She argued that she was changing along with others around her, insisting that even when she returned to her village for a holiday there were mostly students around and stressing that she belonged to a first generation of people with higher education in her region and ethnic group. S., on the other hand, tended to stress the 'efforts' she made to become beautiful rather than the result. Yet, both women sought to represent 'what people did in our time', rather than just their personal attitudes. Thus, it was 'time' and 'people' rather than individuals which changed. For S. time was mostly static for 'girls like her', whilst for P. the times were dynamic and full of political changes for Bashkir youth.

Yet, it was P. who questioned the 'positive victory' of modern (western) dress over ethnic (traditional) styles and the idea of a woman's right to express her sexuality through her appearance without losing her 'morality'. P. did not limit herself to a view of traditional (ethnic) culture as unimportant, but questioned Soviet modernisation from the 'subaltern' position discussed earlier. Her acceptance of modern looks during her own youth, seen, for example, in her experiments with dying her hair, was reversed when she discussed her struggle as a school teacher to stop girls wearing make-up to school. She explained how she urged her pupils to wash off their make-up, insisting that there was no need for them to cover their young faces with cosmetics, because one day somebody 'would love them and they would have a family'. In this context then, she stressed traditional (village) understandings of chastity and heteronormativity as represented through girls' 'natural' appearance. Thus, for P., 'standing out' and 'being attractive' was only acceptable when this 'individualisation of beauty' did not threaten broader patriarchal constructions of heteronormativity or damage traditional village morality regarding control over female sexuality. Thus, the 'normative' concepts of femininity which emerge from an analysis of these women's remembered practices demonstrate the complex interplay and mutual reinforcement between 'traditional', 'modern' and 'Soviet' frameworks for understanding women's beauty practices in post-war Soviet Russia.

Conclusions

The material presented here demonstrates that beauty practices in post-war Soviet Russia incorporated a complex combination of elements. Women's beauty practices drew together components which could be attributed to all three norms: western (modern, urban, consumption-oriented), traditional (patriarchal, village) and Soviet (egalitarian, communist, authoritarian). The resulting normative understandings of beauty were not made up of separate elements, but acted as a system of rules and meanings that were internalised and resisted at the same time.

Many modern attitudes to beauty (including personal hygiene and education of taste) were taken from western social and political agendas and incorporated into Soviet discourses about female beauty. These attitudes symbolised ideals of modernisation and progress, yet they were remembered by many respondents as 'genuinely' Soviet norms of new 'cultured' appearance and body care. Yet, this modernisation/westernisation/Sovietisation was also questioned and, sometimes, reinterpreted as a continuation of pre-Soviet colonial politics towards periphery and non-Russian ethnic groups.

Interactions between beauty discourses and beauty practices were particularly complex. On the one hand, particularly in the late 1950s, beauty discourses presented 'western' as the opposite of 'Soviet', particularly with regard to 'modesty' versus 'standing out in the crowd'. On the other hand, this opposition did not often lead to open confrontation at the level of women's everyday practices. On the contrary, discourses on 'good taste' required that women employ multiple tactics in order to distinguish themselves and reappropriate the beauty space (by saving for a 'special' dress or making an 'exclusive' dress at school). Meanwhile 'western' fashion elements (such as Babette's fringe and skirt) enjoyed huge popularity throughout the Soviet Union. Moreover, in the context of a shortage economy, the fact that women had widespread information about 'western' beauty styles and artefacts (such as make-up and nylon stockings) meant that, far from being liberated from the norms of consumption, Soviet women invested enormous efforts and made great sacrifices in order to achieve norms of 'good taste' and 'aesthetic appearance'.

The huge efforts which women put into their 'beauty shift' reinforced traditional (patriarchal) norms, according to which women were expected to constantly improve their 'beauty qualifications'. This 'beauty shift' in addition to their paid employment and in the context of constant shortages of consumer goods, contributed to women's exhaustion. Yet, many women also regarded their beauty skills (sewing, knitting, hairstyling skills etc.) as assets which bolstered their self-esteem and their social position. Thus, the social meanings attributed to a woman's ability to make fashionable (including western-style) dresses and improve her appearance with complicated hairstyles, were comparable with traditional (village) norms concerning woman's personal skills and practices and their use in a patriarchal context. And yet, contrary to assumptions about the inaccessibility of western standards to Soviet women, the results of women's efforts were frequently that their hairstyles, hats and dresses looked very similar to those worn by women in the west.

Thus, in post-war Soviet Russia personal beauty skills tended to reinforce 'western' norms of individuality and fashion rather than the 'Soviet' or 'village' interpretations of modesty as 'not standing out'. Also, despite the importance of 'homemade' beauty, beauty practices were nonetheless linked with money and consumption to a certain extent and so might be seen as an everyday subversion of Soviet norms. However, even whilst everyday beauty practices seem to have gone a long way towards overcoming Soviet discourses on 'modesty' and 'similarity', my interviews with women living in three different cities of contemporary Russia show that some 'Soviet' constructions about beauty and appearance were not seriously challenged and were frequently reproduced in women's representations of 'normative femininity'. Thus, 'doing femininity' in post-war Soviet Russia required knowledge of multiple norms, codes and techniques of beauty and cannot be classified according to any one set of norms and values.

Notes

1. M. Buckley, *Women and Ideology in the Soviet Union* (Hemel Hempstead: Harvester Wheatsheaf, 1989); W. Goldman, *Women, the State and Revolution: Soviet Family Policy and Social Life, 1917–1936* (Cambridge: Cambridge University Press, 1993); G. Lapidus, 'Women in Soviet Society', in D. Hoffman (ed.), *Stalinism: the Essential Readings* (Malden, MA: Blackwell Publishing, 2003); B. Engel, *Women in Russia 1700–2000* (Cambridge: Cambridge University Press, 2004).
2. C. Kelly, *Refining Russia: Advice Literature, Polite Culture, and Gender from Catherine to Yeltsin* (Oxford: Oxford University Press, 2001); N. Lebina and A. Chistikov, *Obivatel i reformy: kartini povsednevnoi zhizni gorozhan v godi NEPa i Khrushchevskogo desiatiletiia* (St Petersburg: Dmitriy Bulanin Publishing House, 2003).
3. S. Bartky, 'Foucault, Femininity, and the Modernization of Patriarchal Power', in R. Weitz (ed.), *The Politics of Women's Bodies: Sexuality, Appearance and Behaviour* (Oxford: Oxford University Press, 1998); S. Bordo, *Unbearable Weight: Feminism, Western Culture and the Body* (Berkeley: University of California Press, 1993); N. Wolf, *The Beauty Myth: How Images of Beauty are Used Against Women* (New York: William Morrow and Co, 1991).
4. H. Medick, 'Missionaries in the Rowboat? Ethnological Ways of Knowing as a Challenge to Social History', in A. Ludtke (ed.), *The History of Everyday Life: Reconstructing Historical Experiences and Ways of Life* (Princeton: Princeton University Press, 1995); M. De Certeau, 'Walking in the City', in G. Ward (ed.), *The De Certeau Reader* (Oxford: Blackwell Publishers, 2000); N. Kozlova, *Sovetskie liudi: stseni iz istorii* (Moscow: Evropa, 2005).
5. H. Garfinkel, *Studies in Ethnomethodology* (Cambridge and Oxford: Polity Press and Blackwell Publishers, 1984).
6. The magazines analysed include: *Rabotnitsa*, 1930s–1960s; *Zdorov'e*, 1955–1960s; *Zhurnal mod*, 1945–1950s; *Zhenskii zhurnal*, late 1920s; and fashion pages from Soviet women's magazines published in Bashkir and Tatar languages.
7. The first stage of fieldwork outside of Moscow was realised thanks to a travel grant from the Moscow Office of the Kennan Institute for Advanced Russian Studies.
8. Europeanised Russian city culture of the late imperial period is incorporated into this category which is politically, economically and culturally, rather than geographically defined.
9. This interpretation of 'western' clearly overlooks diversities within west European contexts, but is implied by distinctions which are frequently alluded to between Russia on the one hand, and 'western liberal tradition', 'western consumer culture', 'gender divisions between public and private spheres corresponding to modernity' and 'western modernity' on the other – see, for

example, D. Hoffman, 'European Modernity and Soviet Socialism', in David Hoffman and Yanni Kotsonis (eds), *Russian Modernity: Politics, Knowledge, Practices* (Basingstoke: Palgrave Macmillan, 2000); M. Liljeström, 'Knowledge and Otherness: Russian Women as Doubled Others', in Ildikó Asztaloz Morell and Helene Carlbäck (eds), *Gender Transitions in Russia and Eastern Europe* (Eslöv: Forlags ab Gondolin, 2005); S. Damkjaer, 'The Body and Cultural Transition in Russia', in Mette Bryld and Erik Kulavig (eds), *Soviet Civilization Between Past and Present* (Odense: Odense University Press, 1998) and Kelly (2001).

10. According to Kelly and Volkov, *kulturnost'* politics 'represented a Soviet variation of the process described in Norbert Elias' classic analysis, "The Civilising Process" '. C. Kelly, and V. Volkov, 'Directed Desires: *Kulturnost'* and Consumption', in Catriona Kelly and David Shepherd (eds), *Constructing Russian Culture in the Age of Revolution: 1881–1940* (Oxford: Oxford University Press, 1998). See also, T. Dashkova, 'Visual'nie reprezentatsii zhenskogo tela v sovetskoi massovoi kul'ture 1930kh', *Logos*, 11/12 (1999): 131–55. On the importance of clothes for creating a 'cultured look' and the links between correct appearance and 'correct understanding' of Soviet ideology see Kozlova (2005), pp. 215–17.
11. A. Lunacharskii, 'Svoevremenno li podumat' rabochemu ob iskusstve odevat'sia?', *Iskusstvo odevat'sia*, 1 (1928): 6.
12. S. Fitzpatrick, *Everyday Stalinism: Ordinary Life in Extraordinary Times* (Oxford: Oxford University Press, 1999), pp. 79–80.
13. See for example the advertisement with the slogan 'Ask anywhere for compact powder and Glavparfumer's lipstick', *Ogonek*, 2 (1939), back page; or A. Koltunovich and L. Zolotoravskyi's 1937 poster 'A range of squirrel mantles is available in soiuzmekhtorg shops', http://www.davno.ru/posters/collections/ads/poster-11.html.
14. N. Semashko, *Puti sovetskoi fizkul'tury* (Moscow: Izdatel'stvo sovetskoi fizkul'tury, 1926), p. 26.
15. S. Zhuravlev and Iu Gronov, 'Krasota pod kontrolen gosudarstva: osobennosti i etapy stznovleniia sovetskoi mody', *The Soviet and Post-Soviet Review*, 32, 1 (2005): 1–92, p. 17.
16. D. Lass and M. Polikarpova, *Ukhod za kozhei litsa* (Moskva: Izdatel'stvo ministerstva kommunalnogo khoziaistva RSFSR, 1954), p. 3.
17. 'Rizhskie modeli', *Zhurnal mod*, 1 (1945): 5.
18. S.Temerin 'Nazionalnye traditsii i sovremennii kostium', *Zhurnal mod*, 2 (1954): 1.
19. M. P. Dem'anovich 'Ukhod za volosami', *Rabotnitsa*, 4 (1949), back page; Nazarova 'Kak ukhazhivat' za litsom', *Rabotnitsa*, 1 (1949), back page, 'Udalenie piaten', 'Chistka tsvetnikh plat'ev', 'Chistka i glazhenie kruzhev', *Rabotnitsa*, 3 (1949), back page; *Molodoi khoziaike* (Saratov: Saratovskoe knizhnoe izdatel'stvo, 1958); *Domovodstvo*, 2nd edition (Moskva: Gosudarstvennoe izdatel'stvo selskokhoziaistvennoi literatury, 1958); M. D. Makover, *Ukhod za zhilishchem, odezhdoi i obuv'iu. Sovety molodoi sem'e* (Moskva: Sovetskaia Rossiia, 1960).
20. See Kelly (2001), p. 318 on the growing number of behaviour manuals.
21. *SSSR v tsifrakh, 1967* (Moscow: Statistika, 1968), p. 144.
22. E. Zubkova, L. Kosheleva, and G. Kuznetsova (eds), *Sovetskaia zhizn' 1945–1953* (Moscow: ROSSPEN, 2003), p. 98.

23. L. Frost, *Young Women and the Body: a Feminist Sociology* (Basingstoke and New York: Palgrave Macmillan, 2001), p. 78.
24. L. Kassil, 'Devushka so vkusom', *Rabotnitsa*, 4 (1958): 27.
25. M. Tikhonov, 'Pricheski', *Rabotnitsa*, 3 (1955), back page.
26. G. Spivak, 'Can the Subaltern Speak?', in C. Nelson and L. Grossberg (eds), *Marxism and the Interpretation of Culture* (Basingstoke: Macmillan Education, 1988), p. 275.
27. See for example 'Modeli obshchesoiuznogo doma modelei', *Rabotnitsa*, 2 (1952): 31; 'Po narodnim motivam', *Zhurnal mod*, 1 (1949): 22–3. The same trends could be seen in the fashion pages of the Bashkir women's magazine *Bashkortostan kyzi*, 3 (1968): 24.
28. S. Temerin 'Natsionalnye traditsii i sovremennii kostium', *Zhurnal mod*, 2 (1954): 1.
29. Kassil (1958), p. 27.
30. A. Blank, 'Vashe novoe plat'e', *Rabotnitsa*, 5 (1957): 24–5; 'Modeli obshchesoiuznogo doma modelei', *Rabotnitsa*, 6 (1958), fashion page.
31. *Kniga poleznikh sovetov* (Minsk: Gosudarstvennoe izdatel'stvo Belorusskoi SSR, 1961), pp. 346–51, 204–5, 731.
32. *Babetta idet na voinu* was a short version of the 1959 French film *Babette s'en va-t-en guerre*.
33. Wolf (1991).
34. Osokina's study of the pre-war period has shown similar forces at play. E. Osokina, *Za fasadom 'stalinskogo izobiliia'. Raspredelenie i rynok v snabzhenii naseleniia v gody industrializatsii, 1927–1941* (Moscow: ROSSPEN, 1997), pp. 154, 235–37.
35. For further discussion of intersectionality see D. Staunes, 'Where Have All the Subjects Gone? Bringing Together the Concepts of Intersectionality and Subjectification', *NORA*, 2 (2003): 100–10 and A. Brah, *Cartographies of Diaspora. Contesting Identities* (London and New York: Routledge, 1996), pp. 14–21.
36. The 'styliagi', young people who followed 'style' in their clothing and appearance, were defined as 'youth-as-victims-of-western-influence' by dominant discourses and as such were viewed as evidence of westernisation, H. Pilkington, *Russia's Youth and its Culture: a Nation's Constructors Reconstructed* (London and New York: Routledge, 1994), pp. 68–9.

2
How to Combine Motherhood and Wage Labour: Hungarian Expert Perspectives During the 1960s[1]

Ildikó Asztalos Morell

Following the 1956 revolt in Hungary, the Stalinist doctrine on women's emancipation was reframed in the context of a wider process of 'consolidation' of political, social and economic relations. Post-Stalinist rhetoric and practice questioned the suitability of women's bodies, with their reproductive functions, for 'masculine' work and argued that women's role in society should be based on 'realistic' assessments of gender difference. Women were to be offered 'suitable jobs' which could accommodate their family roles and maternal duties. Simultaneously, the family's responsibility for providing childcare during infancy was reappraised, reinforcing demands on women's time and energy.

This chapter will explore the ways in which labour market experts promoted this alternative rhetoric and practice through debate on the development of 'suitable jobs' for women. The arguments put forward here are based on an analysis of eight articles published in *Munkaügyi Szemle* (Labour Review) between 1960 and 1968.[2] The journal was the publication of the Research Group of the Ministry of Labour and as such was a key forum for labour market experts to influence the development and implementation of government policies. The views of this group impacted on policy-making processes and thus contributed directly to gendered constructions of the relationship between reproductive and productive roles and to renegotiations of the terms of women's mobilisation as a labour reserve during the post-Stalinist period. As such they were part of the hegemonic discourse of state socialism.

The analysis presented here focuses on these articles as expressions of a power struggle for control of the redistribution of societal resources, be they resources for industrialisation, labour mobilisation or for the expansion of welfare institutions. In more abstract terms, these experts played a key role in the struggle to produce 'winning' definitions of reality, and to determine the ways in which women's desired and perceived societal roles would be seen in the context of industrialisation and labour mobilisation. These experts played their part in the realisation of state development policies and ideological goals by formulating feasible ways of implementing them at the shopfloor level.

All articles dealing with the mobilisation of female labour published during the period under review and in the selected journals were analysed using qualitative methods of content analysis.[3] Firstly, central themes were identified in the articles and then categories of meaning were developed to code key arguments for or against women's mobilisation. These categories and themes were analysed in relation to the key groups of actors identified within the texts. The articles were seen as the experts' interpretations of the views of managers and male workers on the one hand, and of the aims of the political economic elites on the other, as expressed in the official rhetoric of emancipation. Reflections on the views and experiences of women workers themselves were largely absent.

Labour market experts as mediators of the gender contract

The labour market experts who authored these articles were tasked with analysing conflicts at the shopfloor level and formulating policy recommendations in line with the ideological goals of the state. As such they occupied an intermediary position providing a link between state-led ideology and policy-making on the one hand, and shopfloor experiences on the other, the latter being characterised by conflict between ideological goals, managerial concerns and resistance from male workers.[4] Yet, these experts were neither fully co-opted into the political rhetoric of the day, nor directly involved in the day-to-day practices of policy implementation. Able to legitimise their perspectives by referring to 'scientific' analyses, they claimed detachment from both the teleological elite and the managerial technocracy.[5] Nonetheless, the debates analysed here developed at a time when power was shifting towards the technocratic elite, and ideological rhetoric was open to question and revision. In this context, labour market experts allied themselves with the technocracy in discussions of economic reform.[6]

With regard to gender, the views of labour market experts both reflected existing dominant understandings of productive and reproductive roles and contributed to their re-evaluation. These experts made recommendations on how to resolve the challenges brought about by an influx of women, with their reproductive roles and duties, into a labour force organised on the assumption of the male worker, free from reproductive duties, as the norm.[7] They responded to the concerns of male managers and male workers who focused on the difficulties arising from attempts to integrate women into the labour force. By contrast, the views of women, either as workers or as experts, were notable for their absence from these debates.[8] Thus, the shifting balance of power during the 1960s, which gave the technocratic elite increasing influence in policy-making, did not result in greater representation for women. Women were poorly represented or absent from areas with real political influence (such as the Central Committee)[9] meaning not only a lack of just representation, but also that women's interests and issues were not properly expressed or recognised.[10] Women's issues were defined from a male perspective, through the eyes and based on the interests of men as workers, managers, experts or party executives. This stands in stark contrast to women's allegedly privileged position under state socialism and the perception of women and the socialist state as allies.

The mobilisation of women's labour helped to liberate women from economic dependence on men in the private sphere, yet exposed them to inequalities in the public sphere, such as gendered labour segregation and dependence on welfare institutions.[11] Gender inequalities intersect with other structural inequalities, and the reformulation of the gender contract occurring in Hungary in the late 1950s and early 1960s mirrored changing configurations of economic and political power[12] as the command economy gave way to a modified plan economy. This meant both that power was increasingly concentrated in the hands of the technocratic elites and that compromises had to be struck with the working class and the peasantry.[13] Thus, the expert articles analysed here reflect both class and gender conflict which arose in response to the influx of female labour into previously male-dominated areas of the labour market, a process driven by the ideological goals of the cadre elite. In their writings, labour market experts reflect upon, and construct resolutions to this conflict, based on what Goven has termed the reframing and essentialising of the gender contract in the context of a transition from private to public patriarchy.[14] These expert discourses formed part of the ongoing struggle to define reality and to gain influence over policy-making and implementation. Whilst they were ideologically critical, of the Stalinist rhetoric of emancipation, for example, and its emphasis on women's mobilisation into the labour force, these experts were themselves engaged in the formulation of ideology, in this case through the development of alternative rhetoric on women's integration into the public economy. The lack of women's voices in this process is symptomatic of the transition from private to public patriarchy which characterised this process of mobilising women for production. Unfortunately, as a result of the gender bias in available sources, this chapter is not able to redress this balance by giving voice to women's experiences and opinions, exploring women's perception of these debates and their impacts on the realities of women's lives. This will remain an important agenda for future research.

Labour conflict and the post-Stalinist gender regime

The post-1956 regime sought to consolidate power by balancing policies aimed at achieving an agenda of socio-economic development based on the ideologies of state socialism, with policies aimed at containing popular resistance to this agenda. The latter goal aimed primarily at minimising social unrest which was often an expression of both socio-economic discontent and dissatisfaction with policies and practices relating to gender.[15] Pittaway's study of labour conflict, for example, documents male factory workers' resistance to women's entry into male-dominated working environments during the early 1950s. Despite generational and regional conflicts of interest which divided male workers in other contexts,[16] they united against the state-sponsored intrusion of women into these occupations: 'Gendered notions of hierarchy were not merely the exclusive province of the skilled elite but were also to some extent shared by all male workers.'[17] In response, many managers either adapted their efforts to integrate women into the workforce in order to accommodate male opposition, or gave up such attempts altogether. In the period before 1956, other managers and newly recruited women found support amongst party propagandists in refusing to bow to such opposition. However, as Pittaway has highlighted, managing gender-based unrest was integral to containing social and economic unrest. The solutions put forward by the post-1956 regime indicated a shift in gendered perspectives in terms of ideology relating to the spheres of both production and reproduction.

Women's labour mobilisation was still perceived as necessary, but began to be reframed in a gendered discourse of 'suitability'. Whilst officially a discourse of equality still prevailed, a new ideal, or 'secondary discourse', emerged emphasising the primacy of 'naturalised sexual differences'.[18] In this context, women's labour force participation was viewed as inextricably bound up with and defined by their reproductive responsibilities. This was simply considered a matter of 'reality'.[19] Therefore, it was argued, women's integration into paid labour must be enhanced in ways that would not damage their ability to combine paid labour with reproductive duties.[20]

Simultaneously, increasing concern about declining birth rates was voiced as part of the 'demographic debate'.[21] While the ban on abortions secured high birth rates during the Stalinist period, these fell in the early 1960s to Hungary's lowest ever levels.[22] The problems caused by the conflicting demands placed on women as mothers and as workers were blamed, stimulating urgent debate and calls for new solutions to be found.[23] Anomalies and pressures related to women's working lives were to be tackled in the hope that women would be more willing to become mothers and to have larger families as a result.

Efforts made during the 1950s to encourage women to enter male-dominated areas, such as tractor driving, were criticised in the 1960s as examples of dangerous excess.[24] According to the new doctrine of the 1960s, women were only to be recruited to 'male' jobs after careful evaluation had established that these jobs were 'suitable'. Protective legislation was revised in 1966 so that women could be banned from jobs evaluated as 'unsuitable'. These laws were based on essentialist definitions of women's bodies, where reproductive functions and physical strength (or rather physical weakness) were central. Beyond a core group of occupations from which women were universally banned, however, the new laws delegated decisions on evaluation to the workplace. In practice, the decentralised decision-making process was used locally to prevent a threat to 'male' occupations from a possible influx of female labour.[25] In agriculture, for example, recruitment of women to many newly mechanised occupations effectively stopped.[26]

While protective legislation banning women from certain occupations sanctioned a negative relationship between women's reproductive roles and wage labour as mutually exclusive, positive sanctioning of women's reproductive rights aimed to enable women to combine their roles in reproduction and production. In the late 1950s and early 1960s the benefits available to women in relation to their reproductive and caring roles were extended: unpaid maternity leave was lengthened to 20 weeks; women gained the right to take leave in order to care for sick children; and the need for additional daycare facilities was recognised. The new gender regime was epitomised by the introduction of the childcare subsidy in 1967. This meant that mothers of children up to 3 years of age could choose between paid full-time motherhood and wage labour. The allowance was initially restricted to working mothers and provided approximately 50 per cent of a woman's previous wage.[27] The childcare subsidy implied a re-evaluation of women's maternal roles and a shift away from workplace nurseries and towards the family as primary childcare provider during infancy. The plan (which was gradually realised) was that nurseries for young children should be moved from the factory to residential neighbourhoods and places would not expand substantially, whilst kindergartens for children over 3 years old would expand to provide accommodation for all children.

The discourse on suitable jobs for women and the regendering of the labour force

From rhetoric to practice: transforming the gender contract in the context of economic reform

Only one of the eight articles analysed focused specifically on the issue of women's equality in the labour force. Whilst this article argued that young women should be taught the importance of 'preparing themselves to become working members of society',[28] the other seven focused primarily on assessing the feasibility of translating a rhetoric of equality into practice, arguing: 'Real equality can only be reached through full participation, the fullness of which is naturally to be interpreted "realistically", in the societal division of labour.'[29]

During the early 1960s debates on economic reform produced a split between discourses based on the assumption of a resource-limited command economy[30] and those which took a more reform-minded approach. Proponents of the former argued that the economy's labour shortage could only be resolved by expanding the labour force, which would in turn stimulate economic growth. Since, by the 1960s, male labour reserves were close to exhaustion, women were the only available resource. Thus, it was argued that, 'the objective need of the national economy necessarily demands increased rates of female economic activity.'[31] However, there was a mismatch between this view of women as a key labour reserve and the profile of labour shortages, which were concentrated in branches of heavy industry employing predominantly male labour. In other words, the demand for labour was highest in traditionally male occupations: typically low skill, heavy physical jobs, or skilled technical jobs, where women were traditionally not employed. Attempts to integrate newly mobilised women into these areas, therefore, implied a significant challenge to the prevailing gender segregation of labour.

From within a perspective based fundamentally on preserving the planned command economy, two alternative approaches emerged. Proponents of the first argued that the shortage of male labour could be eased by redefining the 'gender' of occupations. Women could not be 'spontaneously' integrated into previously male-dominated areas due to well-documented opposition from both managers and male workers.[32] Instead systematic political and economic pressure would need to be brought to bear and occupations would need to be 'regendered' by managing women's entry to specific areas of the economy:

> If female labour reserves are used properly, for example by means of regrouping workers within the existing labour force, even those occupations which can only be performed by men, could be filled. The question is, whether there are still sizeable labour areas to be found (beyond those labour areas which are already highly feminised) where women could be employed.[33]

Supporters of the second approach argued for gendered development strategies. Thus it was suggested that strategies of economic development should be adjusted to suit the features, and in particular the gender, of the available labour force. Experts argued that the development of the industrial structure itself could be modified in order to take account of the fact that available reserves of new labour were predominantly female. Instead of regendering existing occupations, this would imply, 'the gradual transformation of the industrial structure and the creation of such workplaces, which could employ primarily women.'[34] Nonetheless, the proposed development strategies continued to prioritise male employment. In industrial regions, where there were clear shortages of male labour, new investments should be made in 'women's' branches of industry, yet in agricultural areas, with male labour reserves, investments should prioritise 'male' branches:

> In industrial counties the primary goal should be to increase female labour, and to invest only in a very limited manner in branches requiring additional male labour. If such investments are nonetheless demanded in order better to exploit natural resources, transfers of labour between suitable branches and regions ought to be planned in advance . . . In contrast, in predominantly agricultural counties, strategies for industrial development should aim to increase suitable branches both for women and for men . . . due to the anticipated release of excess male labour from agriculture.[35]

In contrast to these approaches, each of which assumed the basis of a command economy, an alternative position emerged, emphasising the need to increase efficiency and taking a critical view of the mobilisation of female labour per se. This emerging alternative discourse of 'rational labour-use' questioned the feasibility of labour policy based on continuous expansion of the labour force. The objections of these experts were based, at least in part, on a critique of policies aiming to maximise female employment: 'Increasing women's labour force participation per se may not even be economically feasible.'[36] Increased employment of women was criticised in terms of socio-economic feasibility and rationale. Experts questioned the ratio of cost, in terms of the need to expand the service sector in order to replace women's domestic labour, set against the expected surplus value created by women in the labour force:

> The economic costs of the further incorporation of women are sizeable due to the expense of developing childcare institutions. Furthermore, a part of the potential labour force to be mobilised will be consumed by new staffing requirements (childcare personnel, catering personnel, etc.) created by employing women.[37]

Another critique of the command economy focused on strategies of human resource management, which it was argued ought to balance principles of economic planning and voluntarism: 'The reproduction and organisation of a labour force that fulfils society's requirements should evolve by means of wide-ranging complex operations which nonetheless should be the outcome of the conscious acts of individuals based on free choice.'[38] In the same vein, it was argued that local labour force requirements and the principle of voluntarism, rather than a drive to fulfil central quotas, should guide the process of women's integration into the labour force. This argument is in line with the rhetoric of the 1968 reforms, which sought to devolve decisions about increasing the employment of female labour to the level of the enterprise:

> This will offer a mechanism for regulating [women's employment], which can meet two key requirements: women's protection must be a first priority in areas where it is needed, however, there should be no unjustified barriers to the expansion of women's employment. Instead, this mechanism should be flexible enough to adapt to local conditions, technological developments, and shifts in working conditions. In principle, the mechanism gives enterprises control over such decisions. . . . While . . . Ministry of Labour guidelines offer direction, this strengthens the influence of enterprise economic managers and social organisations.[39]

This change did not signal the end of protective legislation. Rather it meant bringing this legislation in line with the principles of the anticipated economic reforms by devolving decision-making to enterprise and shopfloor levels. This strengthened the position of management and (male) workers in defining the terms of women's inclusion.[40]

Thus, during the 1960s two discourses ran in parallel: one arguing for the mobilisation of female labour reserves in various forms, the other calling for alternative approaches including the rationalisation of labour and the devolution of planning. Common to both was the unproblematised association of caring roles with women. The question of whether women's mobilisation was feasible or not, was assumed to revolve around the development of institutional alternatives to women's childcare duties, rather than any challenging of essentialist assumptions about gender roles and responsibilities.

Assessing resistance to women's integration into the labour force

The dual intentions of government regulations – to enhance women's employment in suitable areas, while prohibiting it in 'dangerous' ones – met with dual obstacles at the enterprise level. Enterprises suffering acute labour shortage were eager to recruit and ignored restrictions on women's employment in unsuitable jobs:

> The implementation of legal provisions and protective regulations justly limiting women's physical burden can cause difficulties, especially in old and small workshops, which do not have the equipment and simple machinery required to ease heavy physical labour and for moving goods around . . . It has been impossible to enforce the restriction on women lifting loads of over 20 kilograms, despite various attempts.[41]

Other obstacles worked in the opposite direction, mitigating against an increase in women's employment. In the first instance, managers were to identify suitable jobs where women could be employed: 'The increasing demand for male labour in the workshops was (and still is being) solved by internal regroupings. Men working in jobs suitable for women were replaced by women. The male labour released in this way has been made available to new workshops.'[42]

At this stage, problems revolved around how to define which jobs might be regendered in this way. At the next stage, however, where plans were to be implemented, underlying problems of a more pragmatic nature, including opposition from male workers and managers, surfaced:

> Inappropriate attitudes have to be overcome amongst both women and working men, and above all amongst managers in charge of production . . . [Women's behaviour] gives ground for opposition to increasing women's employment in the workshops. Therefore, managers' preference for getting rid of women who cause such problems can be understood, although it is not approved of.[43]

To allay various concerns, labour experts argued for a 'realistic' position on women's mobilisation and integration into the labour force based on shopfloor experience. The articles analysed here address this issue firstly through discussion of women's alleged characteristics, secondly from a management perspective, and finally, from the perspective of male workers. Each of these aspects of the debate is discussed in more detail below.

Problematising women as workers

One way of explaining resistance to the employment of women in male-dominated areas was by referring to allegedly female qualities and characteristics, which made women's employment problematic. Szoboszlai states that, 'in many factories there is an aversion to employing women. They are not happy to employ women. Instead the factories insist that it is necessary to employ men.'[44] He goes on to call for discussion of the 'real' reasons for this opposition, searching for the reasons in generalising characterisations of women's potential in the workforce. The features discussed by experts can be grouped into four categories: biologically determined characteristics, both physiological and psychological; women's lack of training and skills; characteristics relating to women's societal roles; and finally women's alleged personality traits.

Biologically determined characteristics

The experts put forward paradoxical views concerning the alleged biological origins of gender differences in occupations. This is illustrated by Jenovay's article.[45] He is critical of the 'common' view that 'women can, in general, only carry out light and less complex, low responsibility jobs.'[46] While male occupations requiring physical strength were defined as unsuitable for women, experts warned against generalised assumptions that all women were unsuited to physically demanding occupations. Critical of generalisations which led to evaluations of women as a category with lower labour capacity, Jenovay defined differences in physical strength as relative:

> Women's average physical capacity is less, than men's average. Similarly, there are differences between features of the nervous-system . . . [Yet, many of the jobs done by women] are not at all light physically . . . Work conditions vary greatly . . . there are individual differences between women.[47]

Jenovay argued against the generalised view of women as unsuited to technological occupations. On the contrary, he argued that women's domestic duties develop skills which are crucial to technical occupations:

> The idea that women lack 'technological skills' is also mistaken. At most we can claim that women are underrepresented amongst those possessing these types of skills. Technological, mechanical features dominate the domestic tasks, which are traditionally carried out by women (cleaning, cooking, baking), just like in many areas of industrial labour.[48]

Thus, in their preoccupation with defining those male occupations which might be regarded as suitable for women, the experts in fact challenge the gender coding of abilities required for male occupations. Instead they state that some women might also possess these abilities, citing as evidence the statistical distribution of these abilities within the female population.

In contrast to such relativistic views concerning women's ability to take on men's jobs, Jenovay also identified those occupations which might be seen as particularly suitable for women: 'There are occupations which women are more suited to carry out, in particular, those occupations or jobs which require more precision, patience and humanity.'[49] Thus, both essentialist and relativist views are found within the same article.

In these articles, 'suitability' was most commonly discussed in relation to how women could take over previously 'male' occupations. Neither the bond between men's physiology and male occupations nor that between women's physiology and female occupations was questioned. However, whilst the suitability of men's bodies for female occupations was not discussed, women were identified as possessing allegedly female characteristics which made them especially suited for specifically feminine occupations (see Figure 2.1).

One plausible explanation for this paradox is that the particular position of experts was articulated as independent of both teleological and

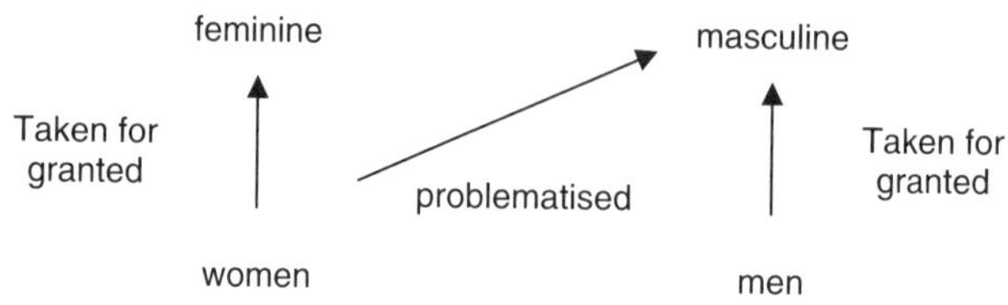

Figure 2.1: Expert analyses of gender 'matching' of occupations

common-sense views. The expert view is grounded in rational arguments and makes reference both to the economic rationality of women's mobilisation in previously male jobs and to 'research' on women's abilities. From the perspective of economic rationality, Jenovay pointed out that women were the only workforce which could still be mobilised to meet labour demand in traditionally male jobs. Jenovay criticised the 'common views' of male workers and managers who opposed the integration of women into male occupations. In contrast, the teleological views of the 1950s pressed for the integration of women into all male occupations. Jenovay formulated a critical position towards these views as well, by relativising women's physiological abilities and defining certain male occupations as more suitable for female labour than others.

In general, these articles sought to assess which male occupations women could perform, and whether views concerning women's alleged primary features would exclude them from these areas. Three main strategies emerged for tackling this dilemma: (a) simply recategorising as 'female', those 'male' occupations deemed suitable for women; (b) adjusting working conditions to suit women's features: a key issue here was the improved use of technology to make jobs physically suitable for women: 'Increased employment of women could be achieved by the mechanisation of heavy physical work, and creation of work-places suitable for women';[50] and finally (c) developing production profiles which would suit women's alleged features. In each case the gendered segregation of occupations remained as a central and unchallenged principle, despite some attempts by experts to question generalisations which emphasise differences between men and women and put them in 'opposite categories'. As discussed above, these relativist tendencies were to enable the recruitment of women into a range of occupations broader than 'common views' considered appropriate, yet narrower than the party propaganda of the 1950s aimed at. In short, it reinforced the acceptability of views arguing for a range of occupations seen as unsuited for women. The definition of the boarders between the two was at issue, not the questioning of essentialist differences per se.

Women's lack of acquired skills

Although a wide range of occupations were officially defined as 'suitable' for women, many of these were slow to employ women. Experts pointed to women's lack of appropriate skills in explaining the low rates of recruitment of women to technologically advanced sectors:

> Even within the postal service there are areas which are already feminised, and areas which could be suitable for women, yet they are filled by men. In the latter areas (technician, book-keeper) the major problem seems to be the lack of skills.[51]

The strategy recommended in this context was to improve women's skills and encourage women to enrol for courses of technical education. However, as it transpired, there were structural issues, which might hinder this solution. Trade schools offering training for 'male occupations' had a very limited number of places, including dormitory space, for female students. Experts suggested that there was considerable silent resistance to the creation of extra places: 'A certain aversion and opposition to the employment of female labour is expressed by enterprises which allocate a very minimal percentage of places in trade schools to be filled by girls.'[52]

Others chose to 'blame the victim' and criticised women for not taking up new opportunities to gain a technical education, guaranteed by the introduction of minimum quotas in training programmes:

> It is of course also true that women seeking employment, as well as employers, adhere to false beliefs . . . For example, now, when we have succeeded in securing a minimum number of places for girls in occupations that can be seen as suitable (such as radio and television technician), there are only enough girls to fill a portion of the allocated places.[53]

It was argued that both enterprise managers and women needed to be motivated to raise women's skill levels in the desired areas:

> Women's disinterest in pursuing leading jobs requiring technological know-how is primarily related to the fact that these positions require regular further education and activities outside of normal work time . . . women's interest in technological subjects and the importance of technology must be more intensively and consistently encouraged.[54]

Women's societal roles

At the enterprise level, arguments against the expansion of women's employment focused predominantly on frustrations caused by women's dual roles, which created organisational difficulties for management. Women were blamed for production deficits: 'Women's frequent absences due to family and health issues, their limited or lower endurance, causes organisational difficulties, large losses and production deficits.'[55] The pressures experienced by managers to find suitable replacement because of unplanned absences to care for sick children were cited as having caused serious difficulties especially in smaller, rural work units.[56]

In another article female labour was described as unreliable. Women's special rights as workers and mothers were problematic for managers, who were under pressure to fulfil state plans and to deliver production figures indicating increased labour efficiency. Employers found women's special rights frustrating:

> The increase in the length of maternity leave,[57] the right to take three years of unpaid leave, the ban on night shifts, the right to take breast-feeding breaks . . . this is precisely where the problems start. The new system of technological staff quotas, with its increased demand for efficiency has been accompanied by a reduction in staff numbers . . . Managers typically react to such measures by seeking to fill their quotas, as far as possible, with male labour.[58]

A 'realistic' attitude towards women's double burden was suggested as the best way to resolve these issues of adaptation. In the articles analysed, the problems caused by family responsibilities were discussed solely in relation to women. Women were blamed for not using the state services available to support working mothers and the solutions offered were further improvement of childcare services (at national and enterprise level) and the mechanisation of household labour. Men's parenthood and their contribution to domestic labour was not problematised in a similar manner. Thus, the experts supported increasingly essentialist understandings of gender.

Essentialising women's personality traits

In some cases women's frequent absences were seen not only as an unfortunate by-product of their dual responsibilities, but as the result of female personality traits. An article describing the situation in the Duna Vasmü steelworks illustrates this point:

> Many women will use every penny to improve their material circumstances. They are not making use of the services that our state provided precisely in order to ease women's double burden (laundries, leasing of household equipment, buying semi-prepared and ready-made food) . . . Most newly employed working women, instead of easing the burden of housework, falsely aim to ease their workload at the enterprise . . . This provokes objections to women's employment.[59]

In the articles analysed, women workers were accused of demonstrating a poor work ethic. Women entering the workforce for the first time were described as prioritising domestic labour and accused of trying to recuperate during working hours by taking frequent sick-leave and looking for undemanding, single-shift positions. It was claimed that women avoided night work and split shifts, seeking instead jobs which could easily be combined with their family duties. By the same token, women's low representation in decision-making positions was explained by women's lack of interest in taking on duties which extended beyond normal working hours or required extra training. This again was linked to women's prioritisation of their reproductive duties. Thus, women's alleged neglect of labour tasks and career options were seen as choices based on personal preferences, as much as they were consequences of their double burden.

Coping with managerial opposition

In response to managerial concerns, experts argued for a 'realistic' approach to the mobilisation of women. Difficulties associated with balancing women's reproductive and productive roles were at the root of most managerial opposition to women's employment:

> As the proportion of female workers increases the number of days leave for which replacement workers have to be employed also increases. Female workers take a higher number of days off on sick-leave than men, because women have to care for sick children. An increase in the proportion of women is also bound to lead to an increase in maternity leave, and unpaid leave.[60]

Such high rates of absenteeism were shown to contradict the specific demands of certain sectors. For example, 'the majority of jobs in the postal service require reliability, precise service and professional know-how. Thus frequent short-term replacements can cause difficulties in delivering the same level of service.'[61] Once again, such difficulties were exacerbated in workplaces with a small number of staff where, 'it is especially difficult if you have a situation where mothers take unexpected leave for unpredictable periods of time. In such cases it can be difficult to find even untrained replacements.'[62]

In developing alternative strategies to cope with these imbalances, experts again called for a 'realistic' position to be taken with regards to women's features within the workforce. What was meant by 'realistic' was that women's reproductive responsibilities must be taken into account:

> We have to acknowledge that women take a substantially larger share of care and domestic duties and that most of these tasks fall on women. A realistic evaluation of this problem and the development of a correct perspective would, to a large degree, facilitate the employment of female workers in larger numbers in the workshops and in productive labour.[63]

As noted above, recommendations for changing the organisation of reproduction focused on increased institutional provision and changing women's behaviour and attitudes.[64] In this context, however, the focus was on developing solutions by changing the organisation of production. One such recommendation was to employ internal labour reserves to cope with the problems caused by women's unexpected absences due to their family responsibilities. Gendered divisions of labour and/or men's lack of responsibility for reproductive duties were not questioned in this context. Another recommendation argued for deflating the value of female labour: 'the leadership could decrease the planned value in measuring per capita production rates.'[65] These proposals implied a further formalisation of women's 'special' status in defining the conditions of their employment on the basis of their reproductive responsibilities. Such adjustments, it was argued, would remove the threat of 'punishment' for not fulfilling the plan from managers employing female labour.

Coping with opposition from male workers

The articles show that opposition from male workers hindered women's employment in previously male occupations. In contrast to the Stalinist ideal, according to which women would compete with men on an equal footing in all areas of employment, women's integration into previously male areas was now to proceed according to a carefully orchestrated and hierarchical plan. As well as establishing which jobs were suitable for female employment, managers had to cope with resistance to women's employment in previously male-dominated areas. The solution put forward was for men who were released from areas deemed suitable for women, to be moved 'upwards' in the internal labour hierarchy and placed primarily in newly opened workshops which were technologically more advanced: 'We intend to employ the released male labour power in occupations requiring further skills and training, where we can ensure increased wages for them.'[66]

Another way of overcoming resistance was via a policy of prioritising the employment of the wives of those workers who had taken part in subsidised housing projects. Such housing projects were part of a strategy to bind a skilled 'core' labour force to the enterprise and these workers were seen as 'stable' and 'reliable'. By employing the wives of 'core' workers it was hoped that reliable women workers would be recruited. The employment of wives and other female family members was also seen as part of a developmental strategy by which housing costs could be kept down, since these women already lived in employee households, in contrast to male workers from the countryside who had no local housing. The employment of female family members also meant that women were more easily accepted by male workers:

> The increase in women's employment was enhanced by permission given to certain workshops and brigades to employ women, whose husbands or other relatives were working in the same brigade or workshop and where the woman's social or other family issues were known. This step helped to win over the support of workers in the brigade . . . Managers' opinions also became more positive, not least as a result of their own workers' responses.[67]

Labour experts problematised women as a special category within the labour force. They objectified women, accepting the perspectives of male workers and managers as 'reality' and offering solutions on this basis rather than seeking to understand women's perspectives and experiences as subjects. In doing so they reaffirmed the naturalised gender order.

Conclusions

This chapter has examined the role of labour market experts in supporting the naturalisation of gender differences in the context of attempts to mobilise and integrate women into the labour force. Labour experts argued for a 'realistic' view of women as workers. This implied an unquestioning association of women with reproductive duties which naturalised women's caring roles and regarded characteristics associated with these roles as innately 'female'. Their analyses and recommendations supported the position of male managers and workers, who were critical of women's entry into previously male occupations, in the context of workplaces organised around the norm of a male worker without caring responsibilities. New, 'realistic' strategies for women's integration into the labour force were to proceed by reasserting the priority of male labour and protecting the interests of male workers. This included ensuring men's primary access to better paid and more highly skilled jobs and ongoing support for the gender segregation of labour which reinforced gendered hierarchies. Thus, experts supported managerial strategies to counteract the threat posed to masculine identities by an influx of women into previously male occupations.

The post-Stalinist shift in economic policy, towards decentralisation and efficiency, coincided with shifts in emancipatory rhetoric and praxis towards naturalising and institutionalising women's caring duties and defining suitable working spheres on this basis. Since the normative wage earner was based on a male worker free from reproductive duties,[68] the influx of women into industrial labour upset the normal functioning of enterprises. Thus, women came to be defined as a deviant category of labour. The difficulties experienced in integrating female wage earners into the labour force demonstrated the incompatibility of the existing systems of production and reproduction. Women's increased labour force participation demanded that both systems be modified, through the increase in childcare institutions, subsidised dining facilities and so on, in the case of the organisation of reproduction, and through the integration of reproductive rights into legislation guiding the organisation of production. However, reproductive rights were codified as maternal rights, reinforcing the segregation of male and female roles and responsibilities, both in the home and at work.

Hierarchical understandings of the relation between male and female jobs were most apparent where alternative ways of pacifying male workers' opposition to women's employment were discussed. Women were to enter the labour force from the bottom. Meanwhile men from those areas to which women could be recruited were to move upwards and be retrained into technologically advanced areas. The lesser value and reliability of female labour was primarily explained on the basis of their family duties and lack of familiarity with wage-labour relations; however, allegedly innate secondary characteristics, such as a lower work ethic and a tendency to avoid demanding jobs, were also mentioned.

The shift in gendered constructions of the organisation of labour, which is reflected in the expert articles analysed here, represents an intersection of class- and gender-based power struggles. In these power struggles, managers gained extended autonomy and control over decisions pertaining to recruitment and the organisation of labour within their enterprises. Working-class men gained power through securing their positions against newcomers and establishing their right to maintain higher positions in the gender- and class-based hierarchy of labour. Managers and working men seemed to have reached a mutually acceptable compromise. Labour experts lent their support to 'realistic' arguments, thus backing managerial/working-class interests against ideologically motivated goals. However, they maintained a degree of professional integrity, by alluding to scientific studies, and warning against generalised essentialist assumptions about women's capabilities. Nonetheless, they failed to problematise the underlying gender contract, accepting instead a view of women's reproductive responsibilities as natural.

Appendix A – Expert articles analysed

J. Balázs, 'A vállalati munkaerö-gazdálkodás vizsgálata és szervezése', *Munkaügyi Szemle*, 3 (1965): 86–91.
L. Berettyán, 'Magyarország területi munkaerö-helyzete', *Munkaügyi Szemle*, 3 (1965): 79–86.
L. Ercsényi, 'Nök foglalkoztatása postai munkakörökben', *Munkaügyi Szemle*, 11 (1966): 430–4.
J. Jenovay, 'A nök foglalkoztatása bövitésének szüksége és lehetöségei', *Munkaügyi Szemle*, 10 (1966): 368–73.
K. Koszó, 'Nök foglalkoztatása a kereskedelemben', *Munkaügyi Szemle*, 9 (1970): 352–8.
O. Pirityi, 'Timár János, Munkahelyzetünk jelene és távlatai', *Munkaügyi Szemle*, 1 (1962): 38.
I. Remenyár, 'A nök fokozott munkába állitása a Dunai Vasmüben', *Munkaügyi Szemle*, 5 (1964): 28–9.
A. Szoboszlai, 'A nök foglalkoztatásáról', *Munkaügyi Szemle*, 7 (1964): 27–8.

Notes

1. Special thanks go to Elisabeth Näsman and Gunilla Dahlkild Öhman at the Department of Sociology at Uppsala University, to Helene Carlbäck at the University of Southern Stockholm, and to Rebecca Kay for their comments and advice on various versions of this chapter.
2. See Appendix A for a full list of articles analysed.
3. S. Kvale, *Den kvalitativa forskningsintervjun* (Lund: Studentlitteratur, 1997).
4. Haney defines three levels in state-led processes: construction of ideology (propaganda and policy-making), implementation (translating the terms of policy into practice) and praxis. On this basis, labour market experts might be seen as 'translators' providing an interface between specific practices and

policy-making; L. Haney, *Inventing the Needy: Gender and the Politics of Welfare in Hungary* (Berkeley: University of California Press, 2002), pp. 7–8.

5. J. Jenovay, 'A nök foglalkoztatása bövitésének szüksége és lehetöségei', *Munkaügyi Szemle*, 10 (1966): 368–73, p. 368.
6. See Szelényi and Konrád on the shift of power from the teleological to the technocratic elite during the reform economic transition of the late 1960s; I. Szelényi and G. Konrád, *The Intellectuals on the Road to Class Power: a Sociological Study of the Role of the Intelligentsia in Socialism* (New York: Harcourt Brace Jovanovich, 1979).
7. I. Asztalos Morell, 'Emancipation's Dead-end Roads: Studies in the Formation and Development of the Hungarian Model for Agriculture and Gender, 1956–1989', *Acta Universitatis Upsaliensis, Studia Sociologica Upsaliensia*, 46 (1999): 485.
8. With the exception of Ferge's time budget study from the 1960s (Zs. Ferge, *A Nök Helyzete A Munkahelyen És Otthon* (Budapest: KSH, 1962)), female experts only started to publish on gender issues from the early 1970s onwards. Yet even then, the majority were sociologists and philosophers, rather than economists. See for example: J. H. Sas, 'A családi munkamegosztásról', in E. Szabady (ed.), *Tanulmányok a nök társadalmi helyzetéröl* (Kossuth: MNOT, 1972); J. Turgonyi, 'Ipari szakmunkásképzés és nöi egyenjoguság', *Társadalmi Szemle*, 1 (1975): 56–68; R. Kulcsár, 'A nök társadalmi mobilitása', in E. Szabady (ed.), *Nök – Gazdaság – Társadalom* (Kossuth: MNOT, 1976), pp. 70–87; A. Heller, 'The Future of Relations Between the Sexes', in A. Hegedüs et al. (eds), *The Humanisation of Socialism: Writings in the Budapest School* (London: Allison and Busby, 1976); A. Vajda, 'A nök beilleszkedése a foglalkozási struktúrába, 1949–1970', *Statisztikai Szemle*, 6 (1976): 672–87; Zs. Ferge, 'Társadalompolitika és a nök', in E. Szabady (ed.), *Tanulmányok a nök társadalmi helyzetéröl* (Budapest: MNOT, 1972). However, it is possible to find even female economists who started to publish on the issue, such as Zs. Kovácsné Orolin, 'A mezögazdasági nöi munkaerö foglalkoztatásának álötalános vonásai', *Közgazdasági Szemle*, 7 (1974): 803–15.
9. E. Fodor, 'Smiling Women and Fighting Men: the Gender of the Communist Subject in State Socialist Hungary', *Gender and Society*, 16, 2 (2002): 240–63.
10. Hernes notes three key arguments supporting women's presence in politics: just representation, women as resources with special experiences, and as representing special interests; H. Hernes, *Welfare State and Women Power: Essays in State Feminism* (Oslo: Norwegian University Press, 1987).
11. Walby refers to six patriarchal structures: paid work, domestic work, state, culture, male violence and sexuality, and explains that these structures manifest themselves in various ways in the process of transition from private to public gender regimes; S. Walby, *Gender Transformation* (London: Routledge, 1997).
12. The relation between the post-Stalinist revision of the gender contract and economic reform politics has been highlighted by a number of studies see: M. Adamik, *Az államszocializmus és a 'nökérdés', 'A legnagyobb igéret – a legnagyobb megaláztatás'*, PhD thesis (Budapest: Budapesti Közgazdaságtudományi Egyetem, Szociológia, 2000), p. 134; K. Kulcsár, *A Családok Helye és Funkcioja a Magyar Társadalomban: Család és Házasság a Mai Magyar Társadalomban* (Budapest: Közgazdasági és Jogi Könyvkiadó, 1971) and Fodor (2002).

13. See for example, Szelényi and Konrád (1979); J. Kornai, *Contradictions and Dilemmas: Studies on the Socialist Economy and Society* (Budapest: Corvina, 1985); M. Pittaway, 'The Reproduction of Hierarchy: Skill, Working-class Culture, and the State in Early Socialist Hungary', *Journal of Modern History*, 74, December (2002): 737–69; I. Szelényi et al., *Socialist Entrepreneurs: Embourgeoisement in Rural Hungary* (Madison, WI: University of Wisconsin Press, 1988); I. Asztalos Morell, 'Rural Women and the Gender Division of Labour in the Post-communist Transition', in J. Starosta (ed.), *Rural Society in Poland and Hungary* (Lodz: Lodz University Press, 1999).
14. J. Goven, 'Gender and Modernism in a Stalinist State', *Social Politics*, 9, Spring (2002): 3–28.
15. Pittaway (2002); Goven (2002).
16. Skilled workers of the older generation, for example, who represented the pre-socialist working-class elite, brought informal pressure to bear on management in protest against the dilution of working-class power by the introduction of new recruits whom they saw as more easy to co-opt into the state's political and economic goals (Pittaway, 2002).
17. Pittaway (2002), p. 24.
18. S. Gal, 'Feminism and Civil Society' in J. Scott et al. (eds), *Transitions, Environments, Translations* (London: Routledge, 1997).
19. See Fodor (2002).
20. Adamik points out that the dilemma of how to combine work and family and the associated pressure to 'choose' one or the other was restricted to women and not seen as relevant to men as fathers; Adamik (2000), p. 134.
21. M. Heller, D. Némedi and A. Rényi, 'Népesedési viták 1963–1986', *Századvég*, 2 (1990): 69–105.
22. See S. Gal, 'Gender in the Post-socialist Transition: the Abortion Debate in Hungary', *East European Politics and Societies*, 8, 2 (1994): 256–86.
23. H. Sándorné, *A GYES-töl a GYED-ig* (Budapest: Magyar Nök Országos Tanácsa, Kossuth, 1986).
24. Jenovay (1966), p. 368.
25. See Pittaway (2002); Asztalos Morell (1999).
26. See Asztalos Morell (1999).
27. However, subsequently, fathers in exceptional family situations appealed successfully to be granted access to the subsidy. Sándorné (1986) mentions approximately 200 cases prior to 1985 when men successfully applied for the subsidy. These men's determination to take on primary caring roles as fathers was viewed as exceptional in this period. They were, thus, the exceptions that proved the rule of childcare as a female domain.
28. Jenovay (1966), p. 369.
29. Ibid.
30. Janos Kornai (1985) argued that development within a command economy is adjusted to the limits of available resources. In this case the gender balance within the available labour force was to set the conditions for development.
31. Jenovay (1966), p. 369.
32. See Pittaway (2002) for an analysis of workplace documentary sources.
33. Jenovay (1966), pp. 369–70.
34. L. Berettyán, 'Magyarország területi munkaerö-helyzete', *Munkaügyi Szemle*, 3 (1965): 79–86, p. 83.

35. Ibid., p. 86.
36. Jenovay (1966), p. 369.
37. Ibid.
38. O. Pirityi, 'Timár János, Munkahelyzetünk jelene és távlatai', *Munkaügyi Szemle*, 1 (1962): 38.
39. Jenovay (1966), p. 372.
40. See also Pittaway (2002).
41. K. Koszó, 'Nök foglalkoztatása a kereskedelemben', *Munkaügyi Szemle*, 9 (1970): 352–8, p. 356.
42. I. Remenyár, 'A nök fokozott munkába állitása a Dunai Vasmüben', *Munkaügyi Szemle*, 5 (1964): 28–9, p. 28.
43. Ibid., pp. 28–9.
44. A. Szoboszlai, 'A nök foglalkoztatásáról', *Munkaügyi Szemle*, 7 (1964): 27–8, p. 27.
45. Jenovay (1966).
46. Ibid., p. 372.
47. Ibid., p. 373.
48. Ibid.
49. Ibid.
50. Berettyán (1965), p. 83.
51. L. Ercsényi, 'Nök foglalkoztatása postai munkakörökben', *Munkaügyi Szemle*, 11 (1966): 430–4, p. 431.
52. Szoboszlai (1964), p. 28.
53. Jenovay (1966), p. 373.
54. Ercsényi (1966), p. 434.
55. Jenovay (1966), p. 372.
56. Ercsényi (1966), p. 434.
57. Paid maternity leave was increased to 20 weeks at the beginning of the 1960s.
58. Szoboszlai (1964), p. 27.
59. Remenyár (1964), p. 28.
60. Ercsényi (1966), pp. 432–3.
61. Ibid.
62. Ibid., p. 433.
63. Szoboszlai (1964), p. 28.
64. For a similar argument see Ercsényi (1966), p. 433.
65. Szoboszlai (1964), p. 28.
66. Remenyár (1963), p. 29.
67. Ibid.
68. See D. Dahlerup, 'Ambivalenser och strategiska val. Om problem kring begreppen särart och jämlikhet i kvinnorörelsen och feministisk teori', *Kvinnovetenskaplig Tidskrift*, 22, 1 (2001): 17–40.

3
Reprivatising Women's Lives: from Khrushchev to Brezhnev

Natalia Vinokurova

Khrushchev's rise to power heralded a period of fundamental political, economic and social change. Political and social liberalisation, following the long years of totalitarian oppression under Stalin, were accompanied by economic growth and a rise in living standards. As a consequence, some of the traditional human values, which had nearly been lost in the preceding difficult decades, gradually began to re-emerge in the Soviet people's consciousness and in the practices of everyday life. A large-scale survey conducted in the 1960s by Soviet sociologist B. Grushin studied the changing opinions and priorities of the urban population and found that, 'undoubtedly, family values take first place.'[1] The increasing preoccupation with and prioritisation of the private sphere, which came to characterise the Brezhnev era of the 1970s, would have been impossible without the foundations laid a decade earlier. This chapter will explore the socio-economic changes of the 1960s and 1970s which acted as precursors to and formed the preconditions for the process of reprivatisation of everyday life.

The arguments presented here are based primarily on analysis of official state statistics and reports. I also draw on qualitative research, conducted over the past 25–30 years, into women's experiences of life in Soviet and post-Soviet Russian society. I conducted over 100 interviews during this period with women and men in Moscow, Ivanovo, Taganrog and Sergiev Posad. These interviews were conducted for a range of sociological studies focusing on a variety of time periods and aspects of women's experiences. Interviews took the form of life-stories and oral histories and thus questions of everyday life and women's experiences of combining motherhood and waged labour were discussed in many of them.[2] In addition, I draw on the results of sociological surveys conducted by a number of Soviet academics and on cultural representations of life in the USSR, during the 1960s and 1970s.

The economic context: women enter the workforce en masse

The Khrushchev era has been characterised as a period of 'economic renaissance'.[3] The famous 'Khrushchev programme' differed from previous programmes in its emphasis on economic modernisation. For the first time economic planning prioritised not only heavy industry, iron and steel production and mining but also the development of automated technology, electronics and instrument engineering. Chemical engineering, the expansion of electrical power networks and technological advances in production became important areas of investment and growth. Scientific achievements were also a priority, particularly in the field of defence: several 'science cities' were established and spacecraft were launched regularly. These technological advances also affected the production of consumer goods: the USSR began to produce refrigerators and vacuum cleaners. Economic development continued in this vein into the 1970s as new technologies were imported from abroad.

Whilst it might be said that these developments came in the wake of international trends towards modernisation, the Soviet experience differed from that of western countries in that economic development was extensive rather than intensive. Technical modernisation, combined with this extensive economic development, demanded an expansion and restructuring of the workforce. New, better educated and more qualified workers were required and considerable investment in education, particularly technical colleges and institutes was ordered in response. Between 1965 and 1975 the number of students specialising in automated technology and electronic engineering increased from 281 000 to 329 000; in instrument engineering numbers increased from 501 500 to 574 000. The number of university students trained for scientific research increased from 279 400 to 368 100.[4]

Science and education became extremely prestigious. Part-time students, teachers and scientists played central roles in a number of popular films, released in the 1960s. For example, the lead characters in the 1965 film *Spring on Zarechnaia Street* (*Vesna na Zarechnoi ulitse*) are an evening-school teacher and her worker-student. Another film, much loved by the intelligentsia, was *9 Days in One Year* (*9 dnei odnogo goda*), released in 1962, which told the story of a group of nuclear physicists. The main character in the play and film *104 Pages about Love* (*104 stranitsy pro liubov*), released in 1964, was also a physicist; however in a 1990s remake of the film the physicist became a journalist reporting on local conflicts: new times demand new heroes.

The desired expansion of the workforce was to be achieved by drawing more women into the labour market. In 1960 the Central Committee decreed that propaganda was required to encourage housewives into productive activity.[5] As the 1960s progressed two-thirds of new recruits to the workforce were female. Eighteen million women entered the labour market, 14 million of whom had previously been housewives. In the early 1960s younger women formed the majority of new recruits; however, from 1965 onwards, women aged 40–49 predominated. In the 1970s the influx of women slowed as the potential female reserve had been absorbed and only school leavers and graduates remained to be recruited. By the early 1970s women constituted 51 per cent of the labour force, and in the RSFSR, 53 per cent, higher than in any other industrialised nation.[6]

These years also established new trends in women's employment and education. The feminisation of certain areas of white-collar work began: nearly half of new female labour recruits flocked to become either engineers or economists. Of course this could not have been achieved without comparable increases in women's education. The proportion of women of working age with higher and/or secondary education more than doubled over the period 1959–70.[7] The proportion of female students increased particularly dramatically in subjects relating to industry, construction and in all the economic specialisms. By 1975, 38.3 per cent of technical students in the USSR were women, compared to 0.8 per cent in the USA, 1.5 per cent in Great Britain, 3.1 per cent in West Germany and 4.7 per cent in Denmark.[8] Forty-eight per cent of design engineers and 59 per cent of technicians were women, and the All-Union Society of Inventors and Innovators had 1 300 000 female members.[9] Higher education gave women access to better jobs. By 1970, 32 per cent of employed women were working in white-collar jobs: 44 per cent of engineers and technicians, 38 per cent of lawyers, 43 per cent of university lecturers, 74 per cent of secondary school teachers, 82 per cent of economists and 66 per cent of scientific and academic researchers.[10]

Yet, even whilst women were contributing significantly to the economic life of the country, and able to get good jobs, they still faced significant barriers when it came to accessing positions in management. In 1959 only 13 per cent of middle and top managers were women. Fourteen years later, in 1973, women still constituted only 9 per cent of directors of industrial enterprises.[11] Even in the most feminised industries the proportion of female managers was low. For example, whilst women made up approximately 75 per cent of secondary school teachers, only 20 per cent of headmasters were women in 1960–1, rising to 29 per cent in 1975–6.[12] The situation in healthcare was very similar: 70 per cent of doctors were women, yet 50 per cent of chief physicians and supervisory personnel were men.[13]

Similar discrepancies can be seen in the earning power of men and women. Soviet labour laws gave strong guarantees to the principle of equal pay for equal work. However, average earnings were much higher in predominantly male industries than they were in those sectors of the economy where women made up the majority of the workforce.[14] In 1975, for example, the average monthly wage in the construction industry, where women constituted only 28 per cent of the labour force, was 176.8 rubles. By comparison, in public health, physical culture and social welfare, where women made up 84 per cent of the workforce, the average monthly wage was 102.3 rubles.[15] Yet, even though their salaries tended to be considerably lower than men's, women's wages were an important contribution to family budgets.

Combining work and family: the impacts of reprivatisation

Over the course of the 1960s and 1970s, the view of work outside the home as a compulsory element of women's lives was finally formulated in state rhetoric and legislation and embedded in popular understandings of family life. The combination of work and family responsibilities, often referred to as women's 'double burden', became the status quo to be inherited by future generations of women. Both men and women came to regard women's work outside the home as a crucial element of gender equality and opinion polls conducted during the 1960s found that only 2 per cent of both men and women thought that women should leave paid employment to be housewives.[16] If these developments are viewed through the prism of the classic alternative, work versus family, it might be expected that the increasing importance of work in women's lives would have to be balanced by a certain reduction in attention to and prioritisation of family life. Indeed statistical evidence of falling birth rates and a rise in the number of divorces in these years seem to bear this equation out, at least in terms of family stability and fertility.[17]

However, the picture is rather different if we look in more detail at the realities of working women's daily lives. Soviet sociologist A. Zdravomyslov identified four lifestyle 'types', based on the ways in which work, family and other interests shaped an individual's day-to-day activities, responsibilities and concerns:

(1) professional activities and interests dominate all other concerns;
(2) family concerns dominate and daily life is organised around these;

(3) personal development is of primary importance and these interests are the most actively pursued;
(4) indistinct interests, unclear boundaries between work and non-work activities.[18]

In the years before and immediately after the Second World War, a significant number of women, who were not employed outside the home, could be referred to as belonging to the second type. In the 1960s, however, working women also began to shift their priorities and lifestyles away from the first type and towards the second. This shift is rather paradoxical since the 'reprivatisation' of women's daily lives was occurring just as their rates of employment and levels of education were on the rise. A study of women's attitudes to domestic activities in Moscow region, conducted by the Institute of Sociology in the 1970s, found that: 'A pronounced willingness to engage in domestic labour is characteristic of women in paid employment, whose domestic activities are focused in households made up of a married couple with children or single parent families with children (both divorcees and widows).'[19] Such studies also found that women's attitudes to their household responsibilities depended greatly on the extent to which these activities were viewed as creative and an expression of the female self. In this respect developments in the wider socio-economic context are crucial to understanding women's everyday practices and attitudes towards their dual roles.

Building family homes: Khrushchev's housing campaign

In the Khrushchev era housing construction had become a key priority for social policy. In the early 1950s the Soviet Union had only 240 500 000 square metres of housing; in the second half of the decade this was almost doubled to 474 100 000 square metres and in the 1960s it reached 1 009 100 square metres.[20] Between 1956 and 1965 100 600 000 people improved their housing conditions.[21] This leap was measured in terms of quality as well as quantity. The 'Khrushchev programme' had declared that families should receive separate flats and the transition from communal housing, barracks and basements to life in individual flats impacted on the whole way of life of millions of families.

Perhaps the most immediately obvious effect of getting a new one-family flat was that it led to a decrease in the number of household members as nuclear families separated from older generations and other adult relatives. In 1970 over 75 per cent of households consisted of either a married couple with or without children or a single parent with children.[22] On the one hand, women in such households lost the potential help of other adult family members and had to shoulder more individual responsibility for the organisation of family life. On the other hand, they were also less subject to the opinions of older family members and neighbours in communal flats and had more freedom to choose their own patterns of behaviour and family relations.

Secondly, but no less importantly, the allocation of individual flats stimulated increased activity relating to their decoration and interior design. After long years spent living in overcrowded communal flats without even the most basic conveniences and where several generations often had to share a single room, women welcomed the opportunity to lavish attention on equipping and decorating their new homes. Frilly lace curtains and glass lampshades replaced the naked lamps and bare windows of communal kitchens. Families purchased furniture and other household goods. A novel written in 1968 describes a house-warming party. The proud tenant of a new apartment shows it off to the guests:

> In the children's room . . . the beds are from Moscow. The table's shared for now. The wardrobe's from the living room set, the rest of which is in the lounge. There's a picture by Shishkin 'Morning in a pine forest'. The carpet is called 'deer'.
> They went into the next room.
> The bedroom furniture is Polish. There are two sprung beds, a full-length mirror, a pouffe . . .[23]

It is clear that the owners are proud of their new furniture and have plans for the further improvement of their flat. The sphere of homemaking, of 'beauty' in all senses of the word, was traditionally considered a female realm, '[women's] worth registered by their domestic material environment'.[24] Thus the task of creating a 'snug home' became a way for women to express themselves and prove their capabilities. The state encouraged women's domestic activities; numerous publications appeared at this time devoted to housekeeping, interior decorating and so on.

One of my respondents from Taganrog spoke of how her father, a communist, had presented her with a book entitled *Housekeeping*, to celebrate her graduation from secondary school. It was 1957, the beginning of the Khrushchev era, and this was the first book on housekeeping anyone in her family had owned. This book included a lot of advice on how to decorate a room within a communal flat:

> A beautiful tablecloth will brighten up your room. During the day it is best to cover the table with a cloth that blends well with the colour

> of other furnishings or with the portiere. When you are having dinner or tea use a white or coloured linen tablecloth . . . Fine lace curtains are the best window coverings . . . Nothing decorates a room better than cut flowers. They look just as good in a crystal vase or a simple earthenware jug.[25]

A year later advice more geared to the needs of people living in individual flats was offered in a new book entitled *Useful Advice*:

> The kitchen can sometimes be used as a dining room, especially for breakfast and supper . . . Do not use heavy, dark curtains at the windows . . .
> Things you should keep in the bathroom:
> a stool, or a lidded box for dirty linen instead,
> a mirror, which should be hung over the wash basin,
> a glass shelf for toiletries (soap, tooth brushes etc.),
> a hanging tidy-bag made of polythene, with sections for your bath cap, scissors, etc.,
> a rubber mat or wooden slatted board.[26]

This book included specific sections dedicated to advice on how to use technical appliances such as a vacuum cleaner or refrigerator. Thus, over the course of a decade new practices, new styles of day-to-day living and new attitudes to consumption had begun to develop.

Rising standards of living and the development of a consumer culture

The 'decline in married women's work', which Tilly and Scott identified as a result of raised living standards and the growth of a middle class in nineteenth-century Europe,[27] did not occur in twentieth-century Russia. Nonetheless, the notable rise in living standards which took place in the USSR during the 1960s and 1970s made a specific impact on women's lives. During the 1970s average incomes continued to rise as did production of modern household appliances. If in 1960 there were 4 washing machines per 100 households, in 1970 there were 52, and in 1980, 76; ownership of refrigerators rose from 4 per 100 households in 1960, to 30 in 1970 and 89 in 1980; corresponding figures for television sets were 8, 52 and 91, and for radios 46, 72 and 92.[28] Yet despite increased production, consumer demand outstripped supply and shortages of these goods grew, sharpening consumer desire further still. One of the many opinion surveys conducted during the 1960s included a question about consumer preferences. The results showed that almost one in five respondents wanted to buy furniture, refrigerators or washing machines.[29] During the Brezhnev era the problem of supplying the population with modern consumer goods was resolved by increasing imports primarily from the countries of the 'socialist bloc'. The emerging availability of imported goods influenced the consumer behaviour of the Soviet people, stimulating their interest in qualitative consumption. Consumer demand also grew for domestically produced high status goods such as crystal ware, carpets and jewellery.

A new culture of consumption linked to the shortage economy developed during these years. It was characterised by conspicuous consumption and consumption of symbolic goods. People made a fetish of imported goods as being of the highest quality but also the most difficult to acquire due to acute shortages. In the 1970s Soviet women dreamt of owning a pair of imported boots, whilst young people were desperate for a pair of jeans. The women whom I interviewed in the 1980s and 1990s often remembered the purchase of a good pair of boots as an important event in their everyday lives. Reminiscing about this era a female author entitled her novel quite simply, *To Buy Boots*.[30] Professor Konstantinov, Deputy Director of the Central Institute for Mathematics and Economics at the Russian Academy of Sciences described this as an 'abnormal consumption syndrome', 'the pressing of goods on people', and discussed the role of goods as both 'stimulant and tranquilliser for young people and women in the late 1970s'.[31]

Finding and 'acquiring' goods played an increasingly central role in daily life and preoccupied women first and foremost. In Russian families men were still considered the main breadwinners whilst women were in charge of managing household budgets and purchasing goods. The majority of husbands delegated power over spending the household budget to their wives. Novelist Barbara Bornycheva had experienced this phenomenon when working as an insurance broker in the 1960s. In one of her essays she described the following scene as typical of what happened when an insurer tried to get money for insurance from a man:

> Men are not of much use to an insurance broker as they seldom have any money . . . Married couples where the man has money and controls the spending of it are very rare. Even those men, whose wives trust them and give them a free rein in spending, avoid interfering in serious money affairs. A man like this will say to me that he has no money but later his wife will complain, 'What do you mean you couldn't pay!' 'I don't know . . .' he tries to justify himself. 'What!? You don't know where the money is kept then?'[32]

In 1965, women spent twice as much time shopping and queuing as men did. Thus, men spent 0.58 and 0.12 hours a day shopping and queuing respectively, whilst women spent 1.14 and 0.24 hours on these activities.[33] In my interviews with women, conducted in the mid-1990s, they frequently reminisced about shopping in the late Soviet era as a primarily female responsibility. For example, an unemployed computer programmer said of her husband, an engineer: 'Just think of it, he had the opportunity to buy a vacuum cleaner at work . . . he turned it down!!! Then I had to search half way around Moscow to get one. . . .' Another woman, who worked full-time in an academic research post, explained that she was responsible for the shopping because, '[My husband] can't stand queuing . . . anyone would think I love it! But I stand in line . . .' So women became 'procurers', supplying themselves and their families with the commodities they needed and desired. Consumption increasingly displaced work as the centre of their attention and interests. In Bornycheva's essay, mentioned above, she writes about a visit to a hospital where she overheard the conversations of female doctors and nurses during their dinner break: 'Where can I get a scarf or a cardigan?', 'What unusually fine stockings that doctor from the physiotherapy department managed to get!', 'A doctor from the X-ray department has a pair of shoes for sale.'[34]

Men appear to have become accustomed to this state of affairs and to have viewed it as 'normal'. In interviews conducted with men and young people in 1980, they frequently talked about women as consumption-oriented and interested in conspicuous consumerism. A 26-year-old graduate, living in Moscow, said of his mother, 'She cared a lot about what things look like. She never bought jeans without a label that they were "made in" somewhere or other. She only dressed me in "made in" clothes.' A divorced husband had the following to say about his ex-wife:

> Basically she's got the right idea. She's reasonably home-oriented. She's very business-like, she really is the leader in the family. Everything we have in the house was bought by her. She might come home in a taxi and say, 'I bought a washing machine' . . . She just makes her mind up and that's that. She's a master at that. The kitchen's a different matter. She has no time for that . . .

Thus, women's contribution to family life, their decision-making power and status in the family increased. Their caring roles were extended to include those linked to the acquisition of consumer and household goods. As the above quotes also illustrate, the gap between official ideology with its disapproving attitude towards demonstrative consumption and philistinism and the realities of people's lived experiences was widening.

Allotments and cars: economic independence and consumption

The early 1970s saw a large-scale distribution of plots of land to the urban population in the form of dachas, co-operative gardens, allotments and so on. This policy was a tacit recognition of the inability of the collective and state farms to provide an adequate supply of food to the population. As a result of the campaign millions of families became more independent economically: a real blow to socialism of the Stalinist school. As far as family life was concerned, this development led above all to a further increase in time and energy spent on domestic tasks and concerns. Yet again, there was a transfer of interests and attention away from formal employment towards the concerns and problems of day-to-day life. It also led to the development of a particular division of roles in family practices linked to the dacha or allotment. Men were primarily responsible for building and repairing structures and 'acquiring' building materials; families worked as a single unit to cultivate their allotments, growing vegetables, berries, fruit and flowers. Supplies were stored for winter. Retired grandmothers spent the summer with their grandchildren in the country, working people turned into commuters every weekend. Heavy bags with food, tools and seedlings were brought from the city. Preserves, vegetables and fruits were brought back. Guests were invited to help in seasonal and building work; open-air parties were arranged. The highly popular film *Moscow Doesn't Believe in Tears*, presents a typical picture of this way of life. The dacha was also a topic which my respondents referred to frequently in interviews, conducted in both 1980 and in the mid-1990s:

> We have a dacha, very close to Moscow and this is also a very important part of my life and the life of my family . . . Yes we have an allotment and my father and I spend a lot of time there . . .

> We had a few apple trees, raspberries, currants . . . I can't imagine life without making jam . . . at least a few jars . . .

The dacha boom gave women yet another set of family responsibilities as the 'suppliers' of products from the allotment, one which was to last for many decades. It also fixed women's and men's family responsibilities on the basis of a model of complementary gender relations. Life had finally discredited Inessa Armand's dream of 'public kitchens and dining halls to replace the family pot'.[35]

A different policy, but one which had some similar consequences to the distribution of plots of land, was the increasingly wide, in Soviet terms, availability of cars made possible by the building of an automobile plant using Italian technologies in the 1960s. As a result, the production of

Soviet-built cars had risen to 1.2 million cars by 1975, compared with only 344 200 in 1970. By 1980, one in ten families owned a car.[36] Once again, families gained greater economic independence and people's interests were oriented further towards consumption and away from the concerns of public production.

Men were generally responsible for everything connected to the ownership of a family car. They became the family driver, were responsible for repairing the car, for getting hold of spare parts, for building garages and so on. These activities led to the development of informal networks of men with cars. One of my respondents, interviewed in Moscow in the mid-1990s, told me about her husband and his motorist friends. Their family had a car and a garage in the garage cooperative not far from their house:

> My husband never nursed the children as much as he 'nursed' that car . . . He spent all his weekends at the garages . . . There was a 'pack' of them who got together there . . . One of them would be lying under the car, another three hanging about, helping. It was lucky that one of our neighbours worked at the factory . . . he helped out with spare parts . . . Sometimes they made their own . . . You couldn't get anything at the time, and anyway we never had any money to spare . . . When we sold the car after the accident he did not want to sell the garage . . . I wanted to sell, we could have got a fair bit for it, [but] they started to meet up in the empty garage to play chess . . . they turned it into a clubhouse.

Thus in many ways, wider car ownership also contributed to a complementary model of gender relations.

Work or family: resolving the contradictions

This section will explore the ways in which individual women, their families and the state sought to resolve the contradictory demands caused by the increase in women's employment, on the one hand, and the increasing pressure to provide for their families' day-to-day needs on the other, in the context of a shortage economy where consumer goods and services were in particularly short supply.

Social policy

Soviet social policy consistently aimed to support women to combine the burdens of work and family. Nonetheless, there were differences between the Khrushchev and Brezhnev periods in this respect. The main achievement of the Khruschev era in this area was the building of kindergartens and nurseries and the allocation of subsidised childcare places. In 1940, the Soviet Union had 46 000 pre-school educational establishments; by 1965 this number had increased to 91 900, and 102 700 by 1970.[37] A system of continuous pre-school education had been created incorporating both nurseries and kindergartens. Impressive progress was also made in the development of facilities and activities for schoolchildren during the summer vacation. In summer 1964 and 1965 4 500 000 schoolchildren spent the summer vacation in 7900 pioneer camps. In 1966, there were 628 such camps in Moscow district alone and 539 000 children spent their vacations there. In addition, 5000 Moscow schoolchildren spent their vacations in special children's sanatoria, 6000 in sports camps, 9000 on organised camping holidays and 110 000 pre-school children spent the summer at kindergarten 'dachas'.[38]

The Khrushchev era also saw the creation of women's councils in the workplace. Although the official aim of these councils was 'to maximise the effectiveness of women's labour',[39] they were also concerned with helping women to resolve domestic issues. First and foremost they helped women to organise childcare, schooling and summer vacation activities for their children.

The remainder of social policy measures introduced by the state in this era, such as increasing benefit payments and allowances for working mothers, did not have a direct impact on easing women's double burden. A survey conducted by Grushin during the early 1960s found that 62.6 per cent of men and 63.5 per cent of women considered that increasing the number of kindergartens and other childcare facilities was the most important measure the state could take to achieve more equality between the sexes. Only 2.3 per cent of men and 3.3 per cent of women in the same survey said that increasing the benefits and allowances available to mothers would make a significant difference in terms of gender equality.[40]

In the Brezhnev era issues relating to women's emancipation and the pressures of the double burden 'were peripheral in comparison with other state concerns'.[41] Gender policies took on a patriarchal, slogan-based nature: the Communist Party of the Soviet Union declared its support for woman as 'participants in the labour process, mothers, carers and housekeepers'.[42] Demographers began to support the idea of a 'return to the home' for women. Labour experts suggested measures to improve women's working conditions, but none of their suggestions was particularly radical.[43] They tended to focus on easing the demands of women's labour participation through reduced working hours, longer lunch breaks and the introduction of part-time work, on improving working environments by improving lighting and introducing fitness breaks, and on improving workplace facilities to lighten women's domestic burden, for example through the provision of catering services, clothing repair services and the production of semi-prepared foods. Finally, measures were suggested for the improvement of healthcare services and so on. Some of these measures began to be incorporated into women's work contracts. In addition, local trade unions were directed to care for women and their special needs, particularly via the allocation of trips to children's summer camps, provision of rest homes for workers' holidays and the organisation of domestic services. The government also introduced a number of measures to facilitate the combination of work and vocational studies,[44] and to ban women from jobs where working conditions were deemed hazardous to women's health. Of the measures introduced at this time, the one which had perhaps the greatest immediate significance for women's everyday life was the establishment of after-school groups and the provision of a range of domestic services in the workplace. A network of centres providing after-school care and activities for children was set up, catering for approximately half a million schoolchildren in 1970.[45] 'The General Directions of Economic Development of the USSR in 1976–1980' emphasised once again the need to expand the system of children's educational establishments, and the provision of domestic and personal services.[46] Yet, despite such proclamations and increases in provision, neither the system of pre-school childcare facilities nor the provision of consumer services were ever enough to satisfy demand in the Soviet era.

Informal factors

In the Brezhnev period informal factors came to play a very important role in allowing women to successfully combine the burdens of work and family. The informal economy and strong informal networks have long been generally characteristic of Soviet and Russian society and play a crucial and often dominant role when times are hard. This can be seen as a mechanism of adaptation; indeed the Soviet sociologist Levada has described the Soviet people as 'homo adaptivus'.[47]

The Soviet work ethic

The first informal factor used by women to help them cope with their increased burdens was the practice of dealing with domestic issues during working hours. In the Brezhnev era, the system itself encouraged workers to see their workplaces as a 'source of personal reward'. Put simply, it encouraged them to steal, to use factory equipment or working time to pursue private interests.[48] The demands of labour discipline had been relaxed everywhere, in line with changing standards of labour practice. In my interview with Professor Konstantinov, mentioned above, he reflected that, 'it was an objective process with serious consequences: the relaxation of labour regulations in the workplace was followed by a general let-up in the norms of social life, morality, culture.'[49] Similarly, opportunities for the purchase of desirable goods depended not so much on earned income as on other, informal factors. Wage-levelling reduced people's motivation to work hard, and women in particular were lacking in motivation, since for the most part they did not expect to be promoted or to see their salaries increase significantly due to gender discrimination in the workplace. This was particularly marked in the fields of management and intellectual or creative work. For example, amongst scientists, 75 per cent of men aged 26–30 had been promoted, as opposed to only 25 per cent of women in the same age group. In general, women lagged at least two to three years behind men in their prospects for promotion.[50] The result was a slump in women's interest in work and further training. A decrease in motivation for work was also seen amongst men. However, they found an outlet in increased activity in the shadow economy which was almost entirely absent amongst women in the 1960s and 1970s. By the end of the 1980s another Soviet sociologist, Rakovskaia, estimated that:

> The country's labour reserves included at least two generations of women with low-level motivation. Their defining quality was indifference to their work. The key factors in seeking employment for them were proximity of the workplace to where they lived, convenient working hours and the opportunity for minimal input of labour.[51]

It became common practice for women to use part of their working day for domestic tasks, for example, by taking a prolonged lunch break, in order to do the shopping, to visit the hairdresser, to do the laundry and so on. It was not uncommon for women to telephone home frequently during the day to check on their children or to contact bureaucratic institutions and offices in order to resolve personal and family issues. Sometimes women just used the workplace as a chance to catch their breath and replenish their energy: 'work is the only place where you can relax', became an infamous anecdote of the time. Bornycheva's essay, mentioned above, paints a stereotypical picture of the ways in which women employed in the state bureaucracy might spend their working days:

> They shuffle and reshuffle their papers. In a corner at the front sits the boss, usually a man, facing his subordinates, like the conductor in

> front of his orchestra. As long as he's there, it's mainly silent and well-behaved. All heads are bent over their work. But he has only to leave the room and the talking and activity starts up. The employees (who are mainly women) do their hair and check their makeup. They make phone calls, have a chat. They call home to find out what everyone's doing, whether they've done everything they were asked to, they give new instructions and orders. Just like anywhere they show each other what they've bought.[52]

It was at this time that the stereotype of women in white-collar jobs who really did nothing at work gained wide currency. Both men and children readily believed it. A male respondent interviewed in 1980 had the following to say about women's employment issues:

> If you take the average level, well a lot depends on what line of work a woman goes into. Suppose she chooses medicine, or maths, or engineering. A person in medicine is always working with people, it's a lot of responsibility. But someone who goes into engineering, well they can spend all day doing nothing, if it's a woman, she might spend all day knitting let's say.

Working hours were also used for discussing politics, books, magazines and films. Intellectual women greatly valued the opportunities for social life afforded by the workplace. A young woman spoke about her mother in these terms:

> Mum's main preoccupation was always the family. It took all her energy. She works too . . . It's like something she does on the side . . . the main thing for her there is the social interaction. It's a chance to get away from her domestic duties, to break the monotony.

Like any stereotype, such views were clearly exaggerated, and many women worked very hard and efficiently. Nonetheless, these opinions were not without some grounding. Soviet people's growing prioritisation of everyday concerns and private life and their loss of interest in work were particularly evident at that time, especially amongst white-collar workers.

It is also significant that female labour was concentrated in those sectors where working hours were shorter. Between 1965 and 1975 the proportion of women in branches of industry, agriculture and transport with a working week of 40 hours or more, fell from 47.9 per cent to 44.5 per cent. Simultaneously the proportion of women rose in sectors such as education, healthcare and culture, where the working week was shorter (33–39 hours) and the regime lighter.

Sharing the burden? Men in the home

The second informal factor supporting women was the increasing involvement of men in domestic activities. This was a slow but clear trend. There was considerable popular support for the idea of increasing men's involvement in the home even during the Khrushchev era. Soviet surveys conducted between 1960 and 1964 asked the question: 'What measures are needed, in your opinion, to end women's inequality in the family?' 54.3 per cent of men and 59 per cent of women answered that husbands and children taking a share in the burden of household duties was the most important factor. Certainly in absolute terms women spent much more time on housework and family responsibilities than men. However, the general reduction in time spent on domestic labour at the end of the 1960s and beginning of the 1970s was also much greater for women, as shown by time budget surveys conducted at the time, as discussed below.

In the 1960s the domestic activities which men were most commonly responsible for included: gardening, household repairs, preparation of fuel stocks, carrying water and building work. However, men also participated in their children's upbringing and education, especially playing with children. Time budget studies indicated that men spent as much time with their children as women did. In interviews which I conducted with divorced men in the late 1970s and 1980s they frequently spoke about domestic arrangements and the division of childcare responsibilities in their former marriages:

> My wife was ill for some time after the birth of our child, so I did all the laundry myself in that period. Afterwards we did everything together. Well, after all, my wife was at work from 8.30 in the morning until 7 at night. Our eldest son was at school. I collected our little girl from the kindergarten . . . in the evenings I'd help the lad with his homework.

> I took charge of our daughter's upbringing. And I did it my way. We tried to spend the evenings together although she went out with her friends a lot too. She's my clever girl . . .

During the 1970s men also began to take a share in typically female work such as cleaning the apartment. The more technical appliances the family had, the more readily men took part in this activity. Sociologists also noted an increasing tendency for families to spend their leisure time together and that women's leisure time was increasing more rapidly than men's.[53]

A time budget survey conducted in Riga at this time shows the most optimistic picture of men's increasing involvement in housework and family duties. Riga, the capital of Latvia, was regarded in the Soviet Union as a model city in the field of culture, leisure time facilities and structures for the support of everyday life. In the period 1968–72, the time women in Riga spent on housework fell by 3.3 hours, in comparison to only one hour for men. The proportion of time spent on specific tasks, within the hours which men and women allocated to domestic duties, was also shifting. Women started to spend proportionally less time on cleaning, washing and ironing. Men on the other hand were spending a higher proportion of their 'housework time' on such tasks: 35 per cent on weekdays and 48 per cent at weekends as opposed to 29 and 32 per cent respectively in 1968. One-third of the men involved in the study did some of the cooking on weekends.[54] In a different survey conducted amongst women engineers, 39 per cent of respondents indicated that their husbands took an equal share in family duties, and 47 per cent claimed that bringing up the children was an equally shared responsibility.[55] Thus, particularly in middle-class, urban households, many men began to take a more active role in the daily care of their children and in housework during the 1970s, as the proportion of their financial contribution to family budgets decreased. This trend continued into the 1980s.

Informal networks and reciprocal support

The third informal factor helping women to deal with the challenges of daily life came from their engagement in informal mutual support networks. These probably hark back to the traditions of communal life in the Russian village where mutual assistance played a significant role in families' survival. Soviet families accumulated this form of shared social capital over many years on the basis of trust, co-operation, mutual aid, and networks of friends, relatives, neighbours, work colleagues and close acquaintances. These informal networks played a particularly important role during potentially difficult periods for families, such as the birth of a child, and offered a flexible variety of support practices.

Relatives were the key source of support for women, helping to resolve the tensions arising from their combination of motherhood and paid work. Grandmothers in particular offered crucial support in this respect. The most common choices of pre-school childcare arrangements were kindergarten or grandmother. My qualitative studies revealed a wide variety of ways in which grandmothers contributed to the care of their grandchildren including: both working and retired grandmothers; those living in extended family arrangements with their children and grandchildren; and those living separately either in the same city or in another city or village. Sometimes grandmothers took care of their grandchildren for several months or even years at a time, sometimes for several days or for a specific number of hours a week. In addition to providing childcare, grandparents frequently offered material support to their children's families, enabling women to take unpaid leave or to reduce their workload even if this meant agreeing to a lower salary. Other relatives also helped in a variety of ways.

Neighbours also played an important role in women's support networks. Perhaps most commonly, elderly female neighbours often helped with household tasks either in exchange for goods and services, or for a small amount of money, or sometimes with no obvious form of payment involved. A new form of neighbourly mutual assistance appeared in the 1970s, when it became quite common for several women to get together and take it in turns to look after each other's children. These arrangements usually involved three to five families and provided a kind of informal alternative to the kindergarten. Such home kindergartens were most often organised by students, postgraduates and women working on a flexitime basis; however, sometimes grandmothers and other relatives also participated, widening the range of women who could take part.

Finally, many women relied on informal networks of mutual support at their workplaces[56] and/or a variety of more rarely occurring networks of mutual assistance[57] to achieve the successful combination of work and family life. Thus, a combination of official state policies and measures on the one hand and informal factors supporting women on the other made it possible to maintain high levels of female employment throughout the late Soviet era.

Conclusion

Khrushchev's socio-economic policy, with its emphasis on improving the Soviet people's standards of living had an important impact on the further development of the country. His promise 'to overtake America' was concerned not only with industrial development but also with living standards and environments. Society was becoming more stable and affluent and having a well-equipped, family apartment, a dacha and a car became symbolic of a 'normal life'. Thus, Khrushchev laid the foundations for further growth in consumption and consumer interests. In the Brezhnev era this prioritisation of private interests and daily life, as well as the development of a consumer culture, became even more pronounced. Although this chapter has not considered in detail the situation in the 1980s and 1990s, it would appear that the increasing dominance of private, 'everyday' interests in the 1960s and 1970s led to the development of a consumption-oriented society in the 1980s. *Perestroika* was as much the result of a widespread desire to match western standards of living as it was the result of a wish to change the political system.

Despite certain increases in men's involvement in domestic life, women bore the brunt of family responsibilities and the burdens of resolving the day-to-day challenges of life in the Soviet Union. It would also appear that they were more strongly inclined towards consumer behaviours than men. As a result, they played a crucial role in the process of reprivatisation of daily life. Simultaneously, however, Khrushchev's reforms led to women's integration en masse into the Soviet labour market and to significant increases in their levels of education and training. As a result, women's contribution to family budgets increased, as did their role in procuring goods and services for the family and they gained influence in their families as a consequence.

Nonetheless, the question of gender equality and egalitarian relations within Soviet families remains complex. On the one hand the expansion of women's roles both within and outside the home and men's increasing involvement in domestic activities would appear to be a big step towards equality, and the end of the patriarchal system. Indeed, Soviet sociologists have suggested that new understandings of proper gender relations became current during the Khrushchev era:

> In particular the idea of women's equality was very popular at that time: it was actively supported not only by female respondents but also by men. It was especially popular amongst younger men. Among younger women these ideas often came to resemble what would later be formulated as various concepts of feminism.[58]

On the other hand some of the trends towards a sharing of domestic duties and responsibilities were more suggestive of a complementary than an egalitarian model of relations between the sexes, whereby men were responsible above all for work at the dacha, mending the car and carrying out repairs in the home. Discrimination in the workplace also continued. Thus the demands on women both in the family and at work increased considerably over the 1960s and 1970s and became hard, if not impossible, to bear. State measures for easing women's dual burdens were insufficient and informal factors played a crucial role in allowing women to combine work and family responsibilities. The patriarchal system might have suffered a serious blow but complete equality had not appeared either.

Notes

1. B. Grushin, *Chetyre zhizni Rossii v zerkale obshchestvennogo mnenia. Ocherki massovogo soznaniia rossiian vremen Khrushcheva, Brezhneva, Gorbacheva i Yeltsina v 4-kh knigakh. Zhizn' 1-aia. Epokha Khrushcheva* (Progress-Traditsia, Moscow, 2001), p. 493 (see also pp. 125–6, 294, 335, 477 for details of the study).
2. The main projects from which data have been drawn in writing this chapter are: 'Grounds for Divorce', 1980; 'Russian Women: Past and Present', 1995–7; 'Women's Adaptations to the Transition Economy', 1996–7; 'A Labor Market in the Making: Women and Men in a Russian Industrial Town', 1998–2000; 'Women in Top Management', 2000; 'Portrait of an Ogonyok Reader', 2003.
3. V. Smirnov, 'Economicheskie prichiny krakha sotsializma v SSSR', *Otechestvennaia istoriia*, 6, November–December (2002): 38; F. Burlatsky, *Khrushchev. Shtrikhi k politicheskomu portretu. Uroki gorkie, no neobkhodimye* (Moscow: Mysl, 1988), p. 68.
4. *Narodnoe khoziaistvo SSSR. 1922–1982. Jubileinyi statisticheskii ezhegodnik* (Moscow: Finansy i statistika, 1982), p. 507.
5. *KPSS v rezolyutsiiakh i resheniiakh s'ezdov, konferentsii i plenumov TsK*, Volume 7 (Moscow: Gospolitizdat, 1960), p. 516.
6. In 1970 the proportion of women of working age in either employment or education stood at 89.7 per cent, having risen from 72.6 per cent in 1959. Consequently the annual accession rate of women to the labour market fell to 2.8 per cent in 1971–5 as compared to 3.9 per cent in 1966–70. *Narodnoe khoziaistvo SSSR v 1961 godu. Statisticheskii ezhegodnik* (Moscow: Gosstatizdat, 1962), p. 574; *Itogi vsesoiuznoi perepisi naseleniia 1970 goda*, Volume 6 (Moscow: Statistika, 1973), pp. 165–9; V. Kostakov (ed.), *Trudovye resursy. Sotsialno-economicheskii kharakter* (Moscow: Ekonomika, 1976), pp. 103–4, 116–17, 120, 125; *Narodnoe khoziaistvo SSSR* (1982), p. 404.
7. *Narodnoe khoziaistvo SSSR* (1982), p. 403.
8. *Trud v SSSR. Statisticheskii sbornik* (Moscow: Finansy i statistika, 1988), pp. 119, 130.
9. *Obrazovanie zhenshchin v SSSR v usloviiakh nauchno-tekhnicheskogo progressa* (Moscow, 1975), pp. 6–15.
10. *Itogi vsesoiuznoi perepisi* . . . (1973), pp. 165–9.
11. Ibid.; *Zhenshchiny v SSSR. Statisticheskii sbornik* (Moscow: Tsentralnoe statisticheskoe upravlenie, 1975), p. 80.
12. *Zhenshchiny i deti v SSSR* (Moscow: Tsentralnoe statisticheskoe upravlenie, 1963), p. 127; 'Zhenshchiny v SSSR', *Vestnik statistiki*, 1, January (1977): 89.
13. *Itogi vsesoiuznoi perepisi* . . . (1973), pp. 165–9.
14. J. Pankhurst and M. Sacks, *Contemporary Soviet Society: Sociological Perspectives* (New York: Praeger, 1980), pp. 236–8; O. Rakovskaia, *Sotsialnye orientiry molodezhi: tendentsii, problemy, perspektivy* (Moscow: Nauka, 1993), pp. 77–9, 89;

K. Katz, 'Gender, Wages and Discrimination in the USSR: a Study of a Russian Industrial Town', *Cambridge Journal of Economics*, 21, 4 (1997): 431–52, p. 446.

15. Data provided directly to author during interviews with statisticians at Tsentralnoe statisticheskoe upravlenie, Moscow, 1985.
16. Grushin (2001), p. 300.
17. *Narodnoe khoziaistvo SSSR za 60 let. Jubileinyi statisticheskii ezhegodnik* (Moscow: Statistika, 1977), p. 74; *Narodnoe khoziaistvo SSSR* (1982), p. 27; *Zhenshchiny Rossii. Statisticheskii sbornik* (Moscow: Goskomstat Rossii, 1995), pp. 27, 34.
18. I. Bestuzhev-Lada (ed.), *Sotsialnie pokazateli obraza zhizni sovetskogo obshchestva* (Moscow: Nauka, 1980), pp. 31–2.
19. T. Karakhanova, 'Otnoshenie k bytovoi deiatel'nosti, ego pokazateli i tipy', in V. Patrushev (ed.), *Otnoshenie k rabote, bytu i dosugu* (Moscow: Institut sotsiologicheskikh issledovanii AN SSSR, 1992), pp. 35–60.
20. *Narodnoe khoziaistvo SSSR* (1982), p. 426.
21. *Narodnoe khoziaistvo SSSR. 1922–1972. Jubileinyi statisticheskii ezhegodnik* (Moscow: Statistika, 1972), pp. 366–70.
22. Kostakov (1976), p. 118.
23. A. Tkachenko, 'Novosel'e', *Novyi mir*, 4, April (1968): 77.
24. S. Reid, 'Women in the Home', in M. Ilic, S. Reid and L. Attwood (eds), *Women in the Khrushchev Era* (Basingstoke: Palgrave Macmillan, 2004), pp. 149–53.
25. *Domovodstvo* (Moscow: Gosudarstvennoe izdatelstvo selskohoziaistvennoi literatury, 1957), p. 7.
26. *Poleznye sovety* (Moscow: Moskovskii rabochii, 1958), pp. 7–8, 39, 42.
27. L. Tilly and J. Scott, 'Women's Work and Family in Nineteenth-Century Europe', *Comparative Studies in Society and History*, 17 (1975): 36–64.
28. *Zhenshchiny Rossii. Statisticheskii sbornik* (Moscow: Goskomstat Rossii, 1995), pp. 34, 74.
29. V. Kantorovich, 'Sociologiia i literatura', *Novyi mir*, 12, December (1967): 167–8.
30. A. Bialko, *Na toi nedele* (Moscow: Octopus, 2005), pp. 3–113.
31. Personal interview conducted by the author, April 1989.
32. B. Bornycheva, 'Den' strakhovogo agenta', *Novyi mir*, 1 (1969): 92.
33. V. Patrushev, *Zhizn gorozhanina (1965–1998)* (Moscow: Academia, 2000), pp. 140, 161–9.
34. Bornycheva (1969), p. 78.
35. I. Armand, *Stat'i, rechi, pisma* (Moscow, 1975), p. 65.
36. *Zhenshchiny Rossii* . . . (1995), p. 74.
37. *Narodnoe khoziaistvo SSSR* . . . (1972), pp. 366–70.
38. N. Dmitrieva, *Zabota o materi i rebenke* (Moscow: Meditsina, 1967), p. 82.
39. O. Tallja, *Zhenskie Sovety – bol'shaia obshchestvennaia sila* (Cheboksary: Chuvashskoe knizhnoe izdateljstvo, 1970), p. 4; A. Miatieva, *Dela i dumy zhenshchin* (Ashabad: Izdateljstvo Turkmenistan, 1973), pp. 5–14.
40. Grushin (2001), p. 300.
41. N. Rimashevskaia, D. Vannoi, M. Malysheva et al., *Okno v Russkuiu chastnuiu zhizn'* (Moscow: Academia, 1999), p. 22.
42. *Materialy XXV s'ezda KPSS* (Moscow, 1976), pp. 85, 217–18.
43. S. Turchaninova, *Professionalnoe obuchenie rabotnits na promyshlennykh predpriiatiiakh* (Moscow: Institut sotsiologicheskikh issledovanii AN SSSR, 1980), pp. 9–11; A. Basalai, *Professionalnaia zaniatost' zhenshchin i ikh kvalifikatsiia*

(Moscow: Institut sotsiologicheskikh issledovanii AN SSSR, 1980), pp. 19–21; V. Zakharov and G. Morozov, *Sotsial'nye aspekty okhrany truda zhenshchin. Professionalnoe obuchenie rabotnits na promyshlennykh predpriiatiiakh* (Moscow: Institut sotsiologicheskikh issledovanii AN SSSR, 1980), pp. 86–9.

44. *Svod postanovlenii SSSR*, no. 17 (Moscow, 1979), p. 346.
45. *Narodnoe khoziaistvo SSSR v 1988 godu. Statisticheskii ezhegodnik* (Moscow: Finansy i statistika, 1989), p. 195.
46. *Osnovnye napravleniia razvitiia narodnogo khoziaistva SSSR na 1976–1980 gody* (Moscow: Politizdat, 1976), p. 70.
47. J. Levada, 'Chelovek prisposoblenny', *Obshchestvennoe mnenie – 1999* (Moscow: Vserossiiskii tsentr izucheniia obshchestvennogo mneniia, 2000), pp. 71–2.
48. J. Millar, 'The Little Deal: Brezhnev's Contribution to Acquisitive Socialism', in T. Thompson and R. Sheldon (eds), *Soviet Society and Culture* (London: Westview Press, 1988).
49. Personal interview, April 1989.
50. T. Kozlova, 'Zhenshchiny v sostave nauchnykh rabotnikov', in Z. Jankova and A. Basalai (eds), *Sotsialnye problemy ratsionalnogo sootnosheniia professionalnykh i semeino-bytovykh funktsii zhenshchiny* (Moscow: Institut sotsiologicheskikh issledovanii AN SSSR, 1980), pp. 34–5.
51. Rakovskaia (1993), p. 77.
52. Bornycheva (1969), p. 86.
53. A. Nestenko, 'Osnovnye tendentsii izmeneniia velichiny i structury svobodnogo vremeni', in V. Patrushev (ed.), *Tendentsii izmeneniia biudzheta vremeni trudiaschhikhsia* (Moscow: Institut sotsiologicheskikh issledovanii AN SSSR, 1979), pp. 70–81. Nonetheless, men continued to have more free time than women. Nestenko points out that by the end of the 1970s working men had an average of 4.6 hours of leisure time per day, as compared to 3.8 hours for women (p. 76).
54. G. Mints and A. Nepomniashii, 'Tendentsii izmeneniia biudzheta vremeni rabotaiushego naseleniia gorodov Latviiskoi SSR', in V. Patrushev (ed.), *Tendentsii izmeneniia biudzheta vremeni trudiaschhikhsia* (Moscow: Institut sotsiologicheskikh issledovanii AN SSSR, 1979), pp. 33–5.
55. E. Safo and G. Subbotina, 'K probleme sootnosheniia professionalnykh i semeino-bytovykh funktsii zhenshchin-inzhenerov', in Jankova and Basalai (eds) (1980), pp. 38–9.
56. See for example Pankhurst and Sacks (1980).
57. For instance, in one family where I conducted interviews, the grandmother's friend, whom she had met in a prison camp, became an 'aunt' to her children and subsequently cared for her grandchildren. In another example a family provided free accommodation to a student from a different city, in return for help with the children.
58. Grushin (2001), p. 335.

4

Wives or Workers? Women's Position in the Labour Force and in Domestic Life in Sweden and Russia During the 1960s[1]

Helene Carlbäck

> Don't forget to pick up the children in time! We exchange these last words in the staircase . . . It is five after seven and of course, I am running . . . I jump on the bus . . . I run and run and on the stairs, I run into Yakov Petrovich. He does not say a word about my being late.[2]
>
> She had been thinking of divorce . . . However, she had no profession to fall back on . . . She had thought that the most important was a stable home, social status . . . It did not seem to be enough, though, with the house they had built. Or the children. Or the social network . . .[3]

The citations above refer to a well-known predicament faced by women in modern times as the public sphere became increasingly open to their involvement in work outside the home. Russian writer Natalia Baranskaia's *A Week Like Any Other*, first published in the late 1960s, illustrates the conflicting situation for a woman rushing between family and work in a seemingly endless rat race. In contrast, *Gates of Paradise*, by Swedish writer Dagmar Edqvist, published some ten years earlier, depicts the frustrated feelings of a housewife looking back at her life which seems suddenly empty and pointless. During the twentieth century, radical changes in gender relations between men and women took place in both Sweden and Soviet Russia. This chapter presents an analysis of public discourses on the question of women and wage labour, as they were expressed in Swedish and Soviet Russian media publications in the 1960s. It will also compare gender practices regarding women's wage labour and the provision of public childcare in these countries based on existing statistical data.[4]

In the analysis presented here, two key publications have been selected for each country. For Sweden these are *Morgonbris* (Morning Breeze), the monthly magazine of the Federation of Social Democratic Women,[5] and *Hertha*, also a monthly magazine and the mouthpiece of the Fredrika Bremer Association,[6] a politically independent women's rights organisation. *Hertha*'s readers were mainly educated, middle-class women, including both housewives and professional women. *Morgonbris*' readers were generally working-class women, including both housewives and women employed in waged labour outside the home. *Hertha* reflected the discourses of a comparatively educated and intellectually conscious group of women, while *Morgonbris*, despite its editors' aim of promoting political consciousness among its readership, carefully mixed this message with articles on homemakers' day-to-day concerns.

The Soviet discourses discussed here are drawn from my analysis of *Literaturnaia gazeta*[7] and *Rabotnitsa* (Woman Worker)[8] magazine. The monthly *Rabotnitsa* had a print run of almost two million copies, while the weekly *Literaturnaia gazeta*, edited by the Union of Soviet Writers, had a print run of 800 000.[9] As the name suggests, the readers of *Rabotnitsa* were predominantly urban women, while *Literaturnaia gazeta*, which did not focus specifically on women's issues, was read by both men and women, mainly educated, urban intellectuals. According to the paper's editors, 75 per cent of its readers had a university education, while only 7 per cent belonged to the working class.[10]

Of course, the analysis of Swedish and Soviet Russian periodicals presented here cannot provide a complete picture of the ways in which women's issues were talked about and thought of in the two societies. However, rather than seek to cover a whole range of opinions on the matter, the aim of this study is to detect changes over time in particular discourses, reflecting the ideas of elite groups, who perhaps had more direct influence over policy-making and ideological developments in both countries.

Clearly, comparative analysis of the Soviet Russian and Swedish press from this era is not unproblematic. Considering the heavy censorship of the Soviet media and the blatant ways in which the Soviet state used the media to propagate its own propaganda, the usefulness of such comparisons might well be questioned. Nonetheless, my preliminary analysis of a sample of publications from the Khrushchev and early Brezhnev periods, including for example *Komsomol'skaia Pravda*, *Literaturnaia gazeta* and *Rabotnitsa* magazine, suggests that a considerable range of opinions were published on questions concerning people's everyday life. The Soviet Russian press of this era made regular reference to opinion surveys and sociological studies on everyday matters, as well as publishing readers' letters with increasing regularity. For example, between 1966 and 1968, the number of readers' letters to *Literaturnaia gazeta* more than doubled, and the editors published a selection of readers' views in the paper's new column: 'Discussion Club'.[11] The question of opinion surveys and the renewed interest in daily life during this period in Soviet Russia will be discussed in more detail below.

The question of whether Sweden and Soviet Russia are appropriate countries for a comparative study of public discourses on the topic of women and their position in the labour force and domestic life must also be addressed. Former state socialist gender regimes are now commonly perceived from a Swedish perspective as systems promoting traditional gender divisions of roles. Yet, the state socialist systems in fact demonstrated the highest level of women's participation in the labour force and developed wide-ranging childcare institutions. Moreover, in earlier periods Soviet Russian norms for gender relations were viewed as role models for radical feminists in Sweden and elsewhere.[12] These shifting and at times contradictory policies, practices and perceptions regarding gender equality in the two countries frame the questions addressed here.

Promoting women's wage labour? Swedish discourses

The Swedish liberal and socialist women's movements of the 1930s had taken a certain interest in Soviet policies regarding women and women's issues. During the 1940s and 1950s this interest waned for a variety of reasons. The political and cultural environment of the Cold War made it virtually impossible for either of the two opposing worlds to admit being influenced by the other. Whilst the Soviet Union was characterised as a 'totalitarian dictatorship' practising 'socialist oppression' in western discourses, from the Soviet perspective the west was guilty of 'capitalist exploitation' and 'imperialist warmongering'. Furthermore, western European states and the US were by this point developing their own welfare systems, robbing the Soviet socialist experiment of some of its significance as an ideal or model for emulation.[13] The prevalence of a housewife ideal in Sweden at this time also prompted a decline in interest in the Soviet system as a model for gender relations: the post-war decade has been labelled the 'genuine age of housewives'. Dominant discourses of gender difference rested heavily on the notion of a specific female talent for caring for others.[14]

In order for women in developed industrial economies to take part in wage labour it was vital that someone shared the responsibility for childcare with them. Analysis of media debates regarding women's responsibilities and duties in Sweden during the 1950s shows that the married professional woman was expected to bear sole responsibility for the home and family, with or without the assistance of a housekeeper. The underlying assumption was that whether or not a married woman chose to work, she was responsible for ensuring that the domestic chores and childcare were performed satisfactorily. Although municipal childcare existed in Sweden at this time, an analysis of the content of *Morgonbris* and *Hertha* suggests that it was not discussed much in public. It was noted occasionally that the development of childcare centres was important in order for women to be able to go out to work, but the issue was far from prioritised. On the other hand, a view of public childcare as 'bad' for children was widely supported by western child psychologists at this time.[15] A Swedish government report, 'Childcare Centres and Preschools', published in the early 1950s, concludes that public childcare is something of a necessary evil: 'From the children's perspective it is of the greatest importance that mothers should have the opportunity to care for and raise them at home, while they are still small and growing.' However, the report does admit that occasionally such centres might offer 'protection and care' to children from 'homes with unsatisfactory housing and environments' and even 'constitute a link in neurosis-preventive childcare'.[16]

Ten to fifteen years later, public childcare enjoyed a much better reputation in Sweden. In fact, public debate on this issue went through a complete revolution in the 1960s. By this time, for example, experts on children's health and psychology had concluded that children whose mothers worked outside of the home were often more able to adapt to going to school.[17] *Morgonbris* and *Hertha* depicted public childcare centres as contributing positively to children's psychological and social development: 'Childcare centres look after children's best interest',[18] according to one author, whilst according to another, the centres made children 'healthy and active'.[19]

In addition, childcare practices had changed. A report presented by the International Labour Organisation in 1963 emphasised that the socialist states in Eastern Europe and the Scandinavian countries had focused on the difficulties encountered by working mothers in the absence of a functioning childcare system.[20] In this respect a considerable change had taken place in Sweden during the 1960s. In 1955, 10 000 children attended public childcare centres. In 1960 the corresponding figure was 10 200 and in 1970, 33 000. Thus, the number had almost tripled over the course of a decade.[21] Yet, demand was still far greater than supply. According to a government study conducted in 1966 nearly 210 000 women[22] (with

350 000 children under the age of six) would have liked to work outside the home if only they could find satisfactory childcare.[23] Furthermore, although the provision of public childcare institutions grew even more rapidly in the following decade, in 1975 only 17 per cent of all children aged between one and six were enrolled at some form of publicly funded childcare institution.[24]

Consistent with this statistical data, in the 1960s, both *Morgonbris* and *Hertha* published a number of articles referring to the USSR and the socialist states of Eastern Europe, stressing the importance of wage labour and the need for expanded public childcare to give women economic independence. This renewed interest in the Soviet model probably tells us as much about what was going on in Sweden, as it does about what happened in Soviet Russia at the time. Radical winds were blowing through Swedish society and it became fashionable to refer to the experiences of the socialist countries.[25] In the first post-war decade, women in Sweden constituted around 25 per cent of the total workforce: a low figure when compared to other industrialised countries.[26] However, in the mid-1950s the proportion of women, especially married women, in the labour market started to grow considerably. The post-war Swedish economy had entered a new stage of development with industrial production expanding rapidly. Various committees, representing employers, as well as trade unions and the state, maintained that the demand for expansion of the workforce would become ever more urgent as this process continued. The Swedish economy was experiencing the effects of increasing labour shortages and housewives began to be described as a 'hidden labour reserve'. Statistical evidence can give us some idea of the speed with which practices changed in terms of the growth in married women's labour force participation during this period. In 1950, 34 per cent of all women worked outside the home.[27] In 1960 the corresponding figure was 39 per cent and in 1969, 47 per cent. These increases were primarily the result of married women entering the labour market: in 1950, 16 per cent of married women were employed outside the home, by 1960 this figure was 26 per cent and by 1969, 48 per cent. Meanwhile the numbers of unmarried women in paid employment actually fell from 68 per cent in 1950 to 66 per cent in 1960 and 44 per cent in 1969.[28]

However, the majority of Swedish married women were not prepared to work full-time, and requests for part-time work were frequently published in the pages of *Morgonbris* and *Hertha*. An article published in 1962, for example, claimed that many more married housewives would enter working life if only employers would look more favourably on the development of part-time positions: 'How often does one hear,

"If only I could get a part-time job, I would be keen to go back to work"?'[29] Nonetheless, aside from a number of specific jobs in the service sectors, many employers, in both public and private sectors, were reluctant to allow their employees to work part-time, as this was seen as disruptive of the routines and organisational habits of the workplace. Trade union representatives, such as the Women's Committee of the Confederation of Trade Unions, were also critical of part-time jobs but for rather different reasons. Demanding part-time jobs was seen as tantamount to accepting that women were a different category of worker, which would justify employers in offering them lower salaries and less job security.[30] Moreover, part-time jobs tended to involve routine work with fewer opportunities for promotion.[31] However, since the majority of married women really only wanted to work outside of the home for part of the day, the committee was forced to concede to the wishes of its members and push for the development of part-time posts.[32]

Such debates aside, economic developments continued to demand a change in the gender composition of the Swedish labour market. As a result, the idea that women should devote themselves entirely to caring for their children and husbands was increasingly challenged. Freedom of choice about whether to work or to stay at home was questioned in the late 1950s, for example by Alva Myrdal,[33] who felt that staying at home was not a serious option for adult citizens, regardless of gender. She took up the issue in *Women's Two Roles – Home and Work*, which she wrote with Viola Klein in 1956.[34] Myrdal had always supported the right, as well as the duty, of both women and men to perform what she called 'socially useful work'. In the 1930s, however, her writings had been strongly influenced by the unemployment crisis, as well as by Sweden's allegedly dangerous demographic situation caused by falling rates of growth in the population.[35] As a result, her writing at that time had focused on how to support women in their duty to be mothers and care for the home and children, as socially useful work. In the late 1950s, however, she placed much greater emphasis on women's need for work outside the home and the need for women in the workforce. Referring to international sociological surveys, she claimed that about half of all married women who wanted to work outside the home were motivated in this wish by their dissatisfaction with domestic work or their interest in productive labour, while the rest claimed economic motives.[36] In Myrdal and Klein's book the tasks of the mother and the professional woman are described as at once closely intertwined and partially separated: as roles which women play at different stages in their lives. Women are seen as having an unquestioned duty to the home and family but only while their children are small. Once maternity leave is over, society should take over the responsibility for childcare by offering day care centres and/or part-time housekeeping and nannies. This would enable women to fulfil their roles as both mother and professional woman without conflict.[37]

Myrdal and Klein were criticised for what was seen as an unfair attack on housewives. A review published in *Hertha* was rather scathing:

> They seem to be unable to hide their contempt for the work of housewives. They also seem to have forgotten that money might be saved on public counselling for maladjusted children and psychologically defective adults if some mothers were not too occupied with their time-consuming work outside the home.[38]

However, these debates in magazines like *Hertha* and *Morgonbris* in the 1950s were mild by comparison to what was soon to come. In the early 1960s, public debate on women's issues became considerably more lively and heated. The discussion of women and work intensified and established gender roles began to be challenged.

The 1960s have attracted considerable attention in recent years from journalists and writers, as well as in academic circles, as a period of radical socio-political change in Sweden and elsewhere.[39] One person often mentioned as having contributed to a discursive breakthrough in the Swedish gender regime is Eva Moberg.[40] A journalist and writer, Moberg was appointed editor-in-chief of *Hertha* in 1960, and a few months later published an article in the anthology *Young Liberals. Nine Contributions to an Ideological Discussion.* Moberg's writing was powerful and combative even in her suggestive, and provocative, title, 'Women's Parole', the meaning of which she explains in the article:

> Woman has only been liberated on the unspoken condition that she continues to consider the care and nurturing of children as her main role. As long as she understands this as her natural role, somehow inseparable from her status as a gendered creature, then certainly, society will recognise her as a free individual.[41]

In Moberg's view, women had been emancipated on this condition, with the support of various regulations that gave them the right to education, political participation and work, but the married woman was not free as an individual unless she was 'socially and economically fully dependant on a man'. Furthermore, she clarified that true emancipation for women could only be achieved if society firmly rejected, rather than confirmed and upheld, 'marriage as a means of economic support'.[42]

In keeping with this view, *Hertha* published an article in 1961, which opened with the following passage, 'Russian women appear to have come furthest in equality with men. They have – not just in theory – the same opportunities for education, career, and work. They are able to complete their studies even if marriage and children come their way.' Finishing her article with the question of whether Russian women were happy or not, the author concluded that both women and men led hard lives in the Soviet Union, but that in exchange women had their independence and were not 'a male appendage'. A Russian woman was 'never a pretty flower, only a plant for every-day use'.[43]

With her outright feminist position which included a strong gender equality programme for the private sphere as well, Eva Moberg was ahead of her time, not least in her position as editor-in-chief of *Hertha*. After she left the magazine in December 1962, her successors distanced themselves from her more radical writing, toning down previous attacks on homemaking and positive references to the Soviet Russian model. In its January 1963 issue, *Hertha* published another article on conditions for women in the USSR. This time the author was a man, M. Slavek, and the content showed signs of a return to Cold War rhetoric. According to Slavek, women's 'alleged equality' held great propaganda value for the Soviet regime, and women's high employment rates were, to a large extent, due to the relative shortage of men in the post-war Soviet Union.[44] Another article in the same issue on the theme of communist countries, entitled 'Communist and Western Ideology', stressed the value of the reformist, evolutionary path chosen by western societies.[45]

To summarise Swedish discourses on women at work and home, I will turn to the Norwegian-Swedish sociologist Edmund Dahlström, who conducted a contemporary analysis of Swedish debates in the 1960s. Dahlström identified three main 'ideologies on sex roles' in Swedish gender discourses in the early to mid-twentieth century: 'romantic', 'classical liberal' and 'Marxist' ideologies.[46]

'Romantic' gender discourses viewed women and men as essentially different, yet complementary to one another. Genetic characteristics meant that man was designed for professional roles and political tasks in the public sphere. Woman, with her inborn predisposition for maternal care, intuition and altruism was assigned to the private sphere of home and family. However, since men and women were equally needed in society, the latter should support women in their role as wives and mothers, guaranteeing them equal access to education, and equal rights within marriage. 'Classical liberal' ideology called for men and women to be guaranteed equal rights to education and professional work, as well as access to political roles. Thus, women would have the same access to the public sphere as men. However, when women married, the rules of liberal gender equality ceased to apply, since they were expected to stay in the private sphere and care for their children and family.[47]

In the Swedish case, both the romantic and the classical liberal discourses formed the ideological basis for ground-breaking legal documents and other reformist texts in the first half of the twentieth century, such as the bill of women's suffrage (1919), new marriage legislation (1920) or the ban on sacking women on the grounds of pregnancy or marriage (1939). From the 1950s onwards, however, 'classical liberal' ideology developed into 'moderate liberal' ideology (again Dahlström's term). According to this, married women should also have access to the labour market and the state had a duty to support them in this endeavour. As mentioned above, Alva Myrdal was one of the proponents of the idea that women had not only a right, but also a duty to perform wage labour, and society should assist her in this by providing childcare facilities. According to Dahlström, public discourses in the 1950s were dominated by the 'moderate liberal' gender ideology reflected in the work of various government committees and official reports tasked with resolving issues concerning women's professional work, equal salaries, education for women and the provision of childcare.

In the early 1960s, however, proponents of a 'radical liberal' ideology, like Eva Moberg, in turn challenged the 'moderate liberal' ideology by claiming that even if legal policies had eliminated the formal barriers to women's emancipation, cultural barriers still prevented them from taking full advantage of these achievements. As far as the labour market was concerned, employers could only be expected to act within existing cultural frameworks including various gender stereotypes. Especially in a free market system, they were predetermined to discriminate against women, since female employment signalled lower labour productivity due to the caring roles also culturally assigned to women. To counter this it was necessary for men and women to share responsibilities for home and children.

Easing women's dual burden? Soviet Russian discourses

We will now turn to Russian and Soviet discourses and debates on women and wage labour from the same era.[48] Here again I will use Dahlström's 'ideologies on sex roles' which also included Marxist ideology, viewed as the key ideological approach of the socialist countries. Marxism shared the demands of the 'liberal' ideologies that basic human rights and freedoms should apply equally to men and women, including the right to enter the labour market and the public sphere. Marxism, however, extended these rights to married women also, regarding the family as an oppressive institution, permeated by patriarchal practices which for women amounted to domestic slavery and economic and social dependency. Women's access to the public sphere could only be guaranteed by the state and society taking on collective responsibility for domestic chores and childcare.[49] From a contemporary perspective men's absence from the Marxist (as well as the classical liberal) analysis of the conflicting demands of parenthood and wage labour is striking. Only the radical liberal gender ideology which emerged in Sweden and western Europe in the late 1960s and 1970s, and which would soon absorb strong elements of Marxism, offered any serious scrutiny of men's roles and behaviour in the private sphere.

As far as gender practices were concerned, extensive industrialisation and the collectivisation of agriculture in the 1930s meant that large numbers of women had already entered the Soviet Russian labour market. The ideal of the full-time housewife and homemaker was not popularised in the USSR as it was in Sweden. Even the so-called (socially useful) housewives' movement of the 1930s, an initiative of the Communist Party leadership, only concerned a small elite, and never developed a wider following.[50] The economic situation following the turbulent 1930s and the Second World War, compounded by the demographic realities resulting from huge losses of predominantly male lives, meant that for most Soviet women work outside the home was a necessity for survival. In addition, the ideological position of the Soviet leadership clearly advocated wage labour for women. By the end of the 1930s, women constituted nearly 40 per cent of the Soviet labour market and this figure rose to 47 per cent by the end of the 1950s.[51] Thus, the underlying assumption of dominant public/official discourse was that every woman was gainfully employed outside the home and that the state had a duty to support these 'working mothers'.[52]

In *Rabotnitsa* magazine, over the first half of the 1960s, a number of themes emerge in relation to the question of women's roles and duties. Firstly, it was taken for granted that women had a firm place in the labour market, and that their work was highly valued. The magazine regularly presented its readers with portraits of working women, occasionally even with the message that in the long run a woman's work was more important to her than a husband.[53] Consequently, housework was not something which a woman ought to devote much time to. One such article celebrates the life of female miner Klavdiya Shevkonova, who worked her whole life through, despite the fact that she could have stayed at home during periods when her husband earned enough to support the family alone. In an interview with *Rabotnitsa*'s journalist the local Comunist Party Secretary of Shevkonova's Ural mining district asks: 'Should she have sat at home, with nothing to do but look at herself in the mirror, waiting for her husband to come home?'[54] Housewives were seldom featured, but on the rare occasions when they did appear in the pages of *Rabotnitsa*, the moral of the story was that housewives could only be seen as socially useful when performing public duties. In a story on Leninski state farm, for example, housewives are depicted running the childcare centre and helping with duties at sowing and harvest times.[55] The message put across in these articles was that housework should not be so time-consuming as to prevent women from working outside the home.

Secondly, with its strongly anti-patriarchal criticism of women's position in bourgeois and traditional societies, Marxism was depicted as the most woman-friendly political ideology. Accordingly, the Communist Party had a duty to protect women's true interests.[56] The Soviet state claimed to strive to alleviate the burden placed on women by their biological constitution. This meant passing labour legislation to support women's employment, supplying families with the necessary childcare facilities, building healthcare facilities for mothers and children as well as a range of communal services, such as cheap laundries, canteens and other facilities to ease women's burdens in their everyday lives.[57] Thirdly, *Rabotnitsa* suggested that women would only receive the recognition and happiness they desired in their private lives as a result of their public sphere activities, namely paid labour. This point is well illustrated by a story, published in *Rabotnitsa* in 1961, about a woman whose husband only began to appreciate her after she had won awards from the state for her excellent work record.[58]

However, *Rabotnitsa* did not only reproduce slogans, offer heroic portraits and optimistic statements about the superiority of Soviet ideology and practice in relation to women's issues. From time to time, the magazine criticised the failures of certain enterprises, farms or districts to implement the well-directed policies of the party-state. A frequent target of such criticism were factory managers who failed, for example, to recognise the needs of mothers with young infants for extra feeding breaks and other time off to allow for childcare responsibilities. An article entitled 'Respect is All We Ask For!', for example, quoted the female employees of a mining company who complained about the management's disrespect for female workers and preference for hiring men, who were regarded as more 'reliable' when it came to work attendance.[59] Attitudes of this kind also acted as an obstacle to women's access to proper vocational training, another pet topic for *Rabotnitsa*.[60]

Towards the end of the 1960s, however, *Rabotnitsa*'s position on the combination of motherhood and wage labour shifted somewhat. Increasingly the magazine published complaints about how difficult it was for women to combine sole responsibility for the home and children with full-time wage labour. One article, 'Housework Hampers Woman', told the far from unusual story of women who did well at work, but were inevitably prevented from advancing any further in their careers as soon as they became mothers. As the author of this article put it, in every factory or engineering department there was always at least one woman about whom people would say: 'She's so good; we had really great expectations of her. But then she got drowned in nappies and saucepans – the usual attack of everyday life!'[61]

Thus, housework, which had previously been depicted as something which almost took care of itself, became a topic for debate in the later 1960s. This shift reflected a renewed interest on the part of the government in issues relating to the daily lives of the Soviet people. Khrushchev's policies of thaw and search for new ways to mobilise citizens to participate in the life of society, encouraged the use of opinion surveys as a way of discovering the concerns and inclinations of the population. Although these studies were generally subjected to a high degree of political control, and certainly cannot be regarded as independent sociological research, this was nonetheless a genuinely new departure. During the 1950s and particularly the 1960s, social sciences, such as sociology and anthropology, were given a new lease of life. Sociological surveys continued to develop under subsequent regimes and one of the most popular trends in Soviet sociology during the late 1960s were time budget surveys.[62] These surveys showed that women spent considerably more time than men on housework, whilst simultaneously working full-time in a professional capacity.

In *Literaturnaia gazeta*, articles on daily life were regularly published with titles such as 'Personal Life' and 'The Individual and the Group', signalling a tendency towards the reprivatisation of daily life.[63] These headings also reflected new economic trends, in particular the introduction of the Kosygin reform of the mid-1960s, which attempted, rather unsuccessfully, to introduce market elements to the Soviet economy.

Thus, whilst the Swedish discussion focused rather narrowly on the expansion of childcare institutions in order to help women to enter the labour market, the Soviet Russian debate centred on both childcare and improving the network of food shops and public laundries. These differences of course reflect real economic and social differences between life in the two countries. In Russia, demands for easier access to consumer goods and other kinds of commercial services, for example, were put forward in the context of a neglected and malfunctioning system of retail distribution, where the population suffered long and tiring queues for the most basic of staple goods. With regard to the provision of childcare services each country had its own historical experience. As discussed above, in Sweden this issue went from being a neglected topic to one of almost iconic status in the late 1960s. In Soviet Russia, the importance of public childcare had been established much earlier. The Communist Party Programme of 1961 declared that it was desirable for children to attend childcare centres, as part of a campaign to encourage collectivism amongst Soviet citizens. Such declarations echoed earlier Soviet debates of the 1920s and 1930s in which children's upbringing was described as too important to leave to parents alone. This signalled a second major expansion of childcare provision, following the initial campaigns of Stalin's industrialisation in 1927–32: over the period 1955–65 the number of childcare centres almost doubled. At that time, efforts had focused primarily on pre-school children aged three years and over. This time, however, infant childcare was the priority, in combination with public after-school activities for older children.[64]

Did the Russian people regard public childcare as desirable? Up until the late 1960s, this question does not seem to have been posed by the Soviet media. This was logical, given that the state's main concern was to mobilise the 'last reserves' of labour, namely the remaining housewives. During the 1960s, almost 70 per cent of newcomers to the labour market were women.[65] However, American researcher Norton Dodge did take an interest in this and his interviews with Soviet Russian families during the mid-1960s led him to believe that people generally accepted the idea of public childcare; his informants told him repeatedly that children in nurseries developed more rapidly than children raised at home. Still, provision was not sufficient to meet the population's needs. With the help of Soviet statistics, Dodge concluded that in 1962, 51 per cent of children aged between three and six years old and living in the cities of the Russian Soviet republic attended public childcare centres. The corresponding figure for the countryside was 12–20 per cent. Dodge estimated that in Moscow the figures were higher; 60 per cent of children aged between three and six years attended childcare centres. However, the numbers of four month to three-year-olds attending childcare centres were considerably lower,[66] and the lack of spaces in childcare centres was mentioned repeatedly in *Rabotnitsa* and *Literaturnaia gazeta*.

Rabotnitsa took a predominantly quantitative approach to the question of public childcare in the 1960s. The magazine criticised the discrepancy between demand and supply, but rarely considered the quality of provision. In other words, the question of whether public childcare was actually good or bad for a child was not often discussed. On the contrary, experts simply asserted that childcare centres had a positive influence on children. For example a professor of medicine quoted in the article 'Both the Family and the Nursery' asserted that nurseries were just as much a 'blessing' for children as they were for mothers. Qualified nursery nurses – with skills that mothers could hardly aspire to match – trained the children both psychologically and physically.[67] In *Literaturnaia gazeta*, however, a cautious critique of the quality of childcare centres started at the very end of the 1960s, becoming more frequent and outspoken during the 1970s.[68]

Furthermore, new solutions were beginning to be proposed to the problem of women's dual burden. In *Literaturnaia gazeta*'s new 'Discussion Club' a lively debate began on this topic in 1967: 'As long as women are forced to work for money they will have a double burden, regardless of any efforts to make men wash the nappies, scrub the floors and cook the dinner', claimed an article by the novelist Eduard Shim, entitled 'Off to Work, Girls!' (*A nu-ka, devushki*!). The title referred to a well-known poster from the Second World War, depicting a young woman energetically taking hold of a wheelbarrow, heavily laden with bricks. After the incredible losses of working-age men, there had been nothing left for women than to go out to work, claimed the author. Now, in 1967, however, more than twenty years after the end of the war, the author asked himself whether it was really still necessary for women to push wheelbarrows, to carry hods laden with mortar, and to lay pipes. His provocative conclusion questioned the need for women to work at all: 'The problem of women's heavy burden – considering that she has both home and work on her mind – will probably only really be solved when women no longer have to think about how to support themselves.'[69] Thus, suddenly, female wage labour was perceived by some as outdated. A developed society could afford to pay for housework, or even make it possible for men to support their wives and families.

Thus, the author suggested a rather radical solution in the Soviet Russian context, namely that women should stay at home. An alternative, less provocative solution, put forward by the same author was to shorten the working day for women. This issue had been talked about for a long time in Sweden, as discussed above. In contrast to the Swedish debate, however, the length of the working day for women had not been widely debated in Soviet Russia.[70] It would remain a taboo subject at official levels until the mid-1980s, although in everyday life, various strategies were employed to shorten women's working days.[71]

Did Shim's proposal signal new trends in Soviet Russian gender politics or should we regard it more as wishful thinking? When *Literaturnaia gazeta* discussed the dual pressures of professional work and family life for women, the underlying assumption was that every woman was employed outside of the home. In the late 1960s, a number of voices in the Soviet Russian discussions of this issue began to express rather nostalgic attitudes, with men longing for a woman's care at home. Letters to the editor from male readers in 1967, for example, contained phrases like, 'Women are supposed to adorn the hearth of the home, like flowers adorn the meadow' or lamentations in the vein, 'Earlier a woman would surprise her husband with a tasty dish, nowadays she surprises him by not cooking anything at all.'[72]

Views like these did not go undisputed, however. Readers' letters began to flood in and their writers' views on whether women should 'be granted' the opportunity to stay at home instead of going out to work differed mainly along gender lines. Female readers protested by stressing that motherhood was not a profession: 'For us women, work is the dearest and most important thing we have', 'One might as well produce a questionnaire with the heading "Do you want to be a parasite or a full worthy citizen?" and then distribute it to women.'[73]

Conclusions

This chapter has identified a range of public discourses from the 1960s on the question of women and wage labour in Sweden and Soviet Russia. I argue that in many ways the two countries' approaches to the question 'women – wives or workers?' can be compared, despite the profound differences between their socio-economic and political systems. In fact, a blend of gender ideologies – liberal, romantic and Marxist – formed the basis of policies and discourses in both countries, although, in Sweden, liberal ideologies and in Soviet Russia, Marxist ideology dominated the public discourses on gender. The romantic discourse, which attributed a special caring aptitude to women, had an influence in both countries. Thus, in both Sweden and Soviet Russia the main responsibility for caring roles in the home and family fell to women, regardless of the level of their involvement in wage labour, and in both countries, public discussions paid increasing attention to the problems caused by this dual burden during the 1960s.

Of the two countries, Sweden experienced the strongest discursive shift, when established norms concerning married women's primary attatchment to the private sphere were questioned in rather revolutionary ways. In Soviet Russian debates, the most commonly recommended solution was to increase the provision of public services. Women's emancipation had been officially declared many years previously and women's right to work in the public sphere was proclaimed as an important achievement of the Soviet state. However, towards the end of the decade a more questioning approach was taken to the realities of women lives: torn between work and home. The need to improve production of consumer goods and to expand service networks was increasingly acknowledged.

Interestingly, just as voices in the Swedish public debate were increasingly questioning obstacles to women's participation in professional work on an equal footing with men, the opposite tendency could be observed in Soviet Russian debates. Thus, for example, *Literaturnaia gazeta* published articles questioning the fact that women took part in wage labour to the same extent as men. Nonetheless, the discourse of the working mother continued to overshadow any 'wishful thinking' about women taking care of men for many years, and this latter discourse only came to the fore from the 1980s onwards.

Notes

1. Thanks go to Lars Ohlsson and Zhanna Kravchenko for assistance with collecting newspapers and summarising articles in St Petersburg and Moscow and to Peter Isotalo for his help with translations into English.
2. N. Baranskaia, *Nedelia kak nedelia* (Columbus, Ohio: Slavica Publishers, 1989).
3. D. Edqvist, *Paradisets portar* (Stockholm: Albert Bonniers förlag, 1958).
4. The data presented here have been gathered and analysed as part of an ongoing research project, undertaken in collaboration with Swedish, Hungarian and Russian scholars, 'Parenthood versus wage labour. Emancipation rhetorics and gender practices in Soviet Russia and Hungary 1955–1985'. The project is financed by the Foundation for Baltic and East European Studies at Södertörn University College, Stockholm. A number of other aspects of women's work, such as wage differences between men and women, women's opportunities for vocational training and other kinds of education, and various aspects of occupational segregation in Sweden and Soviet Russia have also been analysed in the wider project. These are not dealt with here, and will be addressed in future publications.
5. Founded in 1920, after the establishment of voting rights for women in Sweden.

6. Founded in 1884 and named after one of the first Swedish polemicists on women's issues: the writer and journalist Fredrika Bremer.
7. *Literaturnaia gazeta* has been used by other authors analysing gender discourses and ideologies in the Soviet Union; see for example, G. Lapidus, *Women in Soviet Society. Equality, Development and Social Change* (Berkeley: University of California Press, 1978).
8. *Rabotnitsa* has also been used as a key source for several recent studies on Soviet women's issues. See for example, L. Attwood, *Creating the New Soviet Woman: Women's Magazines as Engineers of Female Identity, 1922–53* (Basingstoke and New York: Macmillan and St. Martin's Press, 1999); Y. Gradskova, 'Soviet People with Female Bodies. Performing Beauty and Maternity in Soviet Russia in the mid-1930s–1960s', Stockholm: Södertörn Doctoral Dissertations, 16, 2007.
9. Like most Soviet publications both *Rabotnitsa* and *Litgazeta*, as it was affectionately known by its readers, had a much wider readership than suggested by their official print runs. It was common for subscriptions to be shared amongst families and acquaintances or held in the reading rooms of libraries and institutions. A Russian colleague has informed me that some people even made extra money by 'subletting' their copy of *ditgazeta* for short periods of time.
10. 'Nashi chitateli', *Literaturnaia gazeta*, 52 (1968): 14.
11. The newspaper reported that it had received 22 500 readers' letters in 1966, and that this figure had risen to 51 000 by 1968.
12. See for example, H. Carlbäck, 'Vision och verklighet. Kvinnan, familjen och staten i det tidiga Sovjetryssland', in H. Blomqvist and L. Ekdahl (eds), *Kommunismen. Hot och löfte. Arbetarrörelsen i skuggan av Sovjetunionen, 1917–1991* (Stockholm: Carlssons, 2003). For a comparative analysis of marriage legislation in Sweden and Soviet Russia during the 1920s, see H. Carlbäck, 'Tracing the Roots of Early Soviet Russian Family Laws', in I. Asztalos Morell, H. Carlbäck, M. Hurd and S. Rastbäck (eds), *Gender Transitions in Russia and Eastern Europe* (Stockholm: Förlags AB Gondolin, 2005).
13. For a discussion on the significance of the existence of the USSR for the development of welfare programmes in the west, see E. Hobsbawm, *Age of Extremes: the Short Twentieth Century, 1914–1991* (London: Joseph, 1994), pp. 7–8.
14. See for example L. Sjöstedt (ed.), *Den osynliga historien. Kvinnornas historia* (Stockholm: Forskningsrådsnämnden, 1993), p. 102.
15. A. Hatje, 'Triangeldramat mor, barn och industri', in A. Baude and C. Runnström (eds), *Kvinnans plats i det tidiga välfärdssamhället* (Stockholm: Carlsson i samarb. m. Arbetslivscentrum, 1994).
16 'Daghem och förskolor. Betänkande om barnstugor och barntillsyn avgivet av 1946 års kommitté för den halvöppna barnavården', *Statens offentliga utredningar, Socialdepartementet, Stockholm*, 15 (1951): 137–40.
17. *Kvinnorna och arbetsmarknaden. Fördomar, fakta, framtid* (Stockholm: Arbetsmarknadsstyr, 1971), p. 52.
18. M. Hofsten, 'Förskola åt alla barn', *Morgonbris*, 2 (1968): 12–13.
19. E. Kokk, 'Fördubblade daghemsplatser', *Morgonbris*, 9, (1968): 16.
20. 'Hur många kvinnor arbetar?', *Morgonbris*, 6 (1965): 21.
21. *Kvinnan i Sverige i statistisk belysning* (Stockholm: Arbetsmarknadens kvinnonämnd, 1970), p. 62.
22. There were roughly 2 500 000 women, aged 16–66, in Sweden at the end of the 1960s.

23. *Kvinnorna och arbetsmarknaden* (1971), p. 47.
24. C. Bergqvist and A. Nyberg, 'Welfare State Restructuring and Child Care in Sweden', in S. Michel and R. Mahon (eds), *Child Care Policy at the Crossroads: Gender and Welfare State Restructuring* (New York: Routledge, 2002), p. 288. This number increased substantially in subsequent decades to finally reach very high figures by international standards.
25. Not only women in Eastern Europe and Soviet Union were of interest: *Morgonbris* and *Hertha* also carried frequent reports on women's issues in Cuba, Vietnam and Algeria especially in the latter half of the 1960s.
26. However, a study conducted by the Swedish Confederation of Trade Unions in 1960 found that in comparison to many other countries, a large proportion of Swedish women worked outside the home, but since they often had part-time and/or short-term jobs this was not registered in the general census. J. Norling, *Kvinnan och förvärvsarbetet* (Stockholm: På uppdrag av LO:s kvinnoråd, 1960), p. 15.
27. These Swedish statistics classified anyone over the age of 14 who had worked for more than one hour in a given week as employed outside the home.
28. *Kvinnan i Sverige* (1970), p. 33. These decreases were mainly due to a rapid increase in the number of young women entering further and higher education.
29. 'Kvinnorna – den stora arbetskraftsreserven', *Morgonbris*, 10 (1962): 23.
30 Y. Waldemarson, 'Att föra kvinnors talan. LO:s kvinnoråd 1947–67', in C. Florin, L. Sommestad and U. Wikander (eds), *Kvinnor mot kvinnor. Om systerskapets svårigheter* (Stockholm: Norstedt, 1999), pp. 91–2.
31. *Kvinnorna och arbetsmarknaden* (1971), p. 36.
32. Waldemarson (1999), p. 91.
33. Alva Myrdal, 1902–86, was a politician (social democrat), diplomat and author of several books on women's, family and other social issues, as well as on disarmament and peace negotiations. For a recent biography see Y. Hirdman, *Det tänkande hjärtat. Boken om Alva Myrdal* (Stockholm: Ordfront, 2006).
34. A. Myrdal and V. Klein, *Women's Two Roles – Home and Work* (London: Routledge & Kegan Paul, 1956). Viola Klein is also the author of several articles on Soviet and European marriage and other gender-related issues.
35. At the request of the Swedish government, Myrdal and her husband, Gunnar Myrdal, published a study 'Crisis in the Population Question', A. Myrdal and G. Myrdal, *Kris i befolkningsfrågan* (Stockholm: Bonnier, 1934). The book would draw considerable attention in years to come. Contemporary critics pointed above all to the tendency towards strong state interference in citizens' private life. Later critics would also note the emphasis on methods of social engineering and the eugenic aspects of the book. See for example, Y. Hirdman, *Social Engineering and the Woman Question: Sweden in the Thirties* (Toronto: Canadian Scholars' Press, 1994). G. Broberg and N. Roll-Hansen (eds), *Eugenics and the Welfare State* (Ann Arbor: Michigan State University Press, 1996).
36. Myrdal and Klein (1956), pp. 89, 100–5.
37. Ibid., pp. 43–59, 179–80.
38. M. Bürki-Romdahl, 'Den moderna kvinnans janusansikte', *Hertha*, 5 (1956): 18.
39. An example of recent scholarly interest in the 1960s are the various seminars that the Institute of Contemporary History at Södertörn University College, Stockholm has arranged since 1998 on topics like 'The 1960s and Sexual

Emancipation', 'May 1968 and the New Radical Women's Movement' and others. See also the programme of the forthcoming international and interdisciplinary conference 'New World Coming – the Sixties and the Shaping of Global Consciousness', in Toronto, Canada in 2007.

40. See for example E. Elgán (ed.), *Kvinnorörelsen och '68. Aspekter och vittnesbörd* (Huddinge: Samtidshistoriska institutet, Södertörns högskola, 2001).
41. E. Moberg, 'Kvinnors villkorliga frigivning', in Hans Hederberg (ed.), *Unga liberaler. Nio inlägg i idédebatten* (Stockhom: Bonniers, 1961), pp. 68–86.
42. Ibid., pp. 72, 77.
43. M. Vinberg, 'Gift i Sovjet och orienten', *Hertha*, 6 (1961): 14.
44. M. Slavek, 'Kvinnans villkor i Sovjetstaterna', *Hertha*, 1 (1963): 16.
45. M. Wohlin, 'Kommunistisk och västerländsk ideologi', *Hertha*, 1 (1963): 27.
46. E. Dahlström, *Analys av könsrollsdebatten. En bearbetning av Edmund Dahlströms inledningskapitel i SNS-skriften Kvinnors liv och arbete* (Stockholm: Studieförbundet Näringsliv och samhälle, 1964), pp. 3–4.
47. Ibid., pp. 2–3.
48. For major existing studies on Soviet gender relations in this period, see for example: Lapidus (1978); M. Buckley, *Women and Ideology in the Soviet Union* (Ann Arbor: University of Michigan Press, 1989); M. Ilic, S. Reid and L. Attwood (eds), *Women in the Khrushchev Era* (Basingstoke: Palgrave Macmillan, 2004). For an overview of works on gendered questions specifically related to wage labour, see K. Katz, *Gender, Work and Wages in the Soviet Union: a Legacy of Discrimination* (Basingstoke: Palgrave Macmillan, 2001).
49. Dahlström (1964), pp. 2–3.
50. For a detailed examination of the *obshchestvennitsa* movement see M. Buckley, 'The Untold Story of Obshchestvennnitsa Movement in the 1930s', *Europe-Asia Studies*, 48, 4 (1996): 569–86.
51. L. Denisova, *Zhenshchiny russkikh selenii. Trudovye budni* (Moscow: Izdatel'stvo dom 'Mir Istorii', 2003), p. 20.
52. For a detailed discussion of this term, see for example A. Rotkirch and A. Temkina, 'Soviet Gender Contracts and their Shifts in Contemporary Russia', in A. Temkina (ed.), *Russia in Transition: the Cases of New Collective Actors and New Collective Actions* (Helsinki: Kikimora publications, Aleksanteri Instituutti, 1997).
53. I. Sterin, 'Iz zavtrashnego dnia', *Rabotnitsa*, 4 (1960): 5–7.
54. K. Kuznetsova, 'Prosto Klava', *Rabotnitsa*, 6 (1961): 3–4.
55. A. Volkova and V. Piugina, '25 let spustia', *Rabotnitsa*, 8 (1961): 4–6; A. Volkova and V. Piugina, '25 let spustia', *Rabotnitsa*, 9 (1961): 22–4.
56. G. Lifshits, 'Nachinalos' eto tak', *Rabotnitsa*, 1 (1960): 6.
57. Editorial: 'I razumom i serdtsem', *Rabotnitsa*, 10 (1961): 2–3.
58. V. Gerasimova, 'Shchast'e', *Rabotnitsa*, 12 (1961): 1, 8.
59. N. Azerskaia, 'My khotim odnogo: chtoby nas uvazhali!', *Rabotnitsa*, 9 (1961): 14–15.
60. See for example Azerskaia (1961); E. Cherepakhova, 'Ekho domostroia', *Rabotnitsa*, 3 (1965): 14.
61. T. Aleksandrova, 'Dom meshaet zhenshchinam', *Rabotnitsa*, 4 (1968): 16.
62. Soviet sociologists also took part in a range of international comparative studies of this type; see for example: J. Zuzanek, *Work and Leisure in the Soviet Union: a Time-Budget Analysis* (New York: Praeger, 1980).

63. See also Vinokurova, this volume, for a discussion of the 'reprivatisation' of life under Khrushchev and Brezhnev.
64. N. Dodge, *Women in the Soviet Economy: Their Role in Economic, Scientific, and Technical Development* (Baltimore: Johns Hopkins University Press, 1966), pp. 78–87.
65. Vinokurova, this volume, p. 65.
66. Dodge (1966), pp. 76–87.
67. 'I semia i iasli', *Rabotnitsa*, 5 (1969): 24.
68. Lapidus (1978), pp. 242–7.
69. E. Shim, 'A nu-ka devushki', *Literaturnaia gazeta*, 5 (1967): 12.
70. A. McAuley, *Women's Work and Wages in the Soviet Union* (London: Allen & Unwin, 1981), p. 202.
71. Katz (2001), pp. 95–7.
72. L. Kuznetsova, 'Tak chei zhe udel kukhnia?', *Literaturnaia gazeta*, 28 (1967): 12.
73. L. Kuznetsova, 'Nosha ne po plechu', *Literaturnaia gazeta*, 7 (1967): 11; Kuznetsova, 'Tak chei zhe udel kukhnia?', p. 12.

5
Heroine Mothers and Demographic Crises: the Legacy of the Late Soviet Era

Sue Bridger

The figure of the 'Heroine Mother', a woman who had borne ten or more children, took her place in Soviet propaganda in the wake of the catastrophic losses of the Second World War. In 1944, a draconian piece of family legislation which made divorce virtually impossible simultaneously instituted a range of honours for the mothers of large families.[1] By the 1970s, however, a quarter century after the death of Stalin, the 'Heroine Mothers' could be easily dismissed as an anachronism. As the 1944 law was superceded by the more humane family legislation of the 1960s, these 'Heroines' of an earlier pronatalist policy appeared to be simply a leftover from the Stalinist past. Though the array of orders and medals on offer to mothers of five or more children still remained, their relevance to the majority of the population was increasingly doubtful. Their presence, if it was felt at all, appeared to be largely confined to the obligatory tables in the annual statistical yearbooks. Indeed, so rare were the holders of these awards that most people outside the territories of the Soviet Central Asian republics were unlikely ever to have met one: in the entire history of honouring mothers in this way in the USSR, only 8000 women received an award, just over 400 attaining the pinnacle of 'Heroine Mother'.[2] It was something of a surprise, therefore, when, in the late 1970s, the Heroine Mothers became the focus of sustained propaganda as the Communist Party leadership once more became concerned at demographic developments.

During the 1960s the impact of urbanisation over previous decades had become very visible. For the first time, the majority of Soviet people were living in cities and towns and this move away from the land was accompanied by a significant decline in the birth rate. In part this resulted directly from the trauma of the Second World War: women in the most fertile age groups in the 1960s belonged to the relatively small wartime generation. This factor was, however, exacerbated by a general move towards smaller families in both urban and rural areas over the course of the decade. The low birth rate and ageing population produced a steep decline in natural growth rates in European areas of the USSR during the 1960s and 1970s. At the same time, the birth rate in the Central Asian republics, although declining, remained at a relatively high level in an area with a much younger population. The implications of these developments were, by the mid-1970s, causing considerable headaches for Soviet planners.

Over the course of the 1970s, demographic change produced an increasing degree of unevenness across the country in terms of labour resources. In the European countryside, out-migration and a declining birth rate were together being seen as a substantial threat to agricultural production. However, the influx of rural migrants to the cities would not in the longer term be enough to offset the overall reduction in urban family size. In terms of fertility rates, the urban population in European areas was no longer maintaining itself at replacement level. The republics of Central Asia, meanwhile, were experiencing substantial growth, primarily in their relatively static rural populations. The result was an enormous labour-surplus region whose population could not be adequately supported on the land and yet which still imported skilled labour from European areas to staff its factories.

Although never openly acknowledged in a state dominated by the concept of the 'friendship of peoples', there was undoubtedly considerable disquiet in the Slav-dominated leadership at the burgeoning of the Asian population in the face of relative European decline. Where fears of ethnic imbalance were voiced, obliquely rather than directly, the potential impact on defence, rather than on internal politics and stability, was the key issue at stake. A piece which appeared in the academic journal *Voprosy filosofii* in 1977 illustrated the point:

> Such unfavourable demographic trends in our country as the drop in the birth rate, the halt in the growth of average life expectancy, the development of irrational migration patterns, the formation of disproportionate age and sex structures in the population in some regions and the systematic rise in the divorce rate all have their impact on the Soviet armed forces. These demographic trends manifest themselves in the size, geographic distribution and national make-up of contingents of conscripts . . . Efforts must be made to surmount and offset the consequences of the country's unfavourable demographic situation and to prevent them from affecting the combat capability and readiness of the Soviet armed forces.[3]

In 1981, the Soviet government announced substantial improvements in maternity leave provisions. Rather than being immediately applicable to the whole country, these were to be phased in over several years on a broad geographical basis from the north to the south of the country. This unprecedented approach at once illustrated both the government's concern to tailor family policy to regional development and the political sensitivities which any such attempt was likely to encounter.

The revival of the Heroine Mother

It was against this background that the centrally based, Russian-language press provided its readers with a return to the theme of the Heroine Mother.[4] Across Russia, where the cities were full of 'only children', parents and newly-weds were invited to consider the benefits of large and extremely large families. As some kind of a concession to reality, much of the writing on the latterday Heroines was confined to the rural press: though rural women were evidently expressing little desire to bear ten children, at least they were more likely to have the space for them. Throughout these features the overriding message was that the family, as Russian parents had come to perceive it, was not a real family at all. 'You need at least three children to make a family,' was a sentiment constantly expressed, usually by women who had already given birth to five or more.

One of the most curious aspects of the 'Heroine Mother' campaign in the late 1970s and early 1980s was its very clear plan of attack. The national rural daily, *Sel'skaia zhizn'* (Rural Life), for example, devoted the bottom half of page four, once a month, to an article with a title such as 'The Greatest Happiness', which would feature a happy and contented Heroine Mother. Somewhere in the piece the woman concerned would invariably make a comment such as this from a Moldavian mother of twelve: 'My wish for you, dear women, is to have as many children as I have and for them to be as good as mine are. Children are a great blessing. I should know, believe me.'[5] The blessing, it was spelled out, was not merely in the pleasure of seeing the children grow but in the effect of this process on the woman herself. 'Happy motherhood, love and respect' from both husband and children in families such as these was portrayed not just as a source of fulfilment but, more improbably, as the key to physical beauty in the woman concerned. The benefits, it was maintained, would be experienced not just by the woman but by her husband too. Letters from women readers, responding to these articles, contained glowing descriptions of how the births of their many children had transformed good-for-nothing men into supportive and loving providers. Couples in search of family harmony were advised first to establish the family and the harmony would surely follow. As one male reader summed it up: 'I feel sorry for couples who put off having children. They get to thirty and they still don't have any. That's often the reason why marriages break up.'[6]

These features illustrating the contented lives of the Heroine Mothers and their husbands, together with the letters from parents of more modest, if still sizeable, families were invariably bolstered by the writings and pronouncements of 'experts'. A small army of doctors, teachers and psychologists was drafted in to the campaign, all of them quite clear about what was best for women and for couples:

> A woman's physiology and mentality are forever directing her towards motherhood. Motherhood inspires her, completes her life and her family happiness. Couples who think that family happiness can be created without children and who take steps to avoid the birth of a child are making a sad mistake;[7]

or what was best for children:

> In large families there's a lot less for us doctors to do. The children grow up healthy. They are better developed both physically and psychologically . . . And it's all because in these families the older children look out for the younger ones. The collective takes care of upbringing;[8]

or even what was best for society at large:

> Children from large families are more hard-working, more independent, more modest and have more respect for their elders.[9]

The notion of the family as a collective, as a microcosm of all that was best in the wider Soviet society was patently a very seductive one for the authors of these articles. It was certainly used many times as a counterpoint to the assumed 'selfishness' of the typical modern couple and their self-obsessed 'only child'.

This emphasis on private and public morality, and the promotion of large families as a catalyst for the improvement of both, reached its apotheosis in articles focusing on specific areas with high concentrations of Heroine Mothers. One such place was the village of Borki in the Kharkov region of Ukraine, featured early in the campaign to promote Heroine Mothers as an example of excellent local social organisation. In this village, both the local collective farm and the rural soviet were systematically providing fuel, building materials, free holidays and trips to children's camps, as well as free food, shoes and clothes for the school-age children of the local 'Heroines'. A 1977 article in *Krest'ianka* (Peasant Woman) magazine featured the presentation to a local woman calf-rearer of a carpet and a fridge, together with a promise of a new house, on the occasion of her elevation to the ranks of the Heroine Mothers, the fifteenth woman in the district to be so honoured. By 1980, in a population of just over 2000, Borki could boast no less than 152 large families and a staggering 28 Heroine Mothers. More remarkable still was the fact that some of these women apparently held leading positions on the collective farm – the chief zootechnician, for example – whilst some belonged to 'dynasties' of Heroine Mothers in which mother, daughter and daughter-in-law had all produced over ten children. All of this, the articles were keen to point out, produced a very particular local 'moral climate' in which family breakdown was almost unknown.[10]

Whilst features such as these were relentlessly turned out in the rural press they were by no means confined there. In the late 1970s and early 1980s, features on large families could be found in the unlikeliest places. Even the front page of a national daily such as *Izvestiia* might highlight a photograph of such a family for no other reason than its size and its members' love of hard work.[11] Whilst the families featured in this way more often than not lived in rural areas, their stories of collective endeavour and straightforward morality were undoubtedly intended to have far wider application. In the final years of the Brezhnev era the press campaign was complemented by feature films on general release which sought to convey the same message. One such film, *Twenty Years On* (*20 let spustia*) which toured Soviet cinemas in 1980, told the story of a class reunion where the former classmates, now in their late thirties, described their achievements to each other. The last to tell her tale, an unassuming woman who begins by saying she has achieved very little, ends by simply inviting in her family. The final shot of the film shows her proudly surrounded by her ten children, the clear implication being that she has achieved more than any of them. In press features aimed at an urban female readership, the delivery of the message latterly became somewhat more subtle, though scarcely less relentless. Through 1979 and 1980 in particular, *Rabotnitsa* (Woman Worker) magazine, for example, filled page after page with heavily illustrated features on children, with 'mother and child' line-drawings and paintings, interviews with the mothers of the famous and the mothers of exemplary workers, articles on young families and advice on stronger marriages or features for husbands on how to be a good family man.

If the media swung headlong into the promotion of Heroine Mothers as a means of resolving the country's demographic dilemmas, a rather more sober approach was simultaneously emanating from the academic community. Throughout the 1970s a substantial number of works by demographers and sociologists alike sought to establish correlations between people's notions of an ideal family, the number of children they wanted themselves and the number they actually had. Much of this material showed a very high correlation over time between intentions and reality in all major groups in the population. Before the campaign to boost the birth rate had even got into its stride, surveys were revealing that over 40 per cent of women in major cities would not consider having even a third child whatever the circumstances.[12] It was apparent, therefore, that people often had a clear idea of what constituted the 'right' number of children for a family to have, but did not want such a family for themselves. Given this state of affairs, expending newsprint on descriptions of Heroine Mothers appeared to be a particularly futile activity. Evidently, a rather different approach would be needed if attitudes such as these were to be changed.

Strengthening the family: less heroism, more realism?

The fundamental premise behind the 1981 maternity provisions was the need to promote the three-child family. As the birth of a third child was regarded as decisive for the reproduction of the population, changes in maternity benefits concentrated incentives on the first three children born to a family, with a view to bringing birth rates in the European USSR up to the crucial replacement level. At the same time, the decision not to raise benefits for fourth and subsequent children marked a decisive shift away from past pronatalist policy and sent a clear message to the families of the southern republics. Heroine Mothers might have been a suitable focus for the Russian-targeted press but they were not to be fêted in quite the same way outside the areas of declining births. The beauty of the promotion of the three-child family lay in its simplicity and its apparent egalitarianism. Abandoning the emphasis on very large families, the Soviet government quickly found expert opinion to support its new stance that a family of three was the optimum domestic 'collective'. It was a position which appeared, unlike the Heroine Mother propaganda, to have at least some grounding in reality for urban Russian families. At the same time, the promotion of the three-child family was intended to discourage successive births in the rural south on the grounds of state concern for child health.

In addition to increasing benefits and leave to parents, the 1981 legislation declared the state's interest in 'strengthening the family as one of the highest moral values of socialist society' and, to this end, in increasing and improving popular literature on childcare, marriage and demographic issues.[13] These provisions gave a boost to the production of a whole series of studies by sociologists and demographers which analysed attitudes towards the family and offered strategies for increasing births and enhancing family stability. The consensus emerging from much of this work was that there was very little point in directing propaganda at people who had already produced children: the key group in terms of increasing population were more likely to be still at school. As some writers were pointing out, the predominance of only children in urban families meant that many young people had very limited experience of being with small children or caring for them. Some were suggesting, therefore, that the process of changing attitudes needed to begin in childhood itself. It was proposed that links should be forged between schools and nurseries as well as visits to families with babies and an opportunity for schoolchildren to learn special games suitable for the very young. In this way, it was hoped, a fondness for and understanding of small children might be fostered in children who lacked this kind of contact in their own families.[14]

Beyond childhood, it was found, changes in attitude could still be effected given appropriate information and discussion on themes related to childcare. A pilot study in Lipetsk ran a course for local college students entitled, 'The Family Under Socialism', questioning the participants about their views on their future family. At the beginning of the course 88 per cent of the girls and 74 per cent of the boys said that they wanted to have only one child. After extensive meetings with psychologists, sociologists and doctors, however, these percentages fell dramatically to just over 1 per cent, with three-quarters of the students stating a preference for two children. Even more impressively, over a fifth were now saying that they wanted three or more.[15] Whether the immediate impact of a course such as this was likely to be translated into long-term action remained, of course, a moot point. Many of the sociologists and demographers contributing to this debate proposed substantial changes in taxation, the development of national counselling services for couples and the provision of extensive sex education and advice, as fundamental issues to be tackled if the state were serious about increasing the birth rate.[16]

The issue of counselling, in particular, was regarded as essential by those who saw the divorce rate, as many sociologists did, as inextricably linked to the question of declining births. It was at this point that those demographers and sociologists who were focusing above all on the issue of population decline, found themselves wading through a moral minefield. One and the same author could frequently be found warning of the need for great sensitivity on family matters and simultaneously suggesting new, draconian measures. A characteristic piece, published in 1986, for example, stressed that all elements of coercion must be avoided and then went on to propose a change in the law to prohibit divorce within three or five years of marriage in order to 'make people think' before getting married.[17] Yet, for some contributors to the discussion, counselling was unlikely to be the answer when the roots of the problem went far deeper in social attitudes. For the demographer, Viktor Perevedentsev, for example, the causes of the low birth rate were inextricably linked to divorce, yet the major cause of divorce, in his view, was inequality. As a result of inequality in the home, women not only ended marriages but also became determined not to produce the children which would make their experience of inequality worse still. Given this state of affairs, the issue of the birth rate was unlikely to be resolved unless young people were provided with teaching which would 'inculcate a sense of mutual responsibility in couples both in their relationships before marriage and within the family'.[18]

During the first half of the 1980s, as proposals such as these were beginning to appear in articles written by academics in the mainstream press, journalists were engaged in a rather different way in promoting changes in attitudes towards childbearing. In the wake of the 1981 legislation, media discourse changed markedly, even in publications aimed at a Russian rural readership. Gone was the clockwork regularity of features on Heroine Mothers. In their place came a new emphasis on femininity and motherhood, on the special nurturant qualities only women could convey and all women were expected to demonstrate. Both rural and urban audiences were treated to a steady diet of features and interviews emphasising female self-sacrifice and fulfilment through domestic duties, all of which reached an annual peak in the saccharine produced by a succession of well-known and invariably male writers for International Women's Day:

> All that is sacred is linked with the Mother who gives life to her sons and sends them out with a blessing on their unknown, difficult and therefore beautiful road. She herself, expecting nothing in return for her boundless efforts and care, stands waiting at the doorstep of their home, believing in the future of her sons and hoping that their road will be long and safe, for the strength and faith of mothers lies in their eternal hope.[19]

If the Heroine Mothers had largely disappeared from the pages of Soviet women's magazines in the early 1980s, the copy which took their place was still a very far cry from Perevedentsev's notion of recognising inequality as a primary factor in the birth rate's decline.

Perestroika and pronatalism

The policy of *glasnost* instigated in the mid-1980s under Mikhail Gorbachev did not simply give rise to a more radical agenda in domestic policy. In its initial phase, one of its more curious results was the way in which certain types of propaganda current in the Stalin era which had been quietly allowed to die a death suddenly enjoyed a brief reflowering. Just as the Stakhanovites saw a temporary renaissance in the journalism of the mid-1980s, so the Heroine Mothers unexpectedly put in a further appearance. Despite the post-1981 shift of emphasis towards the three-child family, these enormous families and their purported benefits were once more back on the journalistic agenda. Interestingly, this phenomenon was not confined to the rural press this time, but spilled over into photo features in magazines such as *Rabotnitsa* where loving parents and their numerous attractive children stared out of the windows of city flats.[20] More pointedly still, these examples were evidently intended as a counterpoint to the upsurge of moral panic over youth deviance and the sudden massive media emphasis on sex, drugs and anti-social behaviour. In the wake of the new accommodation between state and religion in the late 1980s, the church could now be relied upon to provide a moral alternative to the threat of a newly individualistic culture. In relation to the eternal question of the birth rate, priests themselves offered some of the few examples of large and exemplary urban families to be found. Interviews with priests and their wives on the moral aspects of upbringing and the role of religion in the family provided an interesting *perestroika*-style dimension to the long-standing discussion of the innate moral superiority of the large family.[21]

But, inevitably perhaps, it was in the rural press that the Heroine Mother propaganda returned with full force once more. *Krest'ianka* magazine, for example, kicked off the year 1987 with a lead article featuring a Kaluga region village where 72 mothers had received the Stalin-era decorations for producing large families and no less than 22 were Heroine Mothers. In these less stable times it was the moral benefits of such an environment which were especially underlined. Whilst readers were assured that 'children in large families don't get ill', it was clearly rather more important that they did not get into trouble either. The children in these families, it was categorically stated, were less naughty, more hard-working, were not selfish or materialistic and, above all, did not become delinquents. Moral pressure evidently had its part to play: in a curious aside it was observed that, if any young men in this village looked like going off the rails after returning from their army service, parents would resort to the 'tried and tested method' of getting them married off. The mothers of these large families were allowed to retire at 50, though this was evidently a reward rather than a necessity as 'a woman stays young when she has growing children'. Just as in Borki almost a decade before, here was a village, it was claimed, with such a particular moral climate that divorces and family conflicts were unknown.[22]

Just to ensure the point was not lost, a similarly expansive piece appeared in the magazine that same summer. A centre-spread photo feature, it focused on the 'Museum of Motherhood' in a Kurgan region village. There was, the article was at pains to point out, nothing special about the women featured in the museum: 'they just have children, bring them up and work for their future'. Just as before, the links were made between exemplary personal morality and exemplary work for the good of the state. Describing one woman, a mother of eleven, the magazine observed, 'the house is always full of children but she always welcomes others . . . and she is one of the best dairy women on the collective farm'.[23]

Krest'ianka rounded off the year with a piece which featured readers' responses to the questions it had raised. In an era when readers' letters were beginning to be more radical than the pundits of *perestroika*, dissenting voices to the notion that large families were always a blessing and a benefit were given short shrift. Mothers of large families, claimed the author of this piece, know that there is 'no happiness for a woman outside the family' and have a deep intuition that children need large families. In the assumption that a large family equals a happy family, the author opined, 'we all have a feeling of envy when we see large families'. Against this background, the descriptions in readers' letters of the difficulties encountered by large families were roundly condemned as pure materialism. At this stage, any genuine discussion of problems could still be swept aside in a mass of propaganda. Readers were still being assured that children in large families had no psychological problems and that the most beautiful wives were mothers of large families because 'it's nature's way'.[24]

However, if *Krest'ianka*'s journalists sometimes appeared to be living in a time warp, the 'expert' view of the *perestroika* period was often considerably more circumspect. Noting that public opinion in European republics of the USSR was already regarding the three-child family as a large family, some demographers and sociologists were advising that such attitudes could not be ignored when taking measures to increase the birth rate. It was not simply a question of promoting all and any births, but rather of taking a sober look at the overall needs of Soviet families. If women were unlikely to produce a third or often even a second child, it was important to recognise that this was frequently connected to unhappy marriages and the increasing numbers of divorced women in their thirties. Another significant factor was secondary infertility created by a reliance on abortion as the major means of birth control. At the same time, the trend towards rising numbers of births to women under twenty was not necessarily something to be welcomed. This, in the view of certain authors, was indicative of a looser sexual morality, producing ill-considered, early marriages and unplanned, unwanted children. What was needed, they believed, was better sex education and a much-improved provision of contraception: in the longer term, the phenomenon of early marriage and early childbearing was unlikely to produce the desired three-child family in significant numbers. Indeed, it might well serve simply to reinforce the negative factors already observed.[25]

In the era of *glasnost*, the issue of public opinion and, especially, of the questioning of the Stalinist legacy was becoming increasingly important. It was something which journalists were now actively seeking out and requiring specialists to respond to, not simply to parrot the party line, but to engage in informed debate. Amongst many 'round table' discussions in the media at this period, the weekly, *Nedelia*, invited a whole roomful of academics, politicians and even the winner of a Lithuanian 'best father' competition to debate how best to support and foster the modern family. The discussion hinged upon readers' letters to the paper expressing the need to ditch the entire post-1944 system of medals and awards for motherhood. As one reader put it, 'A neighbour of ours has brought up two splendid sons, she's a grandmother now, she's gained a doctorate, she's a chemist and she's spent the last five years looking after her father who's paralysed. Isn't she a heroic woman?' Or, as another observed, 'we're emancipated women, who says we're supposed to have ten children?'[26]

The question of the medals could be readily agreed by *Nedelia*'s specialists. After all, the motherhood medals rewarded the mere matter of giving birth and had nothing to say about the issue of upbringing. As far as this was concerned, the experts thought, both parents should be equally rewarded by, for example, a 'Heroine Family' or 'Model Family' award in a move to 'liquidate the injustice' of the system as it stood. For some, however, the very words, 'heroine' and 'heroism', had far too much of a ring of the discredited past about them: giving birth was one thing, being a 'heroine' was something very different. The problem with this line of thought, however, was twofold: it was not at all clear how rewarding excellent upbringing was going to encourage anyone to have more children, and the notion of judging 'quality' within the family immediately implied more rather than less paternalism on the part of the state. For some of the politicians present, this clearly presented no problem:

> I'd like to remind everyone that the family is a cell of society. The kind of family we have determines what kind of society we have. 'Strong family – strong nation' – this is something we seem to have forgotten. And now we can see the results . . . We shouldn't be rewarding people for having lots of children, but for having strong, healthy families!

Exactly who was going to be responsible for deciding awards such as this was equally self-evident to those proposing such measures. The local 'workers' collective' was an obvious choice, or, better still, the local administration could collect references from the workplace, from schools and from the local social organisations. It was left to the demographers present, themselves insisting on the promotion of the four- or five-child family, to warn that meddling in people's families was fraught with danger, however well-meaning the local 'workers' collective' might be.[27]

Everyday heroism: the other side of the medal

Whilst a good deal of the journalism and, at the very least, some of the expert commentary on the issue of large families and demographic developments changed very little through the *perestroika* period, the advent of *glasnost* did bring one very significant difference. Whatever views the 'experts' might expound in the pages of the press, these could now be far more readily challenged, embellished or modified by readers' voices. However much politicians might wish simply to propagandise, they could no longer avoid a discussion of uncomfortable realities. When those who had produced all the children the state required of them and more began to speak, the result offered a very different picture of society's care and concern for large families.

At first glance, the complaints by parents, usually mothers, of large families might appear nothing if not ungrateful. Throughout the *perestroika* period there were substantial improvements announced in benefits to large families and considerable publicity given to schemes already in place. From 1987, low-income families with three or more children had a right to free places at summer camps and on holidays to health resorts. Where families such as these were headed by a single parent they would also get free school, sports and pioneer uniforms and free breakfasts. From 1988 children under the age of two from low-income and large families would receive free food. In addition, local initiatives to assist large families were now authorised by government decree: some of these were developed in the wake of the 1981 family legislation, others were begun or further encouraged by a Council of Ministers' resolution of 1986 and by a Supreme Soviet resolution of 1990. In Moscow, for example, district councils were placed under an obligation to register families with three or more children under sixteen and to ensure that they received priority access to local shops and services and also priority telephone installation. In addition, women who gave birth to twins were to get priority housing within one year. Finally, the overall level of state benefits to families was increased in line with the minimum wage and the basis of entitlement was developed significantly by the new family legislation introduced in 1990. Additional benefits to large families were to be encouraged but would depend on local authority budgets.[28]

Many of the provisions of the 1990 legislation were undoubtedly intended to respond to the letters which had been appearing in the press since the mid-1980s. The most striking of these were not so much complaints as simply detailed descriptions of daily life in a large family and their attempts to make ends meet. One such letter, which its author, a teacher and mother of five, described as 'some thoughts on large families' was printed in full across half a broadsheet page of *Literaturnaia gazeta* in 1986. In it, she explained how the change in maternity leave entitlement brought about by the 1981 legislation had actually worsened the situation for large families. Nurseries, particularly it would appear workplace nurseries, had begun to operate on the premise that places were now no longer needed for children under eighteen months, the new length of maternity leave. Without a nursery place, it was impossible to go back to work, but the leave was only paid (at a mere 50 rubles a month) for the first year. As a result, women were being effectively forced to take the new full leave entitlement but without any form of pay or benefit for the final six months. The result, for a large family, could be catastrophic.

In the example provided by this family, the husband, a highly experienced engineer, had given up his job in order to earn more as a manual worker, a wage, however, which still barely covered the food bill. His wife, meanwhile, described her tortuous and ultimately fruitless attempts at gaining permission to work from home, her hours spent knitting and her anxieties over selling her work. In 1986, warding off poverty in this way was still enough to merit a criminal conviction and the label 'speculator' at her place of work, as she could testify from personal experience. Priority access to goods and services, meanwhile, was by no means guaranteed, often falling victim to local bureaucracy or unexplained prohibitions. On the ground, far away from the pages of the pre-*glasnost* press, a very different picture of life for large families had been emerging. As this woman observed:

> It's impossible to avoid reading and hearing about how much help large families get. You know, when I had fewer children, I genuinely believed it. But after I had my third, then the fourth and fifth, I lost all my illusions . . . If these problems were solved you wouldn't need propaganda to get women to have even two children.[29]

Whilst there were many readers' letters in this era describing problems with bureaucracy, especially over housing, complaints about a simple lack of money also began to appear. Sometimes, negativity towards large families was being expressed by adults who had themselves grown up with numerous brothers and sisters and remembered the constant humiliations of 'going without' rather than the joys of the happy children's collective. Though these might be dismissed as the unavoidable reality of the harsh post-war years (although usually describing a far more recent past), the descriptions of how relative deprivation might feel in the contemporary USSR were more difficult to gloss over:

> We are permanently short of money in our family. The children would love to eat salami or chocolate when it's in the shops, but look at the prices . . . My sons aren't demanding, they wear whatever we buy them, but I'm a mother and I know that a boy of 18 wants to look better. But fashionable trousers cost 100 rubles.[30]

It is, after all, one thing to experience poverty when everyone else is in the same boat in a land entirely lacking in advertisements. By the late 1980s, however, a lack of money might be experienced very differently when consumerism had recently winged in from the west with its fashion magazines and its smart new shops. Even if these things were absent from the provinces, television ensured that, even in the depths of the countryside, young people were perfectly well aware how their more prosperous peers were living.

Beyond the propaganda, sociological research was beginning to reveal the realities of life for large families in the USSR's final decade. Presenting a survey of families with four or more children, the eminent, Leningrad-based sociologist, Sergei Golod, concluded that there were substantial problems, both economic and social, for these families in the Soviet Union's second city. Whilst the press preferred to publish letters from parents of large families who happened to be teachers or doctors, Golod's survey found that the majority of women in Leningrad with large families were manual workers. Almost a quarter of them had not completed their secondary education. Around half were working as caretakers and cleaners on extremely low pay in order to obtain some kind of flexibility in employment. The dynamics of these families were likely to be rather less favourable than the picture habitually presented in the press:

> However much we talk about 'the atmosphere of the large family', about mutual support and discipline, families like this are the exception rather than the rule. As we know from medical and legal research, having too many children in one family is not such a good thing as it may appear at first sight. Large urban families produce more juvenile crime and a great deal of truancy and poor schooling.[31]

As issues such as these began to be acknowledged for the first time in the Soviet media, they formed part of a picture of increasingly negative public attitudes towards the very concept of the large family.

In conclusion: women and market forces

For the journalists of the *glasnost* era, there was no need to step far from their Moscow offices to witness for themselves the relative poverty of larger-than-average families. By the late 1980s, parents of a mere three children in the country's capital were already describing substantial economic difficulties. In part this was due to low wages but also to the problems women were beginning to experience in finding nursery provision or, if their children were often ill, in holding down a job. Descriptions of cost-conscious managements refusing to employ women as soon as they found out that they had three or more children began to find their way into print. As the principles of 'cost-accounting' and 'self-financing' became more widespread, these innovations of *perestroika* created additional problems for large families: free facilities were becoming increasingly dilapidated and unattractive, whilst the introduction of charges, even if not particularly high, produced expenses which could soon mount up for families on a limited budget. Meanwhile, opportunities which parents of only children took for granted, such as music lessons and sports, were frequently beyond the reach of larger families.

In line with much of the 'career versus home' journalism of the *perestroika* era, the answer to the question of inadequate income was rarely viewed in terms of legal rights or better provision of state or workplace nurseries. Instead, women with large families were often encouraged to see their salvation in home-based employment. Yet, in this sphere too, the reaction of managements to the demands of *perestroika*'s new economic regime often seemed to be viewed as inevitable and unavoidable. For women who took up the new opportunities to work from home, the battle for decent terms and conditions appeared to be lost before the fighting had even begun:

> The ideal work for a mother of a large family is homeworking. There are knitting machines in lots of homes. Women knit (they are usually prepared to forget about their training – it doesn't matter if you're a caretaker or a counter clerk in a workshop, just as long as you can get out of this financial situation somehow). But there are lots of complaints about how homeworking is organised, how badly it's paid and how they are forever threatening to 'take the machine back'.[32]

If cost-accounting principles were already causing problems for women employed or seeking employment in state enterprises, it appeared naïve in the extreme to assume that these same issues could somehow be more readily combated for a far more fragmented and vulnerable female workforce. Instead, the question of exploitation in homeworking, which, as the few existing studies showed, undoubtedly existed, was simply swept aside by the 'work bad – home good' orthodoxy of the *perestroika* years.[33]

Nevertheless, on the question of homeworking, as in so many other difficulties large families encountered, there seemed to be a popular notion that everything would be fine if only the favourite Aunt Sally of *perestroika*, the local bureaucrat, could be sorted out. In practice, any sorting out which had to be done, successfully or not, seemed to be something that fell largely to mothers on behalf of their children. It was something which women themselves recognised:

> The children are forever seeing me snapping at people, getting into rows. It's what they think a Mum is like. But if I didn't do it I wouldn't get anywhere. How can you square these calls to have more children

> with this atmosphere of hostility and censure we live in? . . . 'What did you want to have so many for?' That's the sort of slap in the face you get all the time![34]

In the features and letters of the *perestroika* period, it often seemed to be public attitudes such as these, far more than the financial difficulties, which provided the major cause for complaint.

Yet, as *perestroika* proved unequal to the task of reforming the USSR and the state itself moved towards collapse, it would, inevitably, be the question of money which would loom largest for women such as this in the future. With the advent of far more radical economic change and the devaluation of existing safety nets, families with several children were likely to figure disproportionately among the poor. From the desirable, medium-sized family, a household with three children began to be considered large as the impact of transition made itself felt. In the years which have followed, this shift in public perspective has changed little, if at all. Visiting acquaintances in a Russian provincial town at the end of the country's first decade of independence, three children emerged from the living room to take a look at us as we were shown in: 'Meet our local Heroine Mother!' the hostess' friend declared, and, as the subsequent conversation made clear, she was not entirely joking.

Notes

1. Awards for childbearing began from the fifth child with the 'Motherhood Medal', grade two. The 'Motherhood Medal' grade one was awarded for the sixth child, and thereafter the 'Order of Motherhood Glory', grades three, two and one were awarded for the seventh, eighth and ninth child respectively. The title of Heroine Mother was awarded on the birth of the tenth child.
2. *Zhenshchiny v SSSR 1989* (Moscow: Finansy i statistika, 1989), p. 28.
3. A. I. Sorokin, 'Vooruzhennye sily razvitogo sotsializma', *Voprosy filosofii*, 2 (1977): 11.
4. This chapter is based on an analysis of the 'Heroine Mother' campaign during the final years of the Brezhnev administration and its revival in the mid-1980s with the introduction of the policy of *glasnost*. It draws on journalism in national women's magazines and in the national rural press, placing it in the context of research and comment by sociologists and demographers of the period. Finally, the chapter considers how the huge upsurge in readers' letters to the press during the Gorbachev era impacted on both the campaign and public policy in relation to large families.
5. A. Kharitonova, 'U semeinogo ochaga', *Sel'skaia zhizn'*, 15 August (1979): 4.
6. N. Boroznova, 'Semeinaia garmoniia', *Sel'skaia zhizn'*, 18 August (1979): 4.
7. O. Nikonchik, 'Ne lishaites' schast'ia materinstva', *Krest'ianka*, 1 (1978): 31.
8. *Sel'skaia nov'*, 1 (1980): 34.

9. Ibid.
10. *Krest'ianka*, 4 (1977): 13; *Sel'skaia nov'*, 1 (1980): 34.
11. See, for example, A. Illarionov, 'Bol'shaia sem'ia Andreevykh', *Izvestiia*, 7 September (1982): 1.
12. See, for example, E. K. Vasil'eva (ed.), *Sovetskaia molodezh': demograficheskii aspekt* (Moscow: 1981), p. 34, and V. I. Perevedentsev, 'Vosproizvodstvo naseleniia i sem'ia', *Sotsiologicheskie issledovaniia*, 2 (1982): 86.
13. *Pravda*, 31 March 1981, p. 1.
14. See, for example, A. A. Kostin and B. S. Pavlov, *Molodaia sem'ia: opyt i problemy* (Cheliabinsk: 1986), pp. 88–9; Vasil'eva (1982), p. 7.
15. *Molodozheny* (Moscow, 1985), p. 56.
16. See, for example, Perevedentsev (1982), pp. 86–8; L. A. Golub and L. A. Malich, *Ukreplenie sem'i v sisteme mer demograficheskoi politiki* (Donetsk, 1986), pp. 20–4.
17. Golub and Malich (1986), p. 24.
18. Perevedentsev (1982), pp. 86–8.
19. *Krest'ianka* 3 (1983): 5.
20. See, for example, the cover of *Rabotnitsa* for August 1987.
21. See, for example, L. Kodzaeva, 'Matushka', *Rabotnitsa*, 8 (1989): 25–6.
22. T. Shokhina, 'Vremia i mesto rozhdeniia', *Krest'ianka*, 1 (1987): 5.
23. T. Nalymova, 'Matushka, golubushka . . .', *Krest'ianka*, 8 (1987): 24–5.
24. T. Blazhnova, 'Chem podelish'sia?', *Krest'ianka*, 12 (1987): 8–10.
25. V. Perevedentsev, 'Tretii rebenok – vot chto nam nuzhno', *Literaturnaia gazeta*, 26 October (1988): 2; S. Sidorova, 'Mnogodetnaia sem'ia v zerkale statistiki', *Ogonek*, 26 (1988): 19–20, interview with Sergei Golod.
26. D. Akivis and E. Mushkina, 'Kakaia sem'ia nam nuzhna?', *Nedelia*, 47 (1987): 17–18.
27. Ibid.
28. 'Zabota o mnogodetnykh sem'iakh', *Izvestiia*, 21 October (1986): p. 2; L. Gavriushenko, 'I dlia mamy i dlia rebenka', *Rabotnitsa*, 1 (1988): 34; A. F. Severina and G. A. Zaikina, 'Sluzhba sem'i i voprosy ee dal'neishego sovershenstvovaniia', *Sotsiologicheskie issledovaniia*, 3 (1983): 89; 'O neotlozhnykh merakh po uluchsheniiu polozheniia zhenshchin, okhrane materinstva i detstva, ukrepleniiu sem'i', *Pravda*, 14 April (1990): 1–2.
29. T. Kiseleva, 'V sem'e rodilos' piatero detei. Kak byt'?', *Literaturnaia gazeta*, 1 October (1986): 13.
30. Blazhnova (1987), p. 9.
31. Sidorova (1988), p. 20.
32. D. Akivis, 'Kusaiutsia li zuby darenogo konia', *Nedelia*, 22 (1988): 14.
33. See S. Bridger, R. Kay and K. Pinnick, *No More Heroines? Russia, Women and the Market* (London: Routledge, 1996), pp. 96–101.
34. Akivis (1988), p. 14.

Part II

(Re-)Negotiating Gender, Equality and Difference in the Post-socialist Era: Rights, Participation and Marginalisation

6

'In our society it's as if the man is just some kind of stud': Men's Experiences of Fatherhood and Fathers' Rights in Contemporary Russia

Rebecca Kay

The Russian Family Law, passed in December 1995, uses deliberately gender-neutral language to describe the rights and duties of spouses and parents. Article 62 states explicitly that parents enjoy equal rights and bear equal responsibilities in so far as the care, upbringing and education of their children are concerned.[1] By contrast, Soviet family legislation and social provision were constructed overwhelmingly around the mother–child relationship and focused on enabling women to combine work and motherhood. Parental leave, access to state-funded childcare and benefit payments were aimed at supporting women as working mothers, and fathers were relegated to what has been described as an 'assistant role' within the family.[2] It was not until 1990 that fathers were first mentioned, alongside grandparents and other relatives and guardians, in draft legislation allowing them to take leave to look after a child until the age of three and to claim allowances and payments which had been previously allocated to mothers only. By the time this bill was finally passed into law in April 1992, the Soviet Union had ceased to exist and new economic priorities held sway. Feminist observers, concerned about rising levels of female unemployment, which were widely believed to be linked to women's maternal rights and responsibilities, pointed out that changing the letter of the law only overcame one of the barriers to a fairer division of labour and the sharing of rights and duties between the sexes:

> Stereotypes concerning social roles which have eaten away at our society, stand in the way of this law being put into practice. To this day there has been no evidence of any massive rush of fathers eager immediately to take up this happy opportunity to raise their own children.

> The image of a man who temporarily leaves his job to wash nappies instead is still more likely to generate ridicule than respect.[3]

As this author was pointing out, and as seventy years of Soviet-style 'emancipation' had already amply demonstrated, the translation of equal rights on paper into the realities of men's and women's lives, opportunities and experience has to do with a lot more than simply changing the law.

In many societies, the allocation of roles and responsibilities within families, communities, or at an institutional level continue to be shaped by attitudes towards and understandings of gender. In her study of young, white, working-class men in two British cities for example, Linda McDowell notes that 'gender [is] a social, cultural and economic force' which impacts directly on the identities and life choices of her subjects.[4] Martin Mac an Ghaill and Chris Haywood note that gender roles and relations are 'one of the most contested areas of human behaviour' and are undergoing significant change in late modernity. However, they also point out that, 'whatever the empirical evidence about the changing social realities of women's and men's lives, the question of gender is currently centre stage in terms of how we make sense of the world', and that gender transformations are troubling and often perceived as threatening.[5]

In a society where roles, responsibilities and aptitudes are commonly regarded as divided into rather strict male and female categories, individuals may find it difficult to cross that divide even where it runs counter to personal preferences or individual circumstances. Russian feminist observers have long pointed out that, 'the cult of motherhood has always played an important role in our society.'[6] More recently, Russian sociologists have observed that, 'the exclusion of fatherhood from social discourse in Russia is an absolutely obvious fact.'[7] This chapter seeks to explore the implications of these very different attitudes towards and expectations of male and female parenthood and in particular to examine their impact on the realities of men's experiences of fatherhood and their ability to exercise the equal rights and bear the equal responsibilities which the law ascribes to them as parents. Whilst the arguments and evidence presented here relate to specific local case studies within the contemporary Russian context, many of the issues raised resonate with the findings of a much broader range of studies from both within and beyond the post-socialist region.[8]

Studying men's experiences in contemporary Russia

The arguments of this chapter are based on the findings of a Leverhulme Trust-funded research project 'Understanding Men, Masculinity and

Identity in Post-Soviet Russia', which I conducted in 2002–3 in two provincial areas of Russia: a small town and two surrounding villages in Kaluga region, south-west of Moscow, and the city of Barnaul, capital of the Altai region in western Siberia and home to the Altai Regional Crisis Centre for Men.[9] In-depth ethnographic interviews were the primary method of data collection and were conducted with approximately forty men across the two case-study areas. In Kaluga region, where I spent up to a month at a time conducting fieldwork in a very small community, contact with respondents inevitably became more informal. My interview data were enriched by ethnographic observations gathered during time spent socialising and interacting with men and their families. The range of voices contributing to the study became much wider as a result. In Barnaul, the observation was of a different nature, focusing on the functioning of the Altai Regional Crisis Centre for Men and interactions between Centre staff and clients.

The men who took part in this study were aged between 18 and 75 and, in both case-study areas came from a mixture of rural and urban backgrounds. Their education ranged from basic secondary to postgraduate and they were, or had been, employed in various manual and white-collar, urban and rural jobs in both the state and private sectors. In personal terms, too, the range of respondents' experience was very wide, including men who were unmarried, married, divorced and widowed, with or without children. Amongst the twenty-nine fathers interviewed, eight were raising their children alone.[10] The stories and experiences of these single fathers, whilst in many ways exceptional, are nonetheless instructive in highlighting obstacles to involved parenting which may be experienced in less explicit ways by many men. It is for this reason that these single fathers' stories are given particular attention in the argument which follows.

This chapter also draws on data collected during earlier research, in particular, ethnographic interviews which I conducted with Russian women in 1995–6. This earlier research had examined women's views on gender in order to better understand their interpretations of women's position in post-Soviet Russian society.[11] On reanalysing these interviews I discovered a wealth of fascinating data regarding women's attitudes to men and their expectations of men as husbands and fathers. An important aspect of all the research which I have conducted since the early 1990s, has been an analysis of wider media and public discourses relating to gender in contemporary Russia. Whilst the findings of this ongoing discourse analysis are not directly referred to in this chapter, they form the background and context to many of the arguments presented here.[12]

As discussed below, the ways in which fatherhood and 'male' roles and responsibilities are understood by both women and men, as well as wider, socially constructed understandings and expectations of 'male' and 'female' behaviour and capabilities are reflected in practices at the family, community and institutional levels. It is therefore necessary to view men's stories and comments regarding their experiences as parents within a much broader context of understandings of gender in contemporary Russia.

Gender in Russian society: from Soviet 'emancipation' to post-Soviet essentialism

Over the seventy years of the Soviet Union's existence successive leaders maintained an ideological commitment to women's emancipation, which was to be achieved first and foremost through their full and equal participation in paid labour outside the home. This gender egalitarianism was proclaimed as a crucial aspect of the socialist project. By 1988, over 85 per cent of working-age women were either in full-time employment or studying and 51 per cent of the Soviet labour force was female. The Soviet Union could thus rightfully claim that the proportion of women participating in public labour was higher than that in any other industrialised nation.[13] Yet, other important aspects of gender equality had been neglected in this process. In particular, gendered divisions of responsibilities and rights in the private sphere and an equal sharing between parents of the burdens and rewards of childcare and domestic duties were never adequately addressed. Early suggestions that the domestic sphere would be 'socialised' and that state provision would come to replace women's unpaid duties in the home and family proved to be both economically impractical and culturally unacceptable. In later years, concerns about demographic imbalances and population decline in combination with shifting economic priorities led to various ideological reassessments of the 'woman question' and an increasingly overt pronatalism in Soviet rhetoric, policy and practice.[14]

Motherhood was idealised and celebrated as central to women's lives and identities and increasing emphasis was placed on the crucial significance of women's role in the family. Soviet family legislation and social provision prioritised the mother–child relationship above all else and endless academic books, newspaper articles and policy debates focused on how best to enable women to combine their dual roles of worker and mother.[15] Men, by contrast, continued to be deemed to have only one role: that of worker and builder of communism. Their roles and responsibilities within the family were given minimal attention by comparison and were commonly reduced to the function of breadwinner, a spin-off from their duties to the state as workers. As one Soviet journalist observed in the late 1980s, whilst women received medals for producing large families, the notion that men might be similarly rewarded, or that fathers had a comparably significant role to play, seemed as comic as 'four hefty blokes in tutus doing the Dance of the Little Swans'.[16]

In the 1990s, the public commitment to gender equality previously espoused by the Soviet state was swept away as part of the discredited and 'damaging' ideology of the past. Simultaneously, underlying assumptions about the innate differences between men and women, which had in fact been encouraged and reinforced by the pronatalist campaigns of the late Soviet era, were loudly proclaimed in Russian media and public discourses.[17] Culturally accepted norms in gendered divisions of labour and responsibility, particularly in the family, were put forward to explain and justify these essentialist attitudes. Meanwhile, this renewed essentialism was widely invoked both to keep existing divisions in place and to legitimise new inequalities in the public sphere of paid employment and political representation.[18] Circular arguments emerged along the lines: women do most of the housework and childcare because motherhood is central to feminine identities and women's lives, therefore only women are really capable of looking after children and homes properly. These early post-Soviet discourses neatly illustrate Connell's argument that the success of preconceived ideas about biological determinism lies in their ability 'to reflect what is familiar back as science and justify what many readers wish to believe'.[19]

Numerous studies have discussed the potential of post-Soviet attitudes towards and understandings of gender to undermine women's rights, to encourage discrimination and expose women to the threat of marginalisation, sexual exploitation and violence, particularly in the public sphere.[20] Far less attention has been paid to the potentially negative repercussions for men of post-Soviet attitudes towards and expectations of gender. Rather, men have tended to be viewed either as the 'winners' in a situation where infringements of women's rights are assumed to result in increased power and direct benefits for men,[21] or as pathetic 'losers' who have squandered their advantages and opportunities through their own apathy, irresponsibility and despair.[22] More recently, however, a few studies have emerged examining the detail of men's experiences of post-Soviet transformation. This work has highlighted the nuanced interactions between post-Soviet definitions of masculinity and expectations of male behaviour on the one hand and the realities of the post-Soviet labour market and organisation of family roles and responsibilities on the other.[23]

Gender, essentialism and parenting: assumptions about and expectations of motherhood and fatherhood

The partial reassessment of egalitarian policies and ideology relating to gender which began in the late Soviet period included fears about the impacts on men of women's emancipation. Considerable concern was expressed at men's 'emasculation' and its implications for their attitudes towards home and family life. In this context, absence, disinterest and unreliability, rather than engagement, responsibility and care came to epitomise popular images of fatherhood. The solutions most commonly proposed were either to enhance men's roles as breadwinner and 'head of the family' or for women to take a leading role in providing moral guidance to men and encouraging their engagement in the family through a mixture of flattery, cajoling and manipulation.[24] Yet in an economic and political climate where both men and women were expected to work full-time and women's wages, while often lower than men's, made a highly significant contribution to family budgets, the role of primary breadwinner was likely to be rather symbolic. Since women also tended to control household spending and wield considerable authority in decisions relating to the care and upbringing of children and the organisation of home life, men's position as 'head of the family' was also ambiguous.[25]

The interviews which I conducted with women in the mid-1990s suggested that a lasting and tangible impression of men's potential contribution to family life had been produced by the emphasis on women's role as moral guardians and a negative view of men as infantile. One newly married young woman explained with considerable resentment:

> Women are seen as creatures who have a duty to take a certain moral stance. Always! It is quite simply their duty to bear this in mind. A man of course is also expected to in general. But he is like a naughty child. He can, well, a man is just a little child.

Although she claimed personally to be struggling against such rigid interpretations of male and female duties and morality, this young woman felt strongly that such attitudes were a highly influential element of her socio-cultural environment.

An older woman explained the break-up of her marriage on similar grounds complaining that, 'When I was asked how many children I had,

I always said two – my husband and my baby daughter . . . [O]ur men are infantile.' Clearly this woman was drawing on her own negative experiences in coming to this conclusion, yet as is the case with much stereotyping, she shifted seamlessly from the personal and individual to the general, concluding that all men were the same as her ex-husband. Thus, instead of being viewed as adult partners and potentially reliable and caring parents, in the words of various female respondents, men were explicitly grouped with children as the objects of women's care and attention. As well as provoking resentment amongst women, where they are internalised by men such attitudes may be used to excuse irresponsible and self-centred behaviour leading rapidly to a vicious circle of low expectations and unsatisfactory behaviour.[26]

Comments such as those of the two women quoted above were at least in part a response to well-documented problems resulting from men's heavy drinking, non-payment of maintenance and failure to help around the home. Yet, they also reflected the overriding emphasis on the primacy of women in the private sphere and particularly on the importance of motherhood, which from the 1970s onwards was backed up by increasing support for biologically deterministic attitudes to gender. Just as caring, nurturing behaviour, an automatic love for children and an innate responsibility for and understanding of their needs were described as inherently female; a view of men as naturally disinterested in the very young and almost physically incapable of caring for them was the corollary. Thus, according to Russian sociologist, Ol'ga Zdravomyslova, upbringing of children was characterised in the USSR, by a 'female leitmotiv' and the father's role as it related to caring for and educating children was viewed as, 'problematic . . . even in two-parent families'.[27]

As the unbridled essentialism of the post-Soviet era took hold, this problematisation of men's position as fathers came increasingly to look like marginalisation and even exclusion of men from certain aspects of family life. Whatever the realities of shortcomings in some men's behaviour, the comments of the women whom I interviewed in the mid-1990s suggested that a fundamental incapacity to be adequate parents had come to be viewed as a virtually universal male characteristic and one that it was pointless to try and change. Many of these women were firmly convinced that whilst good parenting came naturally to women, it was not something to which men could even aspire. As one woman put it, 'You can educate a man as much as you like, he still won't be able to bring up a child the way a woman can.' Other women made frequent and categorical statements about men's inherent lack of patience to deal with children and were particularly scathing about their abilities when it came to looking after babies. As a result, they took it as given that children should be with their mothers, especially during their earliest years and that fathers could at best play a secondary role.

Again such assumptions contribute to a kind of circular logic: because women are assumed to be 'naturally' skilled in parenting they are given primary responsibility for the care of young children and spend much time developing and honing parenting skills. In contrast, men, assumed to be awkward and incapable, are kept at one remove from the responsibilities of childcare and as a result are less likely to know what to do if and when they are left in charge of a young child. Such essentialist attitudes are not, however, necessarily restricted to gendered divisions in parenting activities, allocation of responsibilities and development of parenting skills. They may also relate to something much more fundamental in any parent–child relationship: the ability to care. As one mother of two put it, 'A mother's heart aches more for her child.'

'I couldn't live without my kids': men's views on fatherhood

Interviews and interactions with men which took place in the context of my more recent study of men's experiences of post-Soviet change were rather at odds with this portrayal of fathers as remote and disinterested parents. Based on the experience of my earlier research with Russian women, analysis of the Russian press and of existing studies of gender in post-Soviet Russia, I had envisaged at the outset that issues relating to employment, economic change and possibly military service would be of most direct relevance to men's experience and that these would be the areas which they would be most keen to discuss. When designing fieldwork I had made a conscious decision that interviews should be highly unstructured, not least because of the cross-cultural and gender sensitivities involved as a British woman interviewing Russian men. Thus, I made no attempt to ask identical or predetermined sets of questions, nor to prompt men to respond to predefined statements about masculinity or male roles. Each respondent was free to select his own starting point and the themes which he was most interested in talking about. It was particularly striking then that in interview after interview, as well as in many more informal conversations and social interactions, the issue which men raised spontaneously and discussed with the clearest degree of emotional and personal engagement was that of their roles in the private sphere of home and family and their experiences of and attitudes towards fatherhood in particular. Moreover, it was not only men with young children living at home who were keen to talk about fatherhood.

Young men who were not as yet in a settled relationship raised the question of fatherhood as an important issue in their futures. Older men whose children had long since left home talked at length about their experiences as both fathers and grandfathers. Men without children talked about their regrets at having never experienced fatherhood, and those whose marriages had broken down and who no longer lived with their children frequently described this as a deeply traumatic and irreconcilable loss.

This is not to say that men directly challenged the idea that a child's primary and most significant bond is with their mother, nor that each of the male respondents who talked with enthusiasm about their experiences as fathers were eagerly seeking a reversal of gender roles in their own families. Men too have been affected both by the official promotion of what might well be termed a cult of motherhood in the late Soviet and post-Soviet eras and by much longer-standing traditions which have given motherhood a particularly elevated status in Russian culture for many centuries.[28] Many of the men involved in this study viewed a mother's role in the care and upbringing of children as crucial and in many respects irreplaceable. The specific roles they described themselves as fathers playing in relation to their children were also fairly stereotypical: providing materially for the costs of raising a child, passing on practical skills and knowledge, exercising discipline and providing moral guidance. Yet, none of this equated for them to a disregard for or dismissal of the more intimate responsibilities and joys of fatherhood. On the contrary, in virtually every interview with those men who had children and/or grandchildren, whether they were still living with them or not, men spoke at length about the ways in which becoming a father had changed their lives and of how important it was for them to be closely involved in their children's lives, upbringing and development. Moreover, in discussing these issues they made clear that the underlying reason for this involvement were the very strong emotional bonds they had with their children. As one father of two adolescent sons explained this, 'They're my children, it's my blood, if they are doing something I can't not pay attention to them.'[29]

The significance of these relationships frequently emerged through body language, the way a man's face would light up as he talked about his children or grandchildren or proudly showed off their photographs; as one older rural man put it, 'Who can say I haven't achieved anything when I have grandchildren like these?' Observations of men's interactions with their children and grandchildren also indicated that these relationships were important not only to the men in question but to the children as well. During a visit to one man's house he sat on the floor while we chatted to allow his eighteen-month-old daughter to pull herself upright against his knees and take wobbly steps in the protective circle he made with his legs and upper body. On another occasion a man's adult son and grandchildren were just leaving as I arrived. His teenage grandson was already in the car but leapt out again when his grandfather came out of the house and ran down the garden to give him a hug. The old man was clearly delighted, calling after him, 'Come back soon, son', as the boy returned to the car.

It was particularly noticeable, given the strength of popular assumptions that men are incapable of dealing with very young children, how often men chose to speak of the feelings they had had for their children when they were babies: the excitement and trepidation of bringing home a newborn from hospital and the joys of having a toddler about the house. One man who spent several hours showing me cine-films of his daughter's early years, reminisced about collecting her from the maternity hospital:

> Of course they gave her to me, because my wife was exhausted from the birth and hadn't been on her feet for several days. It was very snowy and icy and the streets were so slippery. I was terrified in case I dropped her or slipped. It hadn't felt like that with my son. But for some reason it was always like that with my little daughter.

Yet, however strongly a man may feel about his children, his opportunities for consolidating the relationship he has with them and indeed the long-term sustainability of close contact between father and child are circumscribed by broader social, cultural and institutional practices.

Obstacles to involved parenting for men

(Re-)Negotiating family roles

Within the family, fathers' involvement and day-to-day interactions with their children have to be negotiated in relation to men's other roles and responsibilities and are affected by dominant understandings of gender which influence the expectations and activities both of men and of their female partners. As the fathers involved in this study pointed out, the widespread expectation that men's main duty to the family is to provide for its material needs may physically separate men from their children for prolonged periods of time. As one man put it:

> Well of course today it's possible that fathers are excluding themselves from the family. Because with us, what is it that's expected of a man?

> Wages! You are supposed to support your family. So some men hardly ever see their families, because they don't have any time . . . People work as much as they can, even in several jobs simultaneously if they can.

Whilst this man alluded to the problems of men's long working hours and possible multiple forms of employment, other men in this study talked about how a lack of suitable work and decent rates of pay in the local economy had forced them to take jobs in distant towns or cities. As a result, some had ended up living away from home for days or weeks at a time and this too could not but impact on their relationships with their children. As another father explained:

> I also think that fathers have been a bit pushed out into second place . . . Men are seen as like the breadwinner, and I don't know why, but that's all. He just earns money and that's all. He provides, and as usual it's Mum who tidies up, does the washing and the cooking and does everything else. And sits with the kids and everything. That really is the way it is.

If men are consistently unable to take part in the daily interactions with their children which women engage in as a matter of course, they may also miss out on important emotional and developmental issues and quickly find that they are, at best, one step removed from the heart of family life.

However, even in situations where men are not working and may in fact have more time to spend at home than their wives, the power of normative assumptions about mothers' and fathers' roles may still prevent men from taking on primary or even equal responsibility for the care of their children. In their study of husbands' and wives' responses to male unemployment, Sarah Ashwin and Tatiana Lytkina provide an eloquent analysis of the discomfort which may arise for both men and women when gender roles are reversed. That study found that, 'many women, although they frequently lament and suffer as a result of men's disengagement from the household, inadvertently contribute to its cause' both because they find it hard to accept 'men taking responsibility for the home as adequate compensation for their abdication of the role of main breadwinner', and because 'the ability of the woman to fulfil her duties is also thrown into doubt' by such a role reversal.[30] As Ashwin and Lytkina also point out, it is not only in Russia nor only in response to male unemployment that such issues may arise. Studies in other countries have also shown that role reversal may be seen by women, 'to compromise domestic standards and more important, represent a threat to female power'.[31] Such resistance to change demonstrates yet again the power of gender as a social construct which is internalised and acted out by both men and women in the context of wider social discourses, expectations and interactions. In other words, deviation from accepted social and cultural 'norms' of behaviour roles is uncomfortable. As far as gender is concerned, this discomfort is likely to be greater the more rigid and deterministic dominant discourses and culturally acceptable attitudes to gender are in a particular local context.

Challenging societal expectations

Beyond the direct negotiations of gender roles and responsibilities which take place within the family, men are confronted by wider societal expectations and the responses of friends, acquaintances and even complete strangers to their behaviour as fathers. Precisely because their circumstances were exceptional, the single fathers involved in this study provided clear examples of the difficulties encountered by those who do not conform to social expectations regarding gender and parenting. Widely held social attitudes cast doubts on men's capacity to be good parents and these clearly impact directly on the social environment in which single fathers raise their children. The result may be at best awkwardness and a sense of not 'fitting in' for these men and their families. At worst, there may be a direct questioning of a father's parenting abilities and, by extension, of his right to maintain residential care of his children. As one father explained, 'People ask things like: "Why isn't he with his mum?" I say: "Well, why should he be with his mum?" ' The defensiveness of this response was not hard to understand when measured against other fathers' stories of negative reactions, expressions of disbelief and in one case the suggestion that his children would be better off in a children's home.

Yet, perhaps the clearest illustration of the power of normative social expectations is their ability to influence men's and women's views of and confidence in themselves and their own behaviour. Each of the single fathers interviewed in the course of this study had made an active decision to retain sole residential care of his children, often in the face of considerable opposition. Nonetheless, many of them had clearly also internalised a view that there is something fundamentally female about childcare and in particular about close and affectionate relationships with children. As a result even whilst they strenuously resisted any suggestion that they might not be able to care adequately for their children – 'there's no difference whether their mother does it or I do it' – their descriptions of themselves and their behaviour betrayed a certain uncertainty, ambiguity and discomfort about the gender of their role:

> I can be very affectionate, I can be like mum. I can do everything. I can stroke their heads. I can hug them, like a normal mum . . . When a dad is on his own, they call him *makulichka*. It's like a dad who is being a mum . . . Of course it is hard to live like this. For a man it is hard. For me to take a mother's place in everything, it is very hard of course for fathers.

For many decades, feminist studies of women's incursions into previously male-dominated arenas, in the worlds of business and management for example, have documented the discomfort, doubts in their own abilities and conflicting identities and roles which women often experience as they transgress existing gender boundaries.[32] The evidence here suggests that similar transgressions may be no less troubling for men.

Dealing with official institutions

As offensive and distressing as informal questioning of a father's ability to look after his children may be, the implications of widespread assumptions that a father's care is both inferior to that of a mother and somehow 'unnatural' are potentially far more damaging where they influence the operation of official institutions. As indicated at the start of this chapter, Russian family law and regulations governing social provision in relation to the care of children have been carefully formulated to maintain a gender-neutral position. In principle a father's rights are guaranteed. Nonetheless, representatives of the judiciary and other professionals with responsibility for implementing the law and allocating resources are liable to be influenced by the cultural environment of which they are a part. In a popular handbook on coping with divorce, a leading Moscow lawyer offering advice to parents seeking residential care of their children makes explicit reference to the mismatch between the objectivity of egalitarian legislation and the subjective realities of court practice:

> In Russia at present when cases concerning a child's upbringing are considered they are more often than not decided in favour of the mother. She has to be absolutely incapable of bringing up a child (because of alcohol, antisocial behaviour or destitution) in order for a decision on upbringing and residence to be made in favour of the father. This is despite the fact that he has equal rights in law with the mother and the court is obliged to consider all the circumstances of the case objectively, taking into account the interests of the child.[33]

The stories of those single fathers whom I interviewed in 2002, who had gone through official channels in order to gain or retain sole residential care of their children, illustrated this point further still. In each case, the mother of the children had been imprisoned for drug offences and in one case at least was still in prison at the time of the court proceedings. Nonetheless, men found that they were expected not only to prove that their former wives were unfit to care for the children, but also to demonstrate that they were able to do so themselves. As one man explained:

> There was a long custody battle, but I won in the end. The court decided on the basis of all sorts of tests, psychological tests and so on, I don't even remember them all. They spent a very long time carrying out checks on me, both at work and at home . . . but in the end the court decided that the child should live with me, her father.

The fact that it is difficult to envisage a similar level of checks and psychological testing being carried out on a woman, with no prior record of ill-treatment or neglect, seeking residential care of her own children, demonstrates the suspicion with which men's competence as parents is regarded.

It is not only in the court room however, that fathers may find that the rights which are officially accorded to them by the law are harder to access in practice. Men's access to social provisions in the form of benefits and services relating to childcare is also affected by institutionalised practices and the attitudes and opinions of administrative and professional staff. In this area also there is frequently a challenging mismatch between ideals and realities. The difficulty which those responsible for the design and implementation of programmes of social provision have in viewing men's caring roles in the family as comparable to those performed by women may form part of a mutually reinforcing process of exclusion. Yet, it is also true that in reality, fathers are far less likely than mothers to interact with social service providers, educational establishments and children's health services on a regular basis. One of the single fathers in this study gave a particularly frank response when asked whether he had played an equally active role in his children's upbringing and care before the death of his wife:

> When we were all together as a family, as a father I had to work hard to provide and as for bringing them up – I very rarely got to the meetings at school, their mother did all of that, like most mothers . . . I very rarely went, but now . . . well, they're not all at the same school and there might be an hour's difference between the meetings so I'm running from one to the other!

Conversations with other men confirmed that in a two-parent family men were much less likely than their female partners to deal directly with teachers, doctors or other professionals concerned with the upbringing and early development of their children. As a result, those men who find themselves in the position of sole carer and are therefore bound to interact with official institutions on a regular basis are liable to find that they are at best treated as exceptional and at worse as a nuisance.[34]

The experiences of the single fathers involved in this study had been mixed in this respect. Schools in particular, perhaps as a result of their long-term interaction with the children and deeper understanding of the wider family circumstances, had been very supportive in several cases. Describing his difficult court case over residential care of his two young children, one father said:

> At school they seem to understand me. They even helped me. The school has really helped me a lot. We had to go through several court cases . . . If it hadn't been for the school I wouldn't have done it. With our society I wouldn't have gone through this process, because a mother is a mother. It means taking away a mother's custody rights and divorce, but there was no one to support us in court . . . It was very hard to do it. But the school helped a lot. If it hadn't been for the school it would have been simply impossible.

Yet, even in this man's account of the support he had received, his sense of isolation and the lack of support from other quarters was clear. Indeed this was an issue which he described explicitly as a potential curb on a father exercising his rights – without the support of the school, a battle over residential care would have been unthinkable.

Repeatedly, single fathers expressed surprise at support or help that had been forthcoming and made clear that this was not the norm. Another father, for example, described the difficulties he had encountered in attempting to claim benefits and take leave from work as a single parent of two very young children. His divorce had taken place in 1990 prior to the introduction of new family laws extending parental leave and benefit rights to fathers. Officials at that stage had been prepared to bend the rules in order to help him. Yet he described problems in claiming benefits as ongoing, despite more recent changes in the law:

> There's no law for single fathers like there is for single mothers. They get benefits, but there's nothing for men on their own. They tell you, 'Sorry mate, we haven't got the right to pay you that.' But when I got

> divorced, the Children's Committee [Komissiia po delam nesovershennoletnykh] gave me special leave as a single father – like for single mothers . . . When my wife left my daughter was eighteen months old and my son was five months so they gave me one month's leave. And I got fifty rubles, it was virtually illegal, because they didn't have the right to give it to me – they said, 'we don't have the right to give you this but we're doing it.'

Here as elsewhere the personal perspective and attitude of the staff in question could all too easily become a decisive factor. Where a man's predicament aroused sympathy or admiration he might be helped, in other circumstances he might well not be. Where this is the case, normative expectations regarding gender play an important role and if these combine with practical difficulties involved in dealing with a parent of the 'wrong' sex fathers may find themselves confronted with exceptionally intransigent behaviour. For example, the same man cited above had encountered a far less accommodating response when his son fell seriously ill and he took him to the local hospital:

> He had a high temperature and I took him to one of our hospitals. They said it wasn't allowed for me to stay and tried to send me off to another hospital . . . they just said, . . . 'Fathers aren't allowed to stay here, it's all mums looking after the children, where are we going to put you?' . . . We ended up having a huge row and they wanted to throw me out of the hospital . . . I said, 'No, I'm not going anywhere, I'll stay in the corridor, this child is ill' . . . So I'd had this row with the hospital and I couldn't go into the ward and then literally three days later there was another man with two children whose wife was at work. They let him stay with his two children but they wouldn't let me stay with one.

As the final twist in this tale demonstrates, the treatment men receive may be rather inconsistent. Various factors, including the attitudes of staff on duty, the ways in which men respond to initial challenges to their rights as fathers, and the extent to which their family circumstances conform to wider social norms may all play a part in determining how they are dealt with. Nonetheless, the fact that in circumstances where any parent would be anxious for their child's well-being, medical treatment might be withheld on the grounds of the parent's gender is bound to give cause for concern. In cases where both parents are available couples are unlikely to risk rocking the boat, and so the status quo is further reinforced. This self-enforcing norm has potentially negative repercussions not only for men's rights as fathers. It also reinforces a view of women as primarily responsible for and concerned with the family. The result is that women continue to be overburdened with caring duties, damaging their position in the labour market and perpetuating a view of caring for dependants as a 'naturally' female duty.[35]

Conclusion

The findings of the study upon which this chapter is based show that Russian men are far from indifferent parents. Nonetheless, this research also suggests that men's care 'about' their children does not necessarily readily translate into an equal sharing of the responsibility to care 'for' children. Where roles are reversed or altered and fathers do take on some of the tasks more usually associated with mothers, both women and men may struggle to redefine fixed notions of gender and appropriate masculine and feminine behaviours and identities. The experiences of single fathers offer a particularly clear example of the implications of this struggle, since the realities of their family arrangements require them to fulfil virtually all parenting roles themselves. As a result they are constantly confronting and challenging normative expectations regarding gender and parenting. The single fathers in this study clearly found it difficult to explain their roles as sole carer for their children, and the extremely involved and caring parenting which this required, as masculine. They described themselves as substitute mothers at least as often as they talked about what they did as fathers. Thus, although their experiences and realities on the one hand automatically challenge preconceived ideas of biologically determined gender divisions in men's and women's capacity to be good parents, on the other hand, they continue to conceptualise what they do and their relationships with their children along stereotypical lines as mothering, rather than as a new model for fathering.

At first glance it is surprising that these men's own experiences did not override stereotypes of masculinity and femininity, which are not flexible enough to incorporate the realities of their lives. Yet, my earlier research conducted with women in the mid-1990s, found very similar processes at play. Women whose family lives and careers had not followed the trajectories prescribed by rigid understandings of gender, frequently explained their deviation from this path on the basis of their 'masculine' characters or rather 'man-like mindsets'.[36] This unwillingness to challenge gender norms is less surprising when we consider that gender is more than simply a set of opinions or ideas. Rather it is made up of 'complex dynamics of power and identity . . . that situate men [and women] in relationships of power and inequality'[37] and is enacted, in any society, in the practices, relationships and interactions of individuals, families, communities and institutions. As Connell has pointed out, gender is an extremely powerful social construct and the assumptions of the dominant gender order may well take precedence over pragmatic considerations and practical evidence to the contrary.[38]

Thus, in Russia as elsewhere, men's experiences of fatherhood, their behaviour as fathers, and the relationships they develop with their children, are framed by a range of intersecting factors, of which legal definitions of fathers' rights are only one. Broader societal attitudes towards parenting combined with culturally embedded expectations and understandings of gender have produced a status quo in divisions of roles and responsibilities between mothers and fathers from which individuals and families find it difficult, though by no means impossible, to deviate. Widespread assumptions about the sanctity and irreplaceable nature of the mother–child relationship and the commonly asserted view that a man's primary duty to the family is that of material provision leaves only restricted scope for men to involve themselves in the day-to-day business of active parenting. The result is a social reality where women continue to be much more likely to take primary responsibility for the care of young children and to interact on a regular basis with those social, legal and educational institutions which support families with children. It is, therefore, perhaps unsurprising that such institutions continue to function on the assumption that the key recipients of their services and attention are women and children, even where such assumptions run counter to the more egalitarian provisions laid down by law. The danger is that this social reality and the practices which it engenders, interact with rigid understandings of gender in ways which are mutually reinforcing, self-perpetuating and potentially restrictive for both women and men in terms of their opportunities and choices regarding the balance of family responsibilities and activities outside of the home.

Notes

1. *Semeinyi kodeks Rossiiskoi Federatsii. Ofitsial'nyi tekst po sostoianiiu na 15 marta 2002 goda* (Moscow: Ministerstvo iustitsii Rossiiskoi Federatsii, 2002), p. 23.
2. E. Kochkina, cited in V. Sperling, *Organizing Women in Contemporary Russia: Engendering Transition* (Cambridge: Cambridge University Press, 1999), p. 112.
3. V. Nurkova, 'Papa stiraet pelenki, i eto normal'no', *Delo*, 11 (1994): 6.
4. L. McDowell, *Redundant Masculinities? Employment Change and White Working Class Youth* (Oxford: Blackwell Publishing, 2003), p. 1.

5. M. Mac an Ghaill and C. Haywood, *Gender, Culture and Society: Contemporary Femininities and Masculinities* (Basingstoke: Palgrave Macmillan, 2007), pp. 1–7.
6. O. Lipovskaya, 'The Mythology of Womanhood in Contemporary "Soviet" Culture', in A. Posadskaya (ed.), *Women in Russia: a New Era in Russian Feminism* (London: Verso, 1994), p. 128.
7. T. Gurko, 'Fenomen sovremennogo ottsovstva', in I. Semashko and A. Sedlovskaia (eds), *Muzhchina i zhenshchina v sovremennom mire: meniaiushchiesia roli i obrazy* (Moscow: Institut etnologii i antropologii RAN, 1999), p. 221.
8. See for example I. Smidova, 'Changing Czech Masculinities? Beyond "Environment and Children Friendly" Men', paper presented at 6th European Gender Research Conference, Gender and Citizenship in a Multicultural Context (Women's Studies Centre, University of Lodz, Poland, September 2006); B. Hobson (ed.), *Making Men into Fathers: Men, Masculinities and the Social Politics of Fatherhood* (Cambridge: Cambridge University Press, 2002).
9. The Altai Regional Crisis Centre for Men is an innovative new service provider aiming to develop a framework for the delivery of social support to men in Altai region, western Siberia. For a more detailed discussion of its work see R. Kay, *Men in Contemporary Russia: the Fallen Heroes of Post-Soviet Change?* (Aldershot: Ashgate, 2006), pp. 179–206.
10. This unusually high proportion of single fathers in a relatively small sample was a result of the role played by the Altai Regional Crisis Centre for Men in recruiting respondents. For details of the Centre's work with single fathers and their families see R. Kay, 'Working with Single Fathers in Western Siberia: a New Departure in Russian Social Provision', *Europe-Asia Studies*, 56, 7 (2004): 941–61.
11. For full details of the findings of this earlier research see R. Kay, *Russian Women and their Organizations: Gender, Discrimination and Grassroots Women's Organizations 1991–96* (Basingstoke: Palgrave Macmillan, 2000).
12. For a fuller discussion of this discourse analysis see R. Kay, 'Images of an Ideal Woman: Perceptions of Russian Womanhood through the Media, Education and Women's Own Eyes', in M. Buckley (ed.), *Post-Soviet Women: From the Baltic to Central Asia* (Cambridge: Cambridge University Press, 1997); Kay (2000), pp. 26–82; Kay (2006), pp. 19–44.
13. G. Lapidus, *Women in Soviet Society: Equality, Development, and Social Change* (Berkeley: University of California Press, 1978), p. 88.
14. J. Peers, 'Workers by Hand and Womb – Soviet Women and the Demographic Crisis', in B. Holland (ed.), *Soviet Sisterhood* (Bloomington: Indiana University Press, 1985). See also M. Buckley, *Women and Ideology in the Soviet Union* (Ann Arbor: University of Michigan Press, 1989) for a comprehensive review of Soviet era ideology and policy relating to women and its twists and turns over 70 years of Soviet rule.
15. S. Bridger, 'Image, Reality and Propaganda. Looking Again at the Soviet Legacy', in H. Haukanes (ed.), *Women After Communism: Ideal Images and Real Lives* (Bergen: University of Bergen, 2001). See also Bridger in this volume.
16. D. Akivis, *Ottsovskaia liubov'* (Moscow: Profizdat, 1989), p. 4.
17. See V. Sperling, 'The "New" Sexism: Images of Russian Women During the Transition', in M. Field and J. Twigg (eds), *Russia's Torn Safety Nets: Health and Social Welfare During the Transition* (Basingstoke: Palgrave Macmillan, 2000); Kay (2000).

18. See for example, S. Bridger, R. Kay and K. Pinnick, *No More Heroines? Russia, Women and the Market* (London: Routledge, 1996); L. Popkova, 'Women's Political Activism in Russia: the Case of Samara', in K. Kuehnast and C. Nechemias (eds), *Post-Soviet Women Encountering Transition: Nation Building, Economic Survival, and Civic Activism* (Baltimore: Johns Hopkins University Press, 2004); I. Kozina and E. Zhidkova, 'Sex Segregation and Discrimination in the New Russian Labour Market', in S. Ashwin (ed.), *Adapting to Russia's New Labour Market: Gender and Employment Behaviour* (London: Routledge, 2006).
19. R. Connell, *Gender and Power: Society, the Person and Sexual Politics* (Cambridge: Polity Press, 1987), p. 80.
20. See for example Bridger et al. (1996); Buckley (1997); Kay (2000); Sperling (2000); J. Johnson 'Sisterhood Versus the "Moral" Russian State: the Post-Communist Politics of Rape', in Kuehnast and Nechemias (eds) (2004).
21. B. Silverman and M. Yanowitch, *New Rich, New Poor, New Russia: Winners and Losers on the Russian Road to Capitalism*, 2nd edition (Armonk, NY: M. E. Sharpe, 2000).
22. M. Kiblitskaya '"Once We Were Kings": Male Experiences of Loss of Status at Work in Post-Communist Russia', in S. Ashwin (ed.), *Gender, State and Society in Soviet and Post-Soviet Russia* (London: Routledge, 2000); S. Kukhterin 'Fathers and Patriarchs in Communist and Post-Communist Russia', in S. Ashwin (ed.), *Gender, State and Society in Soviet and Post-Soviet Russia* (London: Routledge, 2000).
23. S. Ashwin and T. Lytkina, 'Men in Crisis in Russia – the Role of Domestic Marginalization', *Gender and Society*, 18, 2 (2004): 189–206; J. Round, 'From Inclusion to Exclusion: Barriers to the "Formal" Post-Soviet Russian Labour Market', *International Journal of Economic Development*, 6, 2 (2004): 76–97; Kay (2006).
24. L. Attwood, *The New Soviet Man and Woman: Sex-role Socialisation in the USSR* (Bloomington: Indiana University Press, 1990), p. 187.
25. Kukhterin (2000), pp. 82–3; S. Bridger, *Women in the Soviet Countryside: Women's Roles in Rural Development in the Soviet Union* (Cambridge: Cambridge University Press, 1987), pp. 99–100. See also Vinokurova, this volume, p. 71.
26. McDowell's study finds similar trends in the relationship between negative labelling and unsatisfactory behaviour in the educational and employment records of white working-class young men in the UK. McDowell (2003), pp. 121–3.
27. O. Zdravomyslova, *Semia i obshchestvo: gendernoe izmerenie Rossiiskoi transformatsii* (Moscow: Editorial URSS, 2003), p. 23.
28. See for example, J. Hubbs, *Mother Russia: the Feminine Myth in Russian Culture* (Bloomington: Indiana University Press, 1988); O. Riabov, *Matushka-Rus': opyt gendernogo analiza poiskov natsional'noi identichnosti Rossii v otechestvennoi i zapadnoi istoriosofii* (Moscow: Nauchno-izdatel'skii tsentr 'Ladomir', 2001).
29. This emphasis on the strong emotional bonds between fathers and their children has been highlighted by other, international studies of fatherhood. See for example W. Marsiglio and S. Hutchinson, *Sex, Men and Babies: Stories of Awareness and Responsibility* (New York: New York University Press, 2002), p. 199; and D. Lupton and L. Barclay, *Constructing Fatherhood: Discourses and Experiences* (London: Sage, 1997), pp. 93–118.

30. Ashwin and Lytkina (2004), p. 199.
31. Ibid.
32. See for example, S. Hite, *Sex and Business* (London: Prentice Hall, 2000), p. xiv; C. Cockburn, *In the Way of Women: Men's Resistance to Sex Equality in Organisations* (Basingstoke: Macmillan, 1991), pp. 169–70. Thanks to Mary Buckley for pointing out this comparison.
33. T. Logushko, *Kak perezhit' razvod* (St Petersburg: Piter, 2002), p. 141. Similar issues have been brought to public attention in the UK by the activities of fathers' rights organisations such as Families Need Fathers and Fathers 4 Justice; Mac an Ghaill and Haywood (2007), p. 71.
34. Similar issues have been noted in studies of social service provision in the UK. Indeed, considerable attention has been paid to breaking the cycle whereby women are much more likely than men to access family services which as a result are focused primarily on supporting women and children and where staff may be inexperienced and/or uncomfortable working with men. See for example H. Buhaenko et al., *What Men and Women Want: a Practical Guide to Gender and Participation* (Oxford: Oxfam, 2004).
35. See chapters by Morell, Vinokurova and Carlbäck, this volume, for a discussion of conflict between women's family responsibilities and their position in the labour market during the period of state socialism. See also Kosygina, this volume, for a discussion of similar issues in the experience of female migrants returning to Russia in the contemporary period.
36. Kay (2000), p. 101.
37. McDowell (2003), p. 9.
38. Connell (1987), p. 66.

7

The Right to be Different? Sexual Citizenship and its Politics in Post-Soviet Russia

Francesca Stella

Equal rights for lesbian, gay, bisexual and transgender (LGBT) people have increasingly been flagged up as the 'main story' in current western debates about sexual citizenzhip.[1] Gay marriage in particular has emerged as the central civil rights cause for western and international LGBT lobbying groups and organisations.[2] Strategies based on claims to rights and visibility for gay people have assumed an international dimension, and their increasing deployment on a global scale has been seen as evidence of 'queer globalisation'.[3] This chapter interrogates notions of sexual citizenship politics from a non-western perspective by looking at debates over sexual citizenship rights and visibility in the Russian Federation.

After briefly sketching out debates on sexual citizenship in academic literature, the first part of the chapter outlines the peculiarities of the political, social and cultural context in which discussions on homosexuality are located in contemporary Russia. While significant changes in the legislation and discursive practices concerning homosexuality have taken place in the past two decades, mechanisms of marginalisation and exclusion of 'other' sexualities are still in place, particularly in the public arena. The chapter goes on to explore the micro level of lesbian community organisations and individual perceptions of gay rights among non-heterosexual women, drawing on empirical data collected for my PhD research on lesbian identities and spaces in contemporary urban Russia. Various strategies adopted by gay and lesbian organisations and grassroots groups for challenging inequalities and marginalisation, as well as women's perceptions of the meaning of partnership rights for same-sex couples, will be explored in the following sections, focusing on how rights claims, visibility and recognition are seen to be conducive to social change. The chapter highlights themes emerging from empirical work conducted within two specific communities, and is not intended to offer a comprehensive survey of views on sexual politics within Russian lesbian activism and the wider community. Rather, in analysing the meanings attached to sexual citizenship, it emphasises contingency and cultural difference rather than universality and sameness, which often feature in discourses on the globalisation of gay rights.

Empirical data, arising from semi-structured interviews and participant observation, were collected during two periods of fieldwork in Moscow and Ul'ianovsk in 2004–5. Semi-structured in-depth interviews were conducted with 62 lesbian and bisexual women aged 18 to 56. In Moscow, which has a lively community and commercial scene, most of my interviewees were women gravitating around community initiatives and events, although some of them were also connected with other settings and social networks, such as internet communities and commercial venues. Ul'ianovsk, a city of 700 000 located in the Middle Volga Region, is significantly less affluent and economically developed than the capital Moscow; the entertainment industry is not well developed, and there is no commercial gay scene nor any formalised community spaces. Most of my interviewees were connected to a queer[4] *tusovka*,[5] meeting informally at local cafés, around the central Ulitsa Goncharova and at monthly gay and lesbian parties organised in a local club.

My interviews focused on issues around queer identity by exploring individual experiences of self-discovery and coming out; access to and use of community spaces and informal networks; and identity management across heterosexualised spaces. Although not specifically covered in the interview schedule, the topic of gay rights surfaced in many interviews, usually when respondents were discussing the local lesbian community. Interviewees usually focused on partnership rights, a topic that featured prominently in media debates at the time, with reference both to Russia and to other European countries. Community initiatives and spaces were explored both through participant observation and through key informant interviews with local activists involved in community and commercial projects.[6] These addressed themes such as the reasons for starting or getting involved in an initiative, the type of activities organised and their target audience, resources available and sources of financial support.

Unworthy citizens? Debates on sexual citizenship in academic literature and in the Russian context

Setting the scene: local and global debates on sexual citizenship

The notion of citizenship has been traditionally understood as a system of rights conferred on and duties required of all members of a national community. However, sociological perspectives have challenged the notion of universal citizenship, noting that systemic forms of inequality and domination have in actual fact marginalised some social groups, while concealing and maintaining the privilege of others. Thus, citizenship can be defined as 'both a set of practices (cultural, symbolic and economic) and a bundle of rights and duties (civil, political and social) that define an individual's membership in a polity'.[7]

A growing body of literature on sexual citizenship explores the connection between sexuality, gender and citizenship, recognising that 'claims to citizenship status, at least in the west, are closely associated with the institutionalisation of heterosexual as well as male privilege.'[8] The debate on sexual citizenship has gathered momentum against the backdrop of legal developments which have brought the issue of gay rights under the spotlight in many European countries. While the topic has gained unprecedented coverage and visibility in the media, western LGBT activism has witnessed a shift in emphasis from identity and community-building to political campaigns concerned with equal rights and visibility, an approach Richardson dubs 'a politics of sexual citizenship'.[9]

Some research, however, has explored the limitations of cultural pluralism and rights discourses in producing meaningful social changes in western societies.[10] It has been argued, for example, that in claiming the right to marriage as its central civil rights cause, the gay and lesbian movement may end up embracing an ideal of respectability, thus claiming a more inclusive ideal of citizenship for the 'good homosexual', but further marginalising the 'bad', disreputable homosexual, who does not fit in with dominant conventions of coupledom and relationships.[11] This approach may reinforce, rather than challenge, the heterosexual institution of marriage. Moreover, by claiming to represent the interests of an undifferentiated LGBT community, and failing to recognise inequalities based on gender, ethnicity and class, gay activism often speaks on behalf of a respectable white, middle-class, male constituency.[12]

Other authors have questioned whether strategies based on rights claims and visibility can be effective in countries where different understandings of citizenship and sexuality are culturally rooted. These scholars call for sexual citizenship politics to be contextualised in a particular political and cultural setting, rather than understood as a global strategy that will infallibly result in the modernisation of 'traditional' societies.[13] They note how, both in popular and scholarly literature on the development of a global LGBT movement, there is a tendency to utilise essentialist notions of gay identity and politics that can be exported across geographical boundaries without much questioning. For example, a booklet produced by the International Gay and Lesbian Association reads:

> The increased visibility of lesbians, gay men and bisexuals, supported by a strong movement, has proved to be a successful formula for confronting and fighting homophobic tendencies in all types of societies. Well-organised groups in many countries have succeeded in at least partially improving our human rights.[14]

In this context, political campaigns based on rights and visibility are applauded and encouraged, and assumed to produce progressive change; such discourse, however, fails to acknowledge how gay visibility can incite violence and produce ruptures in the social fabric, as well as advancing the cause of human rights.

In many former communist countries, the introduction of affirmative legislation protecting LGBT people against discrimination, under the aegis of the EU and the Council of Europe, has been seen as a process bringing these countries closer to the standard of progress and democracy embodied by 'the west'. As Binnie points out, however, little consideration has been given to whether changing the letter of the law has been effective in challenging negative attitudes towards homosexuality.[15] In order to situate my analysis within the Russian discursive landscape, the next section will briefly outline the wider context in which discussions on homosexuality are located in contemporary Russia, as well as old and new mechanisms of marginalisation that affect non-heterosexual citizens.

'An especially personal matter of each citizen': Soviet and post-Soviet boundaries to sexual citizenship

In Soviet Russia, and up to the early 1990s, the stigma attached to homosexuality was reflected not just in the law and in medical practice, but also in the almost complete silence surrounding sexuality and sexual diversity. Male homosexuality was a criminal offence punishable with up to five years of jail, while lesbianism was considered a personality disorder requiring psychiatric treatment and hospitalisation.[16] At the same time, the official discourse located sexual intimacy within the boundaries of monogamous heterosexual relationships, and anything deviating from this was unaccounted for and officially non-existent.[17] This silence affected 'deviant' sexualities above all: the subject was taboo in the Soviet media, only occasionally surfacing in specialised medical literature. However, official censorship concerned sexuality more generally: while, like in most industrialised countries, sexual practices and mores began to change in the

1960s and 1970s, a public and open debate on sexuality – 'whether educational, entertaining, pornographic or philosophical' – was not allowed to emerge in the public sphere until the mid-1980s.[18] This took place in a society where the party-state remained firmly in control of the public sphere and the media, and the private and intimate sphere was only weakly protected against encroachments from the authorities, since individual rights and freedoms were subordinated to those of the collective.[19] The silence surrounding sexuality, and homosexuality in particular, consolidated in Russian culture the notion of sexuality as strictly belonging to the private sphere, and of the latter as a space to be protected from state intrusion and public scrutiny.

From the mid-1980s onwards, with the relaxation of censorship brought about by *glasnost*, an open public debate about sex and sexuality began to emerge, reaching the general public through the popular media. Homosexuality, too, gradually gained public visibility: commercial venues targeting a gay audience began to open in the bigger Russian cities, and the first gay and lesbian associations were created.[20] In the 1990s, anti-sodomy legislation was repealed as part of a broad-ranging reform of the Soviet Penal Code (1993), and homosexuality was struck off the Ministry of Health's classification of mental illnesses (1999). While some areas of the Russian legal system still discriminate against LGBT citizens, the legal and medical provisions that represented major obstacles to the development of a consistent legal defence of LGBT rights have been removed.[21]

These changes offered new opportunities for gay and lesbian people, first and foremost in terms of public representation, spaces of consumption and association. However, mechanisms of social control and exclusion of 'other' sexualities still operate in contemporary Russia. Public debate has reinforced the notion that homosexuality is, and should remain, a fundamentally private concern, and that it is a topic unfit for discussion in the political arena because of its dubious morality and potentially corrupting influence. The Russian nation is implicitly imagined as a heterosexual community, while citizenship status for its 'sexual minorities' is conditional and precarious.

In post-Soviet Russia, the articulation of a public discourse around sexuality largely overlapped with the commodification and commercialisation of sex and erotica, which was a completely new phenomenon for Russian society.[22] The growing presence of 'in your face' sex, sexuality and erotica in the Russian media, and of queer-themed cultural products within it, seem to have produced in recent years a backlash against the new visibility of gay culture, which is often associated with the hypersexualised and trendy images presented in popular culture. Arguments against the media spreading 'debauchery' in contemporary Russian society have been appropriated by nationalist politicians, who have often been very vocal in advocating an end to the 'propaganda of homosexuality'. The allegedly growing popularity of homosexuality is deplored as an example of the pernicious influence of western culture, against which genuinely Russian moral customs should be defended, and homophobic arguments are often justified by the need to boost Russia's declining birth rate, as the country's 'gene pool' is seen as the foundation of its greatness and power.[23]

In April 2002, four nationalist MPs submitted to the Russian Duma a proposal to return to the Soviet law criminalising homosexual behaviour between consenting male adults.[24] The proponents of the amendments insisted that they were not so much concerned with homosexual conduct behind closed doors, but rather with taking a strong stance against the danger posed by the growing visibility of gay culture in Russian society.[25] This was not an isolated episode: shortly afterwards, another deputy proposed that lesbianism be outlawed as well, arguing that the growing popularity of female homosexuality, popularised by the pop group Tatu, was having a negative impact on the country's birth rate.[26] In September 2003, yet another nationalist politician submitted a draft law against the 'propaganda of homosexuality': the proposal, similar to the infamous British clause 28, would restrict public discussion and media coverage of homosexuality.[27]

These initiatives were largely considered publicity stunts in the Russian political community and were not met with any substantial support. According to some observers, they reaffirmed the principle that, whatever individual views on homosexuality may be, the state should not be allowed to interfere with the intimate life of its citizens.[28] However, the institutions repeatedly failed to recognise the relevance of sexuality as an issue of social justice and equality. In May 2004, the Russian Duma ignored the draft law on the recriminalisation of male homosexuality: it was ultimately rejected because over three-quarters of MPs did not take part in the vote. An earlier proposal to make incitement of hatred on the basis of sexual orientation a legal offence, advanced as a response to the homophobic initiatives outlined above, was turned down by a Duma committee on the grounds that 'sexual orientation is an especially personal matter of each citizen.'[29] Overall, public debate on homosexuality seems to reinforce the notion that sexual diversity is, and should remain, a fundamentally private concern, and that it is a topic unfit for discussion in the political arena. By doing so, official discourses in actual fact exclude LGBT individuals from citizenship, and leave them vulnerable to forms of arbitrary discrimination, violence and institutional prejudice.

Far from being confined to the level of symbolic representation, mechanisms of exclusion have very real consequences for queer citizens, particularly when their activities become visible or public. This is especially evident in the restrictions imposed on LGBT activism. While, since the mid-1990s, several community organisations have reported problems in obtaining official registration from the local authorities,[30] it is perhaps the 2006 Moscow gay pride march that most emblematically embodied the tensions and social ruptures over the issue of sexual diversity in Russian society.

The Moscow City Council categorically banned the event, intended as a peaceful manifestation in support of gay rights, claiming to act in the name of the majority of the city's population, and arguing that the march could incite violence against the demonstrators themselves. In the atmosphere of moral panic created by the media, Mayor Luzhkov repeatedly stated that he personally regarded homosexuality as an unnatural phenomenon potentially dangerous for society, claiming that 'if any one has any deviations from normal principles in organizing one's sexual life, those deviations should not be exhibited for all to see.'[31] When an unpublicised alternative to the planned march went ahead, demonstrators were attacked and beaten by members of ultranationalist groups, with the backing of Christian Orthodox groups and the blessing of their religious leaders; the huge police forces deployed proceeded to arrest both the violent mob and the protesters, who were considered guilty of taking part in an 'unauthorised' demonstration.[32]

While Russian legislation remains formally neutral on its citizens' intimate lives and sexual choices, political debates on the new visibility of homosexuality suggest that full citizenship status for LGBT individuals is largely dependent on social and institutional attitudes. In public discourses, the citizenry is implicitly imagined as heterosexual, and sexual minority citizenship is largely confined to the private or semi-private spaces of leisure and consumption. Homosexuality can be tolerated when it is confined to the private space; however, by becoming visible, it does not gain recognition but is forced back into the private sphere.

Spaces of citizenship and spaces of belonging

While highlighting the limitations and conditional status of citizenship for Russian gay people, recent debates about the visibility of gay rights in Russian society also raise questions as to the ways in which meaningful social change can be achieved. There is often an expectation that Russian LGBT politics should follow the lead of western activism, with its emphasis on rights and visibility, in the same way as the country was supposed to follow western models in developing into a democratic capitalist state in the aftermath of the fall of communism.[33]

While non-existent in the Soviet period, owing both to the stigma associated with homosexuality and to the strict control of the party-state over the public sphere, since the early 1990s Russian LGBT organisations and grassroots groups have begun to emerge in the major Russian cities. These associations and initiatives are far less institutionalised than their western counterparts, with no support from the state and limited financial and human resources. Until recently, sexual citizenship politics had been a marginal aspect of Russian LGBT activism, which had tended to focus on the organisation of leisure activities and on community-building.[34] However, both the Moscow gay pride march and recent attempts to push for legal recognition of same-sex couples have brought issues of visibility and rights claims into the spotlight.

Controversies about these high-profile events, which were widely debated at the time when fieldwork was conducted,[35] highlight how the opportunity of claiming equality and symbolic presence in the public and political spheres is a highly controversial issue not just in Russian society, but within the LGBT community as well. The gay pride march, organised by a newly established group of (mainly) gay activists,[36] was supported by a variety of west European politicians, human rights activists and LGBT organisations, and received ample coverage in the western mainstream and gay media alike. What media coverage failed to emphasise, however, was that many among the most established Russian and Moscow LGBT organisations and informal groups did not support the march: while some more or less ignored it, others overtly opposed it and signed a joint letter dissociating themselves from the event.[37] In the letter, the march was described as an irresponsible provocation that might incite violence from religious and extremist groups and result in a general backlash against gay people, in a country that is not 'ready for this kind of event'.[38] Several Moscow community groups joined forces to organise an alternative initiative, the festival of gay and lesbian culture *Raduga bez granits* (Rainbow without boundaries).[39] The gay pride march itself attracted few participants, a significant number of whom were foreign politicians and delegates,[40] giving the impression that the west, rather than the local community, was the main sponsor and preferred interlocutor. The mixed reactions in the gay press and the heated discussions on gay and lesbian internet websites also indicates that the community was highly divided on whether to support the event.[41]

A campaign in support of gay marriage also raised heated debate in the community. In January 2005 the human rights activist (and heterosexual family man) Eduard Murzin and the gay businessman and activist Ed Mishin, leader of the Moscow LGBT organisation *Ia+Ia* [I+I], tried to register their marriage at a Moscow registry office. Even though they anticipated a refusal, their aim was to escalate the case to the Russian Supreme Court and, if need be, to the European Court of Human Rights, on the grounds that the Family Code, in defining marriage as a union between a man and a woman, violates the principles of equality established in the Russian Constitution.[42] This attempt to raise the issue of partnership rights in the political arena, however, seems to be a personal initiative rather than representing the outcome of a wider debate within the Russian LGBT community. Both the mixed responses from the local gay and lesbian press[43] and the unsuccessful attempt to find a genuine gay or lesbian couple willing to register their union[44] seem to indicate that the action failed to engage with the broader community. These debates highlight how political strategies based on visibility, recognition and claims to formal rights may not appeal equally to all sections of the Russian LGBT community. They also raise the issue of whether campaigns claiming rights and raising public visibility can, or should, be made in the name of a whole community. In order to look beyond conventional notions of a homogeneous community, unanimously backing political struggles for formal equality, the nature and aims of Moscow lesbian groups' initiatives are explored. An analysis of the strategies used to challenge inequalities and carve out communal spaces will hopefully add to a more nuanced picture of Russian sexual citizenship politics.

The pursuits of lesbian grassroots groups are still largely restricted to the semi-public and informal sphere of leisure and community spaces. Activists usually emphasised the importance of providing spaces where women can meet and get some support. At the same time, many women involved in these projects downplayed the 'political' side of their initiatives, and in one instance claimed not to engage in politics at all. Strategies based on claims to rights and public visibility were considered with a certain caution. Such approaches, it was felt, would be perceived as confrontational in the Russian context and could potentially antagonise rather than engage the wider society, ultimately worsening social attitudes towards sexual diversity.

Activist Lena Botsman (pseudo.), for example, has been organising a small-scale 'pride', a boat trip on the Moscow river attended by a small group of women carrying rainbow flags, on an annual basis since 2003. Although in principle she supports gay pride marches, she questioned the organisation of the Moscow march, claiming that the difference between a gay pride march and her 'Rainbow over Moscow' event is that the latter takes place in the heart of Moscow but far from the public spotlight, and no political claims are associated with it.[45] This example illustrates how claims to symbolic presence in public spaces are made without necessarily claiming public visibility.

Other informants, although in principle open to the idea of sexual citizenship politics, seemed reluctant to get directly involved in them. Ol'ga Suvorova, leader of the Moscow organisation Pinkstar, stated in an interview:

> I am not a politician. And I am not ashamed of this. To me, what is really important is to make a positive change in lesbians' everyday lives and inner worlds. We need to show and demonstrate to society that we are ordinary, normal people, that we are not sick and dangerous. That we too have families, raise children, work for the good of our families and of society, we practice sports and arts . . . That we do not claim some special rights, just the same as everyone else's. As to politics, that is evil, the way I see it. And evil and aggression generate only more evil and aggression.[46]

The low priority given to political activity by Russian activists can be related to the limitations imposed on discussions of homosexuality in the political arena, and the fears of possible repercussions, explored in the previous section. Moreover, the reluctance on the part of civic organisations to turn to the state as their main interlocutor is a pervasive feature of post-Soviet political life, where the state is perceived as distant and not necessarily as a guarantor of individual freedoms and rights.[47] Indeed, during a discussion group for lesbian women held at the Moscow organisation *Ia+Ia*, when an American guest asked about the importance of gay rights to Russian women, a participant retorted that 'there are no rights in Russia', a comment that was met with murmurs of approval from the audience. Another woman illustrated the point by explaining that, if your partner was dying in hospital, you would have to bribe the doctors to get to see her, but the same would hold true for a heterosexual partner, given the widespread practice among medical personnel of demanding gifts and bribes from patients and their families.[48]

While women involved in community projects often distanced themselves from sexual citizenship politics, and were mostly engaged in the organisation of leisure activities and support networks, claims not to be involved in political activism are sometimes a matter of semantics, and should not be taken too literally. Several projects, while careful not to victimise non-heterosexual women, promoted the idea of getting together on the grounds of a common sexuality and shared experiences of marginalisation. Moreover, many initiatives promoted cultural activities, a fact that was commonly explained by the need to challenge and dispel prevailing stereotypes about 'other' sexualities by providing more authentic representation of lesbian lives, produced by lesbians themselves. These initiatives aimed both to give women the possibility of making informed choices about their intimate lives, and to educate the wider society and make it more tolerant. All these ideas resonate with familiar notions of identity politics.

While communal spaces may not provide spaces of citizenship, given their semi-private character, they certainly aim at providing spaces of belonging. Indeed, in-depth interviews with non-heterosexual women from Moscow and Ul'ianovsk often highlighted the importance of such spaces. While sometimes critical of scene and community spaces, women often talked about the important role of lesbian networks, particularly in their coming-out years. 'Lesbian' space was perceived as providing a supportive environment, allowing women not just to explore their sexuality, but also to exchange experiences, form connections and friendships and ultimately make positive choices about their intimate lives. Interviewees often underlined that such spaces were perceived as impacting on individuals' lives in much more tangible ways than political issues:

> As our beloved Dostoevskii said, 'It's a good thing when people have a place to go', and I also need a place to go, I want people to have a choice, this is the most important thing. If all this didn't exist, if the issue of choice became my problem, back then, in the 1980s . . . I would have taken part [in LGBT activism], I would have been interested in fighting. But now, when this exists, and all that's needed is some organisational work, well, this just isn't for me.[49]

Some of the literature on sexual citizenship emphasises the importance of going public as a political act, and identifies the semi-public sphere as a site of passive consumerism, confining citizenship to the ghetto of the gay scene rather than challenging the marginalisation of 'other' sexualities.[50] Yet findings from this research show that these spaces need not be identified with the commercial scene, and that they may be in some ways sites of resistance, challenging the heterosexualised landscape.

The fact that issues of sexual citizenship politics are divisive highlights the diversity of the Moscow lesbian community. While claims to rights are often portrayed as representing a whole community, the views and opinions of its constituents often go unexplored. For this reason, in the next section I will explore women's perceptions of gay rights, and the meanings they attach to them, focusing in particular on partnership rights, the theme that surfaced most often in interviews. Women's experiences of marginalisation also illustrate how social inclusion is perceived not just as a matter of being granted formal rights, but is primarily identified with social and cultural practices.

'They would still say: what kind of marriage is that?' Perceptions of citizenship and partnership rights in Moscow and Ul'ianovsk

Legal status for same-sex couples emerged from women's narratives not so much as a matter of equality, social justice or access to services and benefits, but as something which was consistently associated with citizenship status. Partnership rights for gay people were seen as a sign of recognition from the state; in a country like Sweden, 'the state doesn't deny the existence, does not close its eyes to the existence of these people.'[51] Official recognition means one's non-heterosexual identity is validated in the public sphere, a recognition associated with visibility and social acceptance from the wider society. Partnership rights were seen as evidence that same-sex relationships are considered not just acceptable, but unremarkable and 'normal'. A society that gives formal recognition to same-sex couples is, in the words of a young woman from Moscow,

> some place like the Netherlands, where this is allowed, where people are tolerant about it, where, if you hold hands with your girlfriend on the streets, they won't point at you and say, look at those lesbians, they won't call you names and insult you.[52]

When the topic of partnership rights emerged, during interviews or in general conversation, it usually elicited a more or less explicit comparison with an idealised west, where such rights were firmly located. Whatever their views on the importance of achieving legal status for same-sex couples, there was little expectation among interviewees that partnership rights would be introduced any time soon in Russia, and the matter was debated as an abstract issue.

The fact that comparisons with the west surfaced so often in interviews may have been prompted by interviewees' awareness of my own west European background; nevertheless, such comparisons show how a certain discourse on sexual citizenship evoked among interviewees strong associations with an imagined 'west'. Not just gay rights, but rights discourses in general, were often linked to a 'culture of rights' alien to Russia, and associated with a more stable and affluent society, where entitlements and access to rights are neatly regulated by the law and the state is able to provide support and services to its citizens. By contrast, in Russia people have to 'make do' and fend for themselves, with little support from formal institutions. Although interviewees tended to paint an idealised rosy picture of gay life in the west, they were not uncritical of this imagined 'other': in some instances western sexual citizenship rights were identified with an excessive permissiveness which may turn into 'moral dissipation';[53] with an incomprehensible fragmentation of society along the lines of minority group interests; or with a laughable and unintelligible political correctness taken to absurd extremes.

Empirical data indicate that the language of sexual citizenship rights and legal change, although not unfamiliar, may sound 'other' or alien to Russian women. Global discourses of LGBT emancipation have traditionally emphasised the importance of the law as a discursive site where social change can be initiated.[54] However, there is a need to acknowledge the cultural diversity of models of citizenship participation, and the fact that the liberal framework of legally defined rights and freedoms may be rather specific to some of them.

Western models of sexual citizenship predicated upon rights claims did not appeal to all interviewees in the same way: some dismissed the issue of legal status as irrelevant and far from their daily lives, others were willing to talk at length about the meanings they attach to such rights. However, there is evidence that such models are, at least to some extent, a cultural reference point, and that they do in some ways influence Russian women's expectations of their places within the citizenry.

As already noted, several women referred to 'the west' as a safe haven for queers, where legal recognition of same-sex couples is a sign of their 'normalisation'. Moreover, two interviewees talked at length about the practical steps they had taken, or were going to take, in order to move to another European country.[55] For both, the legal recognition of same-sex couples was a determining factor in their desire to emigrate.

> The right to marry [for same-sex couples] doesn't exist. And no lawyer, good or bad, can help, if there is no law. Adoption is difficult, inheritance is difficult. We need the state to support us. Why do we want to leave? We want a child and a normal family life. We have to leave. Here we can't do anything, and we don't want to hide in our flat, we would like to live as a normal family.[56]

It was women in a stable, monogamous long-term relationship, who were living with their female partner, or planning to move in with a long-term girlfriend, who most engaged with the issue of partnership rights. Among these women the symbolism of family was very powerful. Both in interviews and in general conversation they referred to their union as 'our family', or 'our same-sex marriage', and one young couple also reported celebrating their commitment to each other with a symbolic rite. When asked to fill in a form with their demographic details, including their marital status, several women queried the concept, and eventually entered *zhenata* (married) as their answer, referring to their lesbian relationship rather than to their official marital status.[57]

In these women's narratives, family rights emerged as important both in themselves and as a sign of recognition from the state. Several women noted how, during their life together, they had come across a number of practical issues that had proved far from straightforward to solve because their union was not legally recognised. Such issues ranged from buying a flat together, to inheritance, to getting a loan from a bank; although some of these matters could eventually be resolved, this could be done only by resorting to expedients, and sometimes by bypassing the law:

> We bought a flat together, we can live quietly here, and society doesn't meddle in our life. But, as it happens, we have to protect our rights somehow 'on the side' [*cherez levoe ukho*]. I mean, when heterosexuals get married, the state rises to protect this basic unit of society [*iacheika*], while, to defend ourselves, we have to think over issues of testament, property, guardianship of children.[58]

The lack of legal protection for same-sex families was also perceived as limiting their potential, particularly with regards to having children together. Several couples expressed the wish to have children, and had looked into giving birth or adopting. However, the lack of legal status for same-sex families was felt to offer insufficient guarantees to couples who want to have children. Combined with other factors, such as financial constraints and the fear that their children may be ostracised by peers, lack of formal rights was perceived as a barrier to starting a family.

Importantly, while family rights may be an end in themselves they were also associated with recognition from the wider society. A recurrent image used to describe same-sex families is that of the basic unit of society (*iacheika*), potentially able to make a contribution to the wider community. However, being denied status and visibility, same-sex couples are marginalised and excluded from the life of mainstream society:

> We would like things to be easy. We'd like social status. And not just concerning children. For example, they give you credit more easily in a bank if you're a family. Of course it is important. As it turns out, we are erased from social life.

> As a couple, we are not morally protected. As a family unit [*iacheika*] we don't exist. But we're here.[59]

Cohabiting couples identified family life as the area in which they felt most excluded from mainstream society, since, by making lesbian families invisible, the state effectively erased them from its citizenry.

While long-term couples valued partnership rights, among other interviewees these did not appeal to everyone in the same way, although most women acknowledged the importance of legal recognition for same-sex couples as a matter of principle. Perhaps unsurprisingly, younger women did not see the issue as particularly relevant to their lives, as they were not necessarily looking to settle down with a partner for the long term. For some younger respondents relationship issues were an open-ended question, and some women saw their sexuality as a 'work in progress'. For many, the legal status of same-sex couples was not a burning issue: official recognition was seen as a mere formality, 'a stamp on your passport',[60] which was not essential in a committed relationship. For others, same-sex relations represented an alternative lifestyle, which allowed more freedom and equality and was at odds with traditional models of coupledom.

However, not only cohabiting couples perceived lack of social status and moral marginalisation of same-sex relations as a problem. Several interviewees highlighted how dominant heteronormative practices and prevailing societal prejudice limited women's choices to start a family with a female partner. While bigger cities, such as Moscow and St Petersburg, were seen to offer a better degree of anonymity and more opportunities, women from Ul'ianovsk stressed the fact that it was relatively uncommon for same-sex couples to live together. Moving in with a girlfriend was particularly difficult for those who did not have an independent living space, and it could potentially attract unwanted attention and scrutiny from the wider community. Indeed, in many women's narratives, the home emerged as an unsafe space, particularly when women were materially dependent on their families of origin, a situation common not just for young women, but for older ones as well, owing to both low living standards in the country and to gender inequalities in income levels. Material support from parents, often crucial for a young couple to establish themselves, could be denied as a sign of disapproval of a certain 'lifestyle'.

Downplaying the importance of abstract rights, many women pointed out that sexual identities are negotiated on a daily basis in private spaces and interpersonal relationships, an area beyond the reach of state intervention. Several women emphasised the point that legal status alone would not make a difference, a reminder of the fact that a more inclusive model of sexual citizenship is not just a matter of legal status, but is intertwined in a complex way with cultural practices and social conventions:[61]

> I just want to say that this will not necessarily solve all our problems. Even if they make this legal three thousand times, and everything will be wonderful, all the same you'll find people, who will remain the same, who will say: well, you got married, but what kind of a marriage is that?[62]

Conclusions

While significant changes have taken place in legislation and public attitudes on homosexuality in the past two decades, mechanisms of exclusion and marginalisation of 'other' sexualities are still in place in contemporary Russian society. By reinforcing the notion that (homo)sexuality is a private matter, and dismissing it as an issue of social justice and equality, official discourses leave LGBT citizens vulnerable to discrimination, violence and abuse. Moreover, such discourses sanction tight control over public and political manifestations of 'other' sexualities, often implying that their public visibility should not be legitimised by state institutions, as it may have a polluting and corrupting effect on the wider society. Thus, by representing the Russian polity as a heterosexual community, official discourses in actual fact exclude non-heterosexual individuals from citizenship, and this exclusion, far from being confined to the symbolic level of representation, translates into everyday practice.

Although campaigns concerned with equal rights and visibility for the LGBT community get wide coverage in both Russian and western media, there is disagreement in the community itself about how to challenge exclusion and promote social change. International LGBT politics celebrate visibility and political claims to equality as a strategy to raise awareness of gay issues in mainstream society. However, some forms of public visibility may be seen as inciting violence and producing ruptures in the social fabric, which ultimately worsen, rather than improve, the social standing of non-heterosexual citizens. In western culture 'law, and more generally, political institutions as the wielders of law, are viewed as the site from which social and cultural transformations of the most fundamental sort will emerge.'[63] However, this principle may not translate into Russian culture, where a different model of citizenship participation exists, and where the state is not necessarily perceived as a guarantor of individual freedoms and rights. Indeed, while legal status for same-sex couples was firmly located in 'the west', interviewees were somewhat sceptical that in the current climate the Russian state would provide recognition and legal protection for its non-heterosexual citizens. Rather than engaging with hostile, or at best unsympathetic, public institutions, several lesbian groups preferred to act from the bottom up, carving out communal spaces and trying to change social attitudes through other means.

Precarious entitlement to public space and lack of formal rights were perceived as a consequence of the marginalisation of LGBT individuals, families and communities. While legal status for same-sex couples was associated with entitlements, visibility and recognition, its lack was seen as the result of deeply rooted social norms and mechanisms of exclusion. Since sexual identities are negotiated on a daily basis in private spaces and interpersonal relationships, legal status would be devoid of any meaning, if not accompanied by radical changes in social attitudes towards sexual diversity.

Notes

1. D. Richardson, *Rethinking Sexuality* (London: Sage, 2000), p. 8.
2. D. Bell and J. Binnie, *The Sexual Citizen: Queer Politics and Beyond* (Cambridge: Polity Press, 2000), pp. 53–61.
3. J. Binnie, *The Globalization of Sexuality* (London: Sage, 2004), pp. 67–85.
4. In an effort to include those whose voices often go unheard in research about sexualities, my sample did not comprise only self-identified lesbians, but also a minority of women who identified otherwise (bisexual, transgender), or who refused to be 'labelled'.
5. An informal social network of friends and acquaintances getting together on the basis of common interests, often for recreational purposes, and hanging out at specific meeting places. H. Pilkington, *Russia's Youth and its Culture* (London: Routledge, 1994), pp. 237–40.
6. All the projects included in my investigation were Moscow-based. They comprised: the Moscow gay and lesbian archive; the lesbian non-profit publication *Ostrov* (Island), a mimeographed literary journal also covering news of interest to the local lesbian community; the weekly non-profit recreational circle *Klub Svobodnogo poseshcheniia* (Open Attendance Club), whose main promoter, Lena Botsman (pseudo.) is also involved in the organisation of festivals of lesbian music and other gatherings; the group *Pinkstar*, which organises self-help

groups for lesbian women and recreational gatherings, as well as the annual lesbian conference *Ona+Ona* (She+She); and the recently founded women's association *Tolerantnost'* (Tolerance), which was planning to open a recreational centre for non-heterosexual women.

7. E. Isin and P. Wood, *Citizenship and Identity* (London: Sage, 1999), p. 4.
8. Richardson (2000), p. 75. See also D. Evans, *Sexual Citizenship: the Material Construction of Sexualities* (London: Routledge, 1993); D. Richardson, 'Sexuality and Citizenship', *Sociology*, 32, 1 (1998): 83–100; J. Binnie, 'Invisible Europeans: Sexual Citizenship in the New Europe', *Environment and Planning A*, 29 (1997): 237–48; J. Weeks, 'The Sexual Citizen', in M. Featherstone (ed.), *Love and Eroticism* (London: Sage Publications, 1999); Bell and Binnie (2000); D. McGhee, 'Beyond Toleration: Privacy, Citizenship and Sexual Minorities in England and Wales', *British Journal of Sociology*, 55, 3 (2004): 357–75; and M. Manalansan, 'Queer Intersections: Sexuality and Gender in Migration Studies', *International Migration Review*, 40, 1 (2006): 224–49.
9. Richardson (2000), p. 8.
10. Bell and Binnie (2000); C. Brickell, 'Whose "Special Treatment"? Heterosexism and the Problem with Liberalism', *Sexualities*, 4, 2 (2001): 211–35.
11. Bell and Binnie (2000), pp. 57–61.
12. See, for example, research that analyses the intersection between sexuality and class, or sexuality and ethnicity: Y. Taylor, 'Real Politik or Real Politics? Working-class Lesbians' Political "Awareness" and Activism', *Women's Studies International Forum*, 28 (2005): 484–94; Y. Taylor, 'Inclusion, Exclusion, Exclusive? Sexual Citizenship and the Repeal of Section 28/2a', *Sexualities*, 8, 3 (2005): 375–80; M. Manalansan, 'In the Shadow of Stonewall: Examining Gay Transnational Politics and the Diasporic Dilemma', in L. Lowe and D. Lloyd (eds), *The Politics of Culture in the Shadow of Capital* (Durham: Duke University Press, 1997).
13. Binnie (2004); M. Manalansan, 'A Queer Itinerary: Deviant Excursion into Modernity', in E. Lewin and W. L. Leap (eds), *Out in Theory* (Urbana and Chicago: Univerity of Illinois Press, 2002).
14. A. Hendriks, R. Tielman and E. Van der Veen (eds), *The Third Pink Book: a Global View of Lesbian/Gay Liberation and Oppression* (Buffalo: Prometheus Books, 1993), quoted in Malananansan (1997), p. 490.
15. Binnie (2004), pp. 75–9.
16. D. Healey, *Homosexual Desire in Revolutionary Russia: the Regulation of Sexual and Gender Dissent* (Chicago: Chicago University Press, 2001).
17. I. Kon, *Lunnyi svet na zare: liki i maski odnopoloi liubvi* (Moscow: Izdatel'stvo AST, 1998).
18. A. Rotkirch, 'What Kind of Sex Can You Talk About? Acquiring Sexual Knowledge in Three Soviet Generations', in D. Bertaux, P. Thompson and A. Rotkirch (eds), *On Living Through Soviet Russia* (London: Routledge, 2004), p. 93.
19. I. Oswald and V. Voronkov, 'The "public-private" Sphere in Soviet and Post-Soviet Society: Perception and Dynamics of "public" and "private" in Contemporary Russia', *European Societies*, 6, 1 (2004): 97–117. O. Kharkhordin, *The Collective and the Individual in Russia: a Study of Practices* (Berkely: University of California Press, 1999). V. Shlapentokh, *Public and Private Life of the Soviet People: Changing Values in Post-Stalin Russia* (New York and Oxford: Oxford University Press, 1989).

20. Kon (1998); L. Essig, *Queer in Russia: a Story of Sex, Self, and the Other* (Durham, NC: Duke University Press, 1999).
21. N. Alekseev, *Pravovoe regulirovanie polozheniia seksualnykh menshinstv: Rossiia v svete praktiki mezhdunarodnykh organizatsii i natsional'nogo zakonodatel'stva stran mira* (Moscow: BEK, 2002).
22. Kon (1998).
23. M. Rivkin-Fish, 'From "Demographic Crisis" to "Dying Nation": the Politics of Language and Reproduction in Russia', in H. Goscilo and A. Lanoux (eds), *Gender and National Identity in Twentieth-Century Russian Culture* (DeKalb, IL: Northern Illinois University Press, 2006).
24. A. Braterskii and A. Mikhailov, 'V Dume povtoriaiut zady stalinskogo prava', *Izvestiia*, 23 April (2002), http://main.izvestia.ru/politic/23-04-02/article17531; K. O'Flynn, 'Deputies Want to Outlaw Gay Sex', *The Moscow Times*, 25 April (2002), http://www.themoscowtimes.com/stories/2002/04/25/002.html.
25. A. Nikonov, 'Duma ne dolzhna stoiat' v poze strausa', *Ogonek*, 21 (2002): 14–15.
26. 'Deputies Add Lesbian Sex to the List of Crimes', *Interfax News Agency*, Moscow, 14 May (2002), available at http://www.gay.ru/english/communty/politics/2002f.htm.
27. A. Popova, 'Gosduma gonit gomoseksualitov v podpol'e', *Rbc Daily*, 19 September (2003), http://www.rbcdaily.ru/news/policy/index.shtml?2003/09/19/45221.
28. I. Kon, 'O normalizatsii gomoseksual'nosti', http://sexology.narod.ru/publ033.html; M. Gessen, 'Mama, mama i ia. Chuvstvovat' sebia chelovekom-nevidimkoi tol'ko izredka byvaet nepriiatno', *Novoe vremia*, 20 (2002).
29. V. Kirzanov, 'Polozheniie seksual'nykh men'shinstv', in Moskow Helsinki Group, *Doklad o sobliudenii prav cheloveka v Rossiiskoi Federatsii v 2004 godu*, available at http://www.mhg.ru/files/dok04/mensh04.doc.
30. The Moscow association *Svoi* (Our people) was repeatedly denied registration, and it was made clear that they would not be allowed to register unless they removed from their statute any reference to the lesbian character of their organisation (Key informant interview N. 4, Moscow, 5 September 2005). (When referring to interviews, numbers are used, rather than real names, in the interest of preserving anonymity.) The expectation, based on the experience of other organisations, that plainly stating their aims would result in a refusal of official registration made founding members of the Moscow association *Tolerantnost'* opt for registration as a women's organisation (Key informant interview N. 3, Moscow, 2 July 2005).
31. 'Pride and Violence: a Chronicle of the Events of May 27, 2006, in Moscow', *Human Rights Watch Briefing Paper*, 1 June (2006), p. 3, available at http://hrw.org/backgrounder/eca/russia0606/index.htm.
32. E. Lomovtsev, 'Nevziraia na orientatsiiu', *Vremia novostei*, 91 (2006), available at http://www.vremya.ru/2006/91/51/153031.html; M. Magovedova, 'Boi-parad', *Novye izvestiia*, 29 May (2006), available at http://www.newizv.ru/news/2006-05-29/47105/.
33. See, for example, the introduction to A. Štulhofer and T. Sandfort, *Sexuality and Gender in Postcommunist Eastern Europe and Russia* (New York: Haworth Press, 2005).

34. P. Le Gendre, *The Gay and Lesbian Community in Russia* (King's Hill, Kent: CAF, 1998); Essig (1999).
35. The main period of fieldwork took place between April and October 2005; Mishin and Murzin's civil action, which is discussed in more detail below, took place in January 2005, while the gay pride march was announced to the press in July 2005.
36. In Moscow, the project was supported by lesbian businesswoman Evgeniia Debrianskaia and by the lesbian website VolgaVolga. See http://www.gayrussia.ru/actions/detail.php?ID=6659 and http://www.lesbiru.com/society/alexeev.html.
37. http://gayclub.ru/gaylife/1560.html?PAGEN_1=2&ID=1560.
38. The letter was sent, among others, to ILGA Europe, the LGBT umbrella organisation which had backed the initiative.
39. http://fest.gayclub.ru/members.htm.
40. Although the ban and the anticipated threat of violence played a part in the levels of participation, according to one source, up to three-quarters of those taking part in the conference preceding the march were foreign guests. See human rights activist Scott Long's live journal, http://washingtonblade.com/2006/redpride/index.cfm.
41. http://lesbiru.com/forum/login.php?redirect=viewtopic.php&t=9689&sid=31e2a75276956c3c240683fc5383bf0d; http://lesbi.ru/talk/lgbt/gay_sumbur2006.html.
42. http://www.gay.ru/society/legislation/marriage/murzin_int.html.
43. See, for example, O. Gert, 'Brak ili ne brak?', *Ostrov*, 22 (2005); R. Zuev, 'Oni delali glupost' i poluchili Gerostatovu slavu', available at http://www.gayclub.ru/right/1477.html.
44. Mishin and Murzin initially looked for a real-life gay or lesbian couple willing to register their union at a local registry office through the website gay.ru/lesbi.ru, but had no success. See http://www.gay.ru/news/rainbow/2005/01/08.htm.
45. Key informant interview N. 4, Moscow.
46. http://lesbi.ru/person/suvorova2005.html.
47. Oswald and Voronkov (2004). See also Turbine, this volume.
48. Fieldwork notes, 11 June 2004.
49. N. 1, Moscow.
50. Evans (1993).
51. N. 48, Ul'ianovsk.
52. N. 1 pilot, Moscow.
53. N. 27, Ul'ianovsk.
54. Binnie (2004).
55. N. 21, Moscow; N. 48, Ul'ianovsk.
56. N. 21, Moscow.
57. *Zhenata* is a gender-specific term and refers to a married woman. For a similar discussion of the symbolism of family in lesbian relationships in the Russian context see N. Nartova, 'Lesbiiskie sem'i: real'nost' za stenoi mol'chaniia', in S. Ushakin (ed.), *Semeinye uzy: modeli dlia sborki*, Vol. 1 (Moscow: Novoe literaturnoe obozreniie, 2004).
58. N. 3 pilot, Moscow.

59. N. 11 and N. 10, Moscow.
60. N. 13, Moscow.
61. See also Kay's discussion of men's rights as parents in this volume.
62. N. 5 pilot, Moscow.
63. L. Cata Backer, 'Queering Theory: an Essay on the Conceit of Revolution in Law', in L. Moran, D. Monk and S. Beresford (eds), *Legal Queeries: Lesbian, Gay and Transgender Legal Studies* (London: Cassell, 1998), p. 185.

8

Russian Women's Perceptions of Human Rights and Rights-based Approaches in Everyday Life

Vikki Turbine

The protracted political, economic and social transformations in former communist states have shown that while formal political rights and freedoms have expanded, this has not necessarily led to the realisation of other fundamental rights.[1] Living conditions for many Russian citizens have worsened since the collapse of the Soviet regime, and criticisms of Russia's human rights record continue to be highlighted by international non-governmental organisations.[2] Although these social and economic changes have affected many people living in Russia, regardless of gender, it has been argued that liberalisation and marketisation created 'two mutually repelling poles – a male dominated pole of wealth, integrated into the hypermodern flow of finance and commodities, and a female dominated (working class) underworld, retreating into subsistence and kin networks.'[3] Thus, the transformation process has arguably had a more negative impact on the lives of women. Women's lack of political representation, discrimination in the labour market as well as chauvinistic attitudes displayed towards women have been identified as the main areas of discrimination against women.[4] In addition, increased rates of domestic violence and the trafficking of women and girls into the sex industry have recently attracted attention as some of the major threats to Russian women's human rights.[5]

A great many women's organisations have emerged over the post-Soviet period to confront these challenges, some located at grassroots level, whilst others have found success nationally and at transnational levels.[6] However, few women's organisations campaign on an overtly feminist platform, since the language of 'women's rights' has been discredited as a result of its appropriation by the Soviet regime, and/or its association with western feminism. Some have suggested, therefore, that the 'gender neutral' appeal of human rights may be more successful for advancing the concerns of women.[7] The relative success of the parliamentary party 'Women of Russia' in the 1993 elections when campaigning on a human rights platform contrasts with their defeat in the 1995 elections where a more feminist stance was taken.[8] The success of the Committee for Soldiers' Mothers (CSM) is another example of where campaigning on a human rights platform has been successfully employed by a women's organisation.[9]

Russian women's organisations that attract foreign funding and collaboration in campaigning tend to reflect international women's human rights priority issues.[10] This has been seen in the crisis centre movement in Russia.[11] It is without question that the issue of violence against women deserves attention; however, it is suggested that many Russian women do not regard this as a priority issue in everyday life, instead having more immediate concerns with lack of childcare, employment and welfare.[12] Despite this, social and economic concerns tend not to attract foreign funding or government support at the national level.[13] This has resulted in a lack of formal articulation of women's everyday priority issues within a human rights discourse, demonstrating a gap between international and local priorities.

Through analysis of data generated in forty-nine in-depth interviews with women living in the provincial Russian city of Ul'ianovsk,[14] this chapter examines Russian women's perceptions of human rights in their everyday lives. This study is important because human rights are a socially constructed concept and meanings remain contingent on time and place, something which is particularly pertinent to contemporary Russia, given the redefinitions of state–society relations in the post-Soviet period.[15] As human rights discourses become increasingly influential in global politics, gaining insights into local understandings of human rights is crucial if human rights are to fulfil their social justice aims globally.[16] This chapter discusses respondents' perceptions of human rights as a concept and in relation to concrete situations. It then explores the factors informing these perceptions and how this impacts on agency. In conclusion, I suggest that respondents were seeking information about rights, but that the potential for rights-based approaches to become the norm remains contingent on wider socio-economic and cultural factors.

Perceptions of human rights in Russia: indicators from public opinion polls and press discourses

A large body of research into Russian public opinion on human rights exists, including data collected by the Russian public opinion monitoring body VTsIOM.[17] In 2004, a VTsIOM poll asked 'Which human rights are most important?' The 'right to minimum subsistence' generated the highest response with 38 per cent of those polled identifying positively with this right.[18] Public opinion poll data have also indicated that a significant number of Russians would be willing to give up civil liberties in return for wages and pensions being paid on time.[19] It could be inferred from these results that the association of human rights with civil and political freedoms is perceived negatively by a population that continues to prioritise social and economic guarantees and entitlements.

The association of human rights with civil and political freedoms is rooted in elite attempts to redefine state–society relations in the post-Soviet period. In this context, the attainment of civil and political freedoms has been repeatedly held up as the key to achieving human rights.[20] As a result, in the post-Soviet period, rights have become 'horizons of possibility rather than self-standing entitlements under ostensible state guarantee'.[21] By contrast, the Soviet regime framed social and economic entitlements as human rights in order to justify a lack of civil and political freedoms.[22] Negative public opinions towards human rights as civil and political rights do not, however, necessarily equate to an out and out rejection of the value of civil and political rights. Rather, civil and political rights are not considered as useful in the resolution of the kinds of difficulties arising from declining living standards.

While opinion poll data suggest an association of human rights with civil and political rights, and thus the dismissal of the relevance of human rights among the public, in reality, perceptions and understanding of human rights are less clear cut. Analysis of selected Russian press sources[23] revealed that the topic of human rights featured regularly on the public agenda during the period of study, and attempts were being made to develop awareness of rights and rights-based approaches[24] through press discourses.[25] More significantly, the local press appeared to be attempting to make human rights appear more relevant to everyday experience by framing social and economic issues,[26] such as problems with communal services,[27] healthcare and education as human rights issues. Rights-based approaches were also advocated as a means of resolving these problems.[28] Given the level of discussion of human rights, it was assumed that the respondents taking part in this study would have some familiarity with the topic of human rights.

Respondents' perceptions of human rights

To gauge levels of familiarity with the topic of human rights, respondents were asked the question 'What do you associate with the term human rights?' Responses to this question reflected the 'duality' inherent in the phrase 'human rights'. Human rights can be understood both as a package of claimable rights, and as an ideal moral standard.[29] Where respondents associated human rights with a tangible set of rights that could potentially be claimed, lists of rights given were predominantly focused on social and economic rights. For example, a retired university librarian in her sixties said:

> In the broadest sense of the word, human rights are the rights to rest and employment, some kind of social support . . . if you want to know which rights we actually enjoy at the moment then we have the right to medical care and education, although a trend towards paying for these services is developing.

Where the term human rights was associated with an ideal moral standard that all human societies should aspire to live by, respondents generally emphasised freedoms. A researcher in her twenties described human rights: 'Human rights are legally observed norms, the rights that grant people some freedoms, but also limit these so that we can all live as part of society.'

These two interpretations of the concept of human rights reflect the coexistence of Soviet constructions of human rights that emphasised social and economic entitlements, with newer post-Soviet constructions that emphasise civil and political freedoms. However, regardless of their understandings of the concept of human rights many respondents conditioned their responses, by arguing that human rights were not relevant in their everyday lives because they experienced 'different kinds of problems'. This indicated additional understandings of 'human rights', where the process of exercising human rights provisions was limited to particular crisis situations.

'I'm not particularly worried about human rights at the moment': human rights, 'crisis situations' and 'civil liberties claims'

Most respondents felt that human rights were not a particularly pressing concern in their everyday lives because human rights were perceived to be more relevant to those experiencing some form of 'crisis'. This implied that when relating human rights to lived experiences, human rights were mainly perceived to be relevant as a form of protection in instances of crisis. A 25-year-old sales manager argued that ordinary people generally did not experience 'crisis' situations in everyday life and therefore human rights were not considered relevant:[30]

> 'Human rights' is an extremely important concept, but I don't feel that in my case these rights are being violated . . . I'm not experiencing some kind of crisis where I could say my rights are not being observed, or someone is violating them. If you were homeless for instance, then of course you would have a sense of this. But if you are just a normal person, then your human rights will hardly ever be violated.

The aforementioned attempts by the local press to frame local social and economic concerns within a human rights discourse did not appear to impact on respondents' perceptions. However, this is a relatively recent development and it may be that the link between human rights and everyday problems is yet to be internalised by respondents, or demonstrated by visible improvements.

Another recurring theme in response to questions about the significance of human rights in everyday life was an association of human rights with the political sphere; an arena that respondents felt was remote from their lives.[31] A single mother in her late thirties who had previously worked as a survey researcher retold her experiences of conducting surveys on the topic of human rights in Ul'ianovsk. She felt that most citizens were not concerned with human rights issues because of their association with high profile cases involving the state or wealthy individuals:

> I don't think the general population is really concerned with these issues; I would go as far to say that they're not even interested in the subject. Take Khordorkovsky's arrest,[32] for instance . . . when I worked as a survey researcher, I had a whole section of questions about Khordorkovsky and human rights . . . like 'are you following the Khordorkovsky court case?' I never met a single person who was. It's just not interesting to anyone – those millionaires have their court cases, but ordinary citizens have their own concerns.

The link between human rights and wealthy individuals pursuing civil liberties claims through the legal process had also linked the process of claiming rights with the legal system, an issue that will be returned to later in this chapter. It appeared that it was not only these specific connotations of the phrase human rights that led respondents to dismiss the significance of human rights in their everyday lives. Existing cultural norms and ascribed gender roles also appeared to have an influence.

Women's human rights: are cultural norms more relevant than human rights provisions?

When respondents were asked to identify which human rights they felt were most important for women,[33] Soviet understandings of human rights were prioritised in relation to everyday life. The human rights identified as most important for women included, reproductive rights (access to abortion and contraception), the right to maternity and child support, women's rights to property in marriage or civil partnerships, and the right to self-realisation. However, the right to employment was identified as the most important human right for women. The aim of this chapter is not to give detailed discussion of the employment issues facing women in Russia,[34] but rather to use the example of respondents' understandings of employment as a human right to illustrate the cultural factors influencing women's perceptions of human rights.

It was unsurprising that the right to work was identified as the most important human right for women, as over the post-Soviet period women were among the first to lose their positions as a result of changes to the state system. Although some women have been able to take advantage of the opportunities for entrepreneurship presented in the post-Soviet period and have been successful in creating new careers, most of the women in this study continued to be concentrated in low paid employment, or were unemployed. Respondents felt that their rights were violated in employment because of continuing cultural expectations that women act as primary carers, but also on grounds of age.[35]

Despite identifying employment as a human rights issue affecting women, the provisions of human rights were not perceived to be relevant because they were not enforced,[36] and did not override pre-existing gender norms. An American Bar Association report found that 'the concept of discrimination against women is not well understood in Russia . . . women generally maintain that their rights are realised equally to those of men. Yet, they also agree that discrimination against women exists in a number of spheres.'[37] The respondents taking part in this study echoed these findings in acknowledging violations of their rights, whilst simultaneously accepting them as 'inevitable' effects of prevailing cultural norms. A 23-year-old woman, working in advertising, felt that attempting to defend her rights was ultimately pointless because cultural norms were more powerful than formal provisions that guaranteed women's rights on paper: 'You don't want to spoil relations [by complaining], and I don't know if I would use anti-discrimination legislation. If I'm being honest, there are instances where it's better just to keep your mouth shut.'

It could also be that the right to work was identified as the most important human right for women as a consequence of Soviet constructions of women's roles as workers and mothers. The continued importance of the Soviet social contract and understandings of human rights are now discussed in order to show how local understandings of human rights both diverge from, and overlap with understandings of citizenship rights.

Human rights are not relevant, but rights are violated: the breakdown of the Soviet social contract and local understandings of rights

Although respondents tended to dismiss the relevance of human rights in their lives, a rights violations discourse was prevalent throughout interviews. It appeared that understandings of rights violations were informed by the withdrawal of Soviet-style citizenship rights, rather than by post-Soviet understandings of the concept of human rights as outlined above. However, attempts to make clear-cut distinctions between understandings of 'human rights' and 'rights' can be difficult. Whilst human rights and citizenship rights have conceptually distinct original aims,[38] similarities between the two exist. Human rights have developed with reference to citizenship rights, and the increasing moral force of human rights discourses in the latter part of the twentieth century has, in turn, impacted on the scope of citizenship rights.[39]

It is particularly difficult to make clear distinctions in the post-Soviet context because elite redefinitions of human rights and citizenship as civil and political freedoms exist alongside Soviet constructions of citizenship and human rights that continue to hold legitimacy. The following extract illustrates what Humphrey calls an 'emotional' attachment to the paternal role of the state. This results in post-Soviet reforms and redefinitions of rights being framed as morally wrong, unjust and as breaking the social contract.[40] An IT support worker in her thirties described a sense of 'abandonment' by the state: 'Before, I had certainty for tomorrow, the state would always know what was happening and I did not feel that the state would abandon me.' Therefore, distinctions that can be made at a conceptual level are muddier in public discourse. For example, a primary school teacher in her late forties felt that the basic right to life was violated, which could be interpreted as both a human rights and a citizenship rights issue:

> You can see for yourself how my rights are violated, my right to the provisions necessary for life is violated . . . we can't find employment and therefore we don't have the means to live . . . in all, I would say

> my rights are violated because I live in this rich country, but I don't receive a single thing from it.

This conflation of understandings of human rights and rights is significant because respondents appeared to be forming similar perceptions about their citizenship rights as they had about human rights. Rights were perceived as lacking in relevance because of their association with 'different types of problems'. In addition, respondents' sense of 'abandonment' by the state, through its failure to protect and uphold the social and economic rights considered legitimate, and experiences of the overly bureaucratic nature of the state, created perceptions of rights-based approaches as irrelevant in attempting to resolve everyday issues.

It is also important to note the influence that past experiences of the limited success of rights-based approaches had on respondents' perceptions of rights. Rights-based approaches require interaction with the state administrative system, but this was characterised as stressful, time-consuming and unproductive. A geography teacher in her late forties explained that even attempting to fulfil basic citizenship obligations such as the renewal of an internal passport[41] resulted in difficulties: 'At the moment it's best to avoid contact with the state. It's one paper for this, then another, then a third . . . and still you get nowhere.' Such disillusionment with the state had led some respondents to explore alternative avenues in which to pursue rights claims, one of which being the legal approach. However, negative or disappointing experiences of the legal approach resulted in the entrenchment of negative perceptions of rights-based approaches because they were perceived as ineffective.

Rights as 'legal entitlements': negative perceptions of the legal system and their impact on perceptions of rights-based approaches

The growth of legal consultancy practices and the prevalence of legal advice in local newspapers and television 'talk shows' highlighted and placed legal approaches to claiming rights on the city's public agenda during the period of study. A part-time budget sector administrator reflected on growing popular interest in legal approaches as a means to resolving everyday issues:

> Perhaps it may become possible to resolve problems by legal means. At the moment there are many programmes on television aiming to help people learn about their rights and how to use the law . . . I've

> noticed just how many people watch and pay attention to these programmes. It may be possible to go through the courts and resolve problems. However, I still think that the majority of the population believe it is those who have money and connections who will win [by using the legal system].

A number of respondents spoke of instances where they felt legal consultations had been necessary. Personal problems, such as dealing with the police or enquiring about alimony or child maintenance claims as a result of relationship breakdown, were areas in which respondents cited legal consultation as an effective potential means to resolve problems. However, others felt that it was possible to use legal means to hold the state to account. A PhD student in her mid-twenties talked about the use of legal approaches to hold the state to account in the provision of social and economic entitlements was setting a precedent: 'At the moment there have been a number of precedents where people have gone to court and won their case, for example to get some entitlement from the state.' These views suggest that respondents were considering rights-based approaches, however, legal approaches to resolve problems were not accessible to the majority of respondents interviewed for this study. It was not only the financial costs of legal consultation that prohibited many respondents from pursuing this approach, but also the time and emotional costs involved in fighting a court case. Respondents felt that this would outweigh any benefits of a victory. An editor of a local magazine in her late forties explained:

> To take a case to court takes a lot of money, and even if you win the case, for example in claiming compensation or pension entitlements, you will not make up the money you have spent on the case. Therefore, even if I wanted to, I couldn't use legal means because I simply don't have the money.

Scepticism about the legal system was entrenched because only those with the ability to pay for services could access services, creating the suspicion that lawyers could be bought. A family and criminal defence lawyer explained:

> There is this suspicion that the courts are for sale; that there is no justice, the process is dishonest and that everyone in the system can be bought or sold. There is an element of truth in these fears, and people talk about it a lot, we have to try and convince people that the legal process can [be used to] protect their rights.

These suspicions were echoed by a female member of the editorial team on the magazine *Sel'skaia nov'*. Despite working for a magazine that provides legal advice and which has an editorial commitment to the promotion of rights-based approaches,[42] the respondent still perceived lawyers as only serving the interests of those with the ability to pay. She felt that even her own son who was a lawyer could not protect his own rights, or those of ordinary citizens as the majority of legal work was for business clients.[43] Without greater access to free legal consultations, it is difficult to envisage how those without disposable financial resources could truly benefit from pursuing rights-based claims through legal approaches.[44]

Even where respondents had been able to access the legal system, a lack of guaranteed resolution, even in the event of an official victory, discredited the effectiveness of this approach. An unemployed single mother recounted her experience of the court system when attempting to claim child maintenance from her ex-husband:

> I went to court and the court demanded that he pay [child maintenance]. However, a year has already passed since the official resolution of the problem and nothing has changed. Although a special service apparently exists to enforce court recommendations, they don't appear to be doing anything.

This chapter has thus far discussed associations of human rights with the civil and political sphere, the conflation of human rights and rights terminology, the experience of lack of realisation of citizenship rights, and the association of rights with legal approaches. In addition, respondents argued that cultural norms reduced the effectiveness of legal norms to protect women's rights. Together, these perceptions and experiences culminated in respondents forming the overall perception that it was not worthwhile pursuing their rights. This resulted in the majority of respondents dismissing even the vocabulary of rights for that of 'everyday problems'.

'Resolving problems' not 'claiming rights'? The role of informal networks in post-Soviet society

Respondents in this study appeared to reject the language of 'rights' for that of 'problems' when discussing how to resolve specific examples of rights violations experienced in everyday life. A librarian in her mid-twenties represented how the negative perceptions and experiences of rights, discussed above, influenced the ways in which people talked about everyday problems:

> Normally I don't think in relation to my rights because I encounter different types of problem . . . although we have rights on paper, it's a little different in real life. Among my friends, well we don't spend time thinking about our rights – it's better just to get on with your life.

I argue that respondents were using a vocabulary of 'problem solving' as a form of coping mechanism. If 'problems' can be resolved without the need to interact with the state or legal systems, stressful, time-consuming, and ineffective processes can be avoided. The vocabulary of problems may also be more familiar to respondents when considering that the most common site of action in everyday life continued to be within informal networks.[45] A researcher in her twenties argued that informal networks are most commonly used to resolve problems because they are regarded as reliable, trustworthy and capable of offering a guaranteed solution, even if only in the short term: 'People resolve problems more easily through friends and acquaintances than by formal approaches . . . they [formal approaches] take too long, involve too much red tape and they don't seem to resolve your problems anyway.'

Informal networks of family, friends and acquaintances were used throughout the Soviet period in order to combat the rigidities of the command economy. Networks and 'blat' facilitated the exchange of goods and information.[46] Operating within informal networks was also a key part of the 'privatisation' of life that took place in the post-Stalin period.[47] In the post-Soviet period, informal networks have been retained in everyday life and offer a strategy to cope with the new obstacles presented by the changes in the state system.[48]

Informal networks operate as a system of 'weak ties' and involve interaction outside of the immediate circle of family and friends. This provides the opportunity to access different resources from different groups and may generate further inclusion and progress.[49] It can therefore be argued that almost every person will have some form of access to a network, and this distinguishes informal networks from systems of personal connections.[50] Rather than regarding operation within informal networks as indicative of atomisation from the state, they can be viewed as an important resource where interaction with state structures has been proven to be stressful and unproductive.[51] In this sense, informal networks can operate as a source of moral support, a forum for discussion of problems, and as a means of accessing information in a trusted and familiar environment.

The practice of using informal networks to access information is now explored in relation to the findings of this study.[52] The data from this study revealed that although respondents generally held negative perceptions of rights-based approaches, some were using informal networks to access information about rights and rights-based approaches.

The role of informal networks in raising awareness of rights and rights-based approaches

An increased awareness of rights issues and interest in rights-based approaches to problem resolution appeared to be developing among some of the respondents in this study. This was revealed in discussions about the variety of means respondents felt were available to them for resolving problems. Although informal networks remained the main site for resolving everyday problems, some respondents were using informal networks to access advice about rights and the process of making a rights claim from friends or acquaintances with legal expertise.

It has been argued that increased awareness of rights can lead to the transformation of existing norms or perceptions of human rights and the empowerment of women.[53] Making enquires about rights issues within the trusted environment of informal networks can be viewed as empowering as they provide a space in which women can explore these issues without experiencing the stresses associated with making contact with state or legal structures. Moreover, the empowerment potential of sourcing information in this way is increased as informal networks often operate as a set of increasing concentric circles. Most people can potentially access this type of information that would otherwise be inaccessible to them, either because of the bureaucracy of the state, or the prohibitive costs of legal consultation. In this respect, there was the potential for informal networks to act as a springboard for respondents to pursue formal approaches.

In contrast to the negative perceptions of the legal profession illustrated above, legal advice accessed through informal networks was perceived as reliable because the contact possessing legal knowledge was made familiar and trustworthy by virtue of the system of recommendations operating within a network. A self-employed matrioshka artist in her early thirties and an unemployed teacher in her late forties were two of several respondents who felt that legal advice obtained through a network was trustworthy:

> I have a female friend who is a lawyer, so I would go to her [for advice]. She's a really good lawyer so I would hope she would offer to help me.
>
> We have a good female friend who is a lawyer; well she is a lawyer and a historian . . . she has used her influence on several occasions to campaign for our rights.[54]

Friends or acquaintances with legal training were also considered to be valuable 'sounding boards' against which to assess the appropriateness of pursuing a rights claim through legal channels for the resolution of a particular problem. For example, a part-time researcher who was experiencing serious problems in attempting to secure citizenship for her second child[55] thought that seeking legal advice was useful in weighing up her options:

> My husband asked a former classmate, who's in her second year of legal training, about our problem and she said it is pointless to go to court. Even if we won, we would only receive one hundred rubles[56] and what's the point of that?

The value of sourcing legal advice via informal networks lies in its relatively stress- and cost-free nature. However, the above extract raises some important questions, both about the quality of legal advice available, and about the appropriateness of legal approaches for the types of rights violations encountered by the respondents in this study.

Consolidating negative perceptions of rights or assessing alternative approaches?

The above example illustrates two points. Firstly, the legal advice was sought from a student in her second year of training, which could result in incomplete or inaccurate advice being given. The independent legal system in Russia is still evolving and newly trained lawyers are therefore continually playing 'catch-up' with changing legislation and professional rules.[57] Analysis of readers' letters appearing in the Russian periodical *Sel'skaia nov'*, also indicated a practice of 'double-checking' legal advice received.[58] Secondly, the advice received focused on monetary compensation as the only possible outcome from a court case. Clearly monetary compensation would be an inappropriate and inadequate resolution of the problem. The respondent's aim in claiming the basic right of citizenship for her child was not financial gain through compensation, but to ensure her child would have entitlement to social welfare benefits, medical attention and schooling in the future. Whilst rights exist as legal entitlements, it could be problematic for a legalistic definition of rights to become entrenched in popular discourses in the post-Soviet context. This study has shown that the types of rights violations or 'problems' respondents often cited were linked to wider moral discourses where the lack of social and economic rights protection arose out of the perceived breakdown of the Soviet social contract. Such wider moral claims, or social and economic rights violations, cannot be easily resolved through a legal ruling.[59]

Conclusions

This chapter has discussed Russian women's perceptions of human rights in relation to their everyday experiences. Respondents' perceptions of human rights demonstrated a wide range of possible understandings of this concept. Respondents variously understood the concept of human rights as an ideal moral standard, a package of rights, a particular form of 'crisis' intervention and also as shorthand for an approach or tool to resolving problems. In contrast, when discussing human rights in relation to lived experiences Soviet constructions of human rights continued to be prioritised. The relevance of Soviet human rights in everyday life was reinforced as respondents simultaneously rejected the relevance of human rights, but discussed everyday issues within a rights violations discourse. The continued legitimacy of Soviet understanding of human rights led to disillusionment with state failure to uphold them, and respondents discussed alternative approaches to claiming rights. Two alternative approaches to the resolution of everyday problems were proposed: legal approaches and informal networks.

Legal approaches promoted in the media had generated interest among respondents, but distrust of the legal profession and the prohibitive costs of legal consultation made this an unfeasible option for many. As a result, most respondents continued to rely on informal networks to talk in terms of 'resolving problems', rather than 'claiming rights'. However, this study also revealed that some respondents were using informal networks to access information about rights, which was described as a new use of an older practice. This new use may have empowerment potential if it enables women to pursue formal approaches. Whilst the benefits of accessing information in a cost-free and trusted environment were apparent, the almost exclusive focus on legal advice raises questions about the extent of this approach's potential to empower women.[60]

Despite accessing this information, respondents tended not to pursue their claims outside of informal networks because of negative perceptions of the legal system and the cost of legal approaches. The legal advice received tended to define victory in terms of monetary compensation, and this may be a blunt tool in the current socio-economic climate. Therefore, the interest in pursing rights-based claims may be fleeting where the focus remains on financial compensation, which has been shown to be ineffective in resolving wider social, economic and gender rights violations. This chapter concludes that the use of informal networks as a source of information about rights can be initially empowering for women, but may ultimately entrench negative perceptions of rights-based approaches where the advice received and anecdotal evidence shared prioritises and at the same time discredits legal approaches.

Notes

1. I. Balfour and E. Cadava, *And Justice for All? The Claims of Human Rights* (Durham: Duke University Press, 2004), p. 287.
2. See for example, Amnesty International's 2003 report *Justice for Everybody: Human Rights in the Russian Federation*, which details a range of human rights abuses in Russia. Available at www.amnesty.org/russia.
3. M. Burawoy, P. Krotov and T. Lytkina, 'Involution and Destitution in Capitalist Russia', *Ethnography*, 1, 1 (2000): 61. They argue that a consideration of class is crucial in gendered analysis of the transformation, as working-class men have also experienced marginalisation in certain sectors of employment and in the home.
4. For a discussion of the affects of transition on women in Russia and the former post-Soviet region see, S. Bridger, R. Kay and K. Pinnick, *No More Heroines? Russia, Women and the Market* (London: Routledge, 1996). Recent scholarship has also focused on the effects the transformation has had on men. See, R. Kay, *Men in Contemporary Russia: the Fallen Heroes of Post-Soviet Change?* (Aldershot: Ashgate, 2006); S. Ashwin and T. Lytkina, 'Men in Crisis in Russia: the Role of Domestic Marginalisation', *Gender and Society*, 18, 2 (2004): 189–206; and Burawoy et al. (2000), p. 61.
5. See Amnesty International's website for more details, www.amnesty.org/russia. See also Buckley, this volume.
6. R. Kay, *Russian Women and their Organisations: Gender, Discrimination and Grassroots Women's Organisations, 1991–96* (Basingstoke: Palgrave Macmillan, 2000).
7. P. Watson, 'Rethinking Transition: Globalism, Gender and Class', *International Feminist Journal of Politics*, 2, 2 (2000): 185–213, pp. 190–2; L. McIntosh Sundstrom, 'Women's NGOs in Russia: Struggling from the Margins',

Demokratisatsiya, 10, 2 (2002): 207–9. However, the 'gender-neutrality' of human rights has been debated. See for example, N. Kaufman and A. Lindqvist, 'Criticising the Gender-Neutral Treaty Language: the Convention on the Elimination of Discrimination Against Women', in A. Peters and J. Wolper (eds), *Women's Rights, Human Rights: International Feminist Perspectives* (London: Routledge, 1995).

8. H. Pilkington, 'Can Russia's Women Save the Nation? Survival Politics of Gender Discourse in Post-Soviet Russia', *Bradford Studies in Language, Culture and Society, Issue 1: Women in Post-Communist Russia* (Bradford: Interface, 1995).
9. For analysis and discussion of the work of the Committee of Soldiers' Mothers see, A. Caiazza, *Mothers and Soldiers: Gender, Citizenship and Civil Society in Contemporary Russia* (London: Routledge, 2002).
10. For a discussion of transnational feminist campaigning and issues prioritised, see S. Walby, 'Feminism in a Global Era', *Economy and Society*, 31, 4 (2002): 533–57.
11. J. E. Johnson, 'Public-Private Permutations: Domestic Violence Crisis Centres in Barnaul', in A. B. Evans Jr., L. A. Henry and L. McIntosh Sundstrom (eds), *Russian Civil Society: a Critical Assessment* (New York: M. E. Sharpe, 2005), pp. 268–9. For a discussion of domestic violence issues in post-Soviet Russia, see J. Hemment, 'Global Civil Society and the Local Costs of Belonging: Defining "Violence Against Women" in Russia', *Culture and Society*, 29, 3 (2004): 815–40. Although the issue of domestic violence was not the main focus of my research, I interviewed the directors of the city's crisis centre for women and families experiencing domestic abuse in order to have a local perspective on the issue, should it come up in interviews.
12. V. Sperling, 'Women's Organisations: Institutionalised Interest Groups or Vulnerable Dissidents?', in Evans et al. (2005), p.169.
13. Sperling (2005).
14. The interviews were conducted as part of fieldwork research for an ESRC sponsored doctoral thesis, which explores women's perceptions of human rights and rights-based approaches in everyday life. Fieldwork was conducted between May and October 2005 in the city of Ul'ianovsk, in the Middle Volga region of the Russian Federation. Respondents who took part in this study were aged between 18 and 65 years, and represented a wide range of occupations and family structures. Where respondents are cited, general demographic details are given to offer context, but have been modified as appropriate, in order to protect anonymity.
15. R. Stones, 'Rights, Social Theory and Political Philosophy: a Framework for Case Study Research', in L. Morris (ed.), *Rights: Sociological Perspectives* (London: Routledge, 2006).
16. Watson (2000).
17. VTsIOM is the transliterated abbreviation for 'Vserossiiskii Tsentr Izucheniia Obshchestvennogo Mneniia' (Russian Centre for the Study of Public Opinion), see www.wciom.ru.
18. VTsIOM, 'Which Human Rights are Most Important', *Russian Life*, 47, 1 (2004): 8.
19. N. Romanovich, 'Democratic Values and Freedoms "Russian Style"', *Sociological Research*, 42, 6 (2003): 62–8.

20. M. Buckley, *Redefining Russian Society and Polity* (Oxford: Westview Press, 1993).
21. Watson (2000), p. 203.
22. M. Hawkesworth, 'Ideological Immunity: the Soviet Response to Human Rights Criticism', *Universal Human Rights*, 2, 1 (1980): 67–84.
23. Press sources analysed included; the Russian periodical *Sel'skaia nov'*; the local newspaper *Simbirskii kur'er*; and *The Current Digest of Post-Soviet Press*. *Sel'skaia nov'* was chosen as it offered an insight into the types of problems and rights issues identified by provincial readers through its letters pages. *Simbirskii kur'er* is published in Ul'ianovsk four times per week, with a circulation of 8000 on weekdays, and 12 000 for the Saturday edition. It is available as an online edition that enables searching and analysis of local issues when not in the field. For further details about this newspaper, see www.ulpressa.ru and www.sk-narod.ru. The focus of my research was primarily on local press discourses, but the *Current Digest of the Post-Soviet Press* (www.currentdigest.org) was also consulted to give an overview of national rights discourses.
24. A rights-based approach involves not only using the language of rights in policy initiatives, but also promoting participation and making rights user-friendly for addressing local problems. See L. VeneKlasen, V. Miller, C. Clark and M. Reilly, 'Rights-based Approaches and Beyond: Challenges of Linking Rights and Participation', *Institute of Development Studies*, 235 (2004).
25. See issues of *Sel'skaia nov'* to consult the letters page, 'Pravovaia neotlozhka', which provides legal advice in response to letters published. For examples of local press discourses on human rights see, 'A molodezh – to razve ne grazhdane?' *Simbirskii kur'er*, 15 July 2004; 'Imeiut li pravo prava narushat'? Uchashchikhsia lishili prava vybora: idti ili ne idti na pravozashchitnyi kinofestival', *Simbirskii kur'er*, 3 April 2004; and 'Dumaem vmeste: komitet po pravam cheloveka', *Simbirskii kur'er*, 8 April 2006. All articles are available online at www.sm-k.narod.ru.
26. International human rights activists have also been pressing for the reintroduction of social and economic rights into human rights discourses. See T. Basok, S. Ilcan and J. Noonan, 'Citizenship, Human Rights and Social Justice', *Citizenship Studies*, 10, 3 (2006): 267–73, pp. 268–9.
27. Communal services, or 'Zhilishchno-kommunal'noe khozaistvo' (GKH), are responsible for the repair and maintenance of housing stock. The recent reform of the system and lack of adequate provision of services has proven controversial. See A. Vasil'ev, 'Shok-eto po nashemy: Reforma GKH dlia liudei ili za chet liudei', *Sel'skaia nov'*, 3 (2006), p. 15.
28. 'Dumaem vmeste: novosti', *Simbirskii kur'er*, 17 December 2005; and 'Tat'iana Sergeeva: shkuru sdai i potrokha', *Simbirskii kur'er*, 24 July 2004.
29. C. J. Anderson, A. Paskeviciute and Y.V. Tverdova, 'In the Eye of the Beholder? The Foundations of Subjective Human Rights Conditions in East-Central Europe', *Comparative Political Studies*, 38, 7 (2005): 771–98, p. 773.
30. As respondents did not characterise the problematic issues in their lives as 'crisis', this dampens the force of 'perpetual crisis' theories that were said to characterise everyday life in Russia in the 1990s. See, F. Pickup and A. White, 'Livelihoods in Post-Communist Russia: Urban/Rural Comparisons', *Work, Employment and Society*, 17, 3 (2003): 419–34, pp. 420–1.

31. For a discussion of the sense of remoteness Russian citizens feel from the political sphere in the post-Soviet period see, R. Rose 'Russia as an Hour-Glass Society: a Constitution Without Citizens', *East European Constitutional Review*, 4, 3 (1995): 34–42. See also Stella, this volume.
32. Khordorkovsky, one of the so-called 'oligarchs', was head of the Russian oil group Yukos, and also had media interests until his arrest in 2003. He was accused of corporate and personal tax evasion, but his supporters believe the arrest was, in fact, politically motivated because he had emerged as a potential challenger to Putin in the 2003 elections. After an eleven-month trial, he was convicted and sentenced to nine years in prison. See 'Khordorkovsky: an Oligarch Undone', *BBC News Online*, 31 May 2005. Available at http://news.bbc.co.uk/1/hi/business/4482203.stm accessed November 2006.
33. Research conducted by local academics in 2003 found that the types of human rights prioritised differed across 'traditional' gender divisions, with women prioritising rights required in 'private' spheres, for example social welfare entitlements and childcare support. Men prioritised those required for 'public activism' such as civil and political freedoms. See 'Ona dumaet o dome, on o svobode. Ul'iainovskie zhenscshini schitaiut, chto segonda sil'no narushaetsia konstitustionoe pravo', *Simbirskii kur'er*, 6 March 2004. Available from www.sm-k.narod.ru.
34. For a comprehensive discussion of the issues affecting women in the Russian labour market see S. Ashwin (ed.), *Adapting to Russia's New Labour Market: Gender and Employment Strategy* (London, Routledge, 2006).
35. Ashwin (2006); Kosygina, this volume.
36. The lack of enforcement powers of human rights norms is frequently cited in debates about the potential of human rights to empower and promote social justice. At present human rights represent an 'unresolvable paradox' whereby they exist as a check on state power, but are at the same time dependent on the state for enforcement. See Balfour and Cadava (2004), p. 287.
37. American Bar Association, 'CEDAW Assessment Tool Report for the Russian Federation', February 2003. Available at www.abanet.org/ceeli/publications/cedaw/cedaw_russia.pdf.
38. See, Basok et al. (2006), pp. 267–8, for a discussion of such distinctions.
39. See A. Brysk and G. Shafir, 'The Globalisation of Rights: From Citizenship to Human Rights', *Citizenship Studies*, 10, 3 (2006): 275–87, for a discussion of the development of human rights in accordance with the pattern of development of citizenship rights.
40. C. Humphrey, 'Inequality and Exclusion: a Russian Case Study of Emotion in Politics', *Anthropological Theory*, 1, 3 (2001): 331–53.
41. Renewal of internal passports is crucial because of the residence permit or *propiska* system. Although the *propiska* system was formally abolished in 1993, registration at a permanent address remains the precondition for the enjoyment of most civil rights and entitlement to social benefits. For a more detailed discussion, see T. Hojdestrand, 'The Soviet-Russian Production of Homelessness: Propiska, Housing, Privatisation', available at www.anthrobase.com/txt/H/Hoejdesrand_T_01.htm, accessed March 2007. Human rights organisations have also voiced their concerns at the way in which the residence system is being enforced in some areas to discriminate against ethnic minorities, or to extort payment. See for example, Amnesty International's

analysis of this trend, available at http://www.amnesty.org/russia/minorities.html, accessed November 2006.

42. Interview with the editor-in-chief, and the letters pages' editorial team of the Russian periodical *Sel'skaia nov'*, Moscow, October 2005.
43. Interview with the editor of letters pages of the magazine *Sel'skaia nov*, Moscow, October 2005.
44. Free legal consultation is not a statutory right in Russia at present, although free legal consultations are available in certain cases. Free legal advice can be obtained by clients of crisis centres through hotlines or consultation, see Johnson (2005), p. 267. Those not using crisis centres can write letters to press services offering legal advice, but there is no guarantee of a response. Some law students offer free legal consultation in order to gain experience, but again such consultations are provided on an ad hoc basis. This practice is discussed in F. F. Dudyrev and V. P. Malkov, 'Iuridicheskie kliniki v Rossii: vozvrashchenie cherez 150 let', *Gosudartsvo i pravo*, 4 (2002): 61.
45. See M. Caldwell, *Not by Bread Alone: Social Support in the New Russia* (Berkeley: University of California Press, 2004); and C. Humphrey, *The Unmaking of Soviet Life: Everyday Economies after Socialism* (Ithaca, NY: Cornell University Press, 2002).
46. See J. Millar, 'The Little Deal: Brezhnev's Contribution to Acquisitive Socialism', *Slavic Review*, 44, 4 (1985): 694–706; and A. Ledeneva, *Russia's Economy of Favours: Blat, Networking and Informal Exchange* (Cambridge: Cambridge University Press, 1998), p. 212, for comprehensive discussions of the ways in which connections and informal networks operated in the Soviet and post-Soviet periods.
47. See Vinokurova, this volume; and V. Shlapentokh, *Public and Private Lives of the Soviet People: Changing Values in Post-Stalinist Russia* (Oxford: Oxford University Press, 1989).
48. Burawoy et al. (2000), p. 47.
49. J. Gibson, 'Social Networks, Civil Society and the Prospects for Consolidating Russia's Democratic Transition', *American Journal of Political Science*, 45, 1 (2001): 51–68, p. 53.
50. Networks based on personal connections within the administration are not available to all and may entrench unequal access to rights. See Ledeneva (1998).
51. R. Rose 'Russia as an Hour-Glass Society: a Constitution Without Citizens', *East European Constitutional Review* 4, 3 (1995): 34–42, pp. 34–6.
52. During the Soviet period, word of mouth remained the most trusted source of information on almost any subject. See Shlapentokh (1989), pp. 172–8. See also, S. Ashwin and V. Yakubovich, 'Cherchez la femme: Women as Supporting Actors in the Russian Labour Market', *European Sociological Review*, 21, 2 (2005): 149–64, p. 160, for a discussion of the ways in which women share information about employment opportunities widely amongst informal networks.
53. K. Nash, 'Human Rights for Women: an Argument for Deconstructive Equality', *Economy and Society*, 31, 3 (2002): 414–33, p. 417.
54. This respondent was a member of a Seventh Day Adventist Church and expressed a sense of being discriminated against on grounds of her religious beliefs. Interview with teacher on sick leave, Ul'ianovsk, October 2005.

55. A query over the mother's registration status at the time of birth (see note 42) left the mother without official citizenship status. This meant the child was technically born to a 'non-citizen' mother and therefore not entitled to automatic citizenship.
56. At the time of the study (May–October 2005), 100 rubles were equivalent to US$5.
57. A family and criminal defence lawyer explained how attempting to keep up with these changes was a stressful element of her job. Interview, Ul'ianovsk, October 2005.
58. See for example, 'Pravovaia neotlozhka', *Sel'skaia nov'*, 11 (2003): 25.
59. H. Englund, 'Towards a Critique of Rights Talk in New Democracies: the Case of Legal Aid in Malawi', *Discourse and Society*, 15, 5 (2004): 527–51.
60. G. Binion, 'Human Rights: a Feminist Perspective', *Human Rights Quarterly*, 17, 3 (1995): 509–26.

9

Doubly Disadvantaged? Gender, Forced Migration and the Russian Labour Market

Larisa Kosygina

In the years following the collapse of the USSR the Russian Federation experienced a significant influx of migrants from the other former Soviet republics. A high proportion of these new migrants came to Russia with their families seeking permanent residence as a result of the political, social and economic situation in the former Soviet republics and due to shifting understandings of cultural and political belonging. In the 1990s, official discourses within Russia represented this migration flow mainly as forced migration.[1]

The glossary on migration issued by the International Organisation for Migration defines forced migration as:

> A migratory movement in which an element of coercion exists, including threats to life and livelihood, whether arising from natural or man-made causes (e.g. movements of refugees and internally displaced persons as well as people displaced by natural or environmental disasters, chemical or nuclear disasters, famine, or development projects).[2]

In the Russian Federation, this broad definition is reduced to the somewhat narrower classification of forced migration as migration caused by persecution or by the threat of persecution 'on the basis of race, nationality, religion, language, and affiliation to a particular social group or political conviction'.[3] Russian legislation divides such migrants into two categories on the basis of citizenship: Russian citizens have the right to apply for forced migrant status, while non-Russian citizens can apply for the status of refugee.

In the period 1992–2003, more than 1.6 million people arriving in the Russian Federation received the status of either forced migrant or refugee. Eighty-five per cent came from the former Soviet republics, mostly from

Kazakhstan and from the other Central Asian republics and the Caucasus.[4] Moreover, it has been estimated that only one in three people who had the right to apply for such status did so successfully.[5] Of the migrants arriving from the former Soviet republics 20.6 per cent were recognised by the Russian government as forced migrants or refugees. Of these 15.5 per cent were recognised as refugees and 84.5 per cent as forced migrants. Women comprised 55 per cent of forced migrants registered between 1992 and 2002 and 53 per cent of refugees registered between 1993 and 2002.[6]

Numerous studies have been conducted into the experiences of forced migrants from the former Soviet republics in the Russian Federation.[7] Migrants' experiences in the Russian labour market have been perhaps one of the most topical themes for such research. Researchers have examined the interactions between labour market experiences and other elements of adaptation, for example, housing and registration (*propiska*).[8] The impacts of local economic structures and conditions in the place of settlement have been analysed[9] as has the role of migrants' educational and professional background in determining their experiences in the Russian labour market.[10] Researchers concerned with a gender analysis of forced migration have also written about forced migrants' experiences of and positions within the labour market of the receiving society.[11] Whilst they explore differences in the labour market experiences of male and female migrants, these studies have not investigated the extent to which such differences correspond with the gendered labour market experiences of the local population. This chapter seeks to fill this gap in the literature by examining the experiences of forced migrants in the context of existing data regarding the gender dimensions of the Russian labour market.

This chapter examines the ways in which dominant beliefs about gender in contemporary Russian society influence the labour market experience of forced migrants from the former Soviet republics and explores a number of other factors which make their experiences more difficult than those of the local population. The arguments presented here are based on the findings of an INTAS-funded research project 'The effectiveness of programs for the integration of forced migrants: a gender perspective',[12] which I conducted in Novosibirsk region (western Siberia) in 2001–3. The aim of this research was to investigate the ways in which the post-Soviet Russian gender order[13] has influenced the implementation of measures prescribed by Russian legislation and Federal Migration Programmes to facilitate the integration of forced migrants into the receiving society. Semi-structured interviews were conducted with migrants who had settled in Novosibirsk region to reveal the ways in which these state-led measures actually affected their lives. Interviews were loosely structured around those key aspects of migrants' experience, which are addressed in the Federal Migration Programmes: respondents were asked about their experiences of housing, acquisition of forced migrant status and residential registration (*propiska*), and also about their experience in the labour market of the receiving society. This semi-structured approach allowed me to gather information about differences between the experiences of men and women. I was interested both in those differences which were a direct result of the implementation of state-led measures and in those which were not affected, or at least only indirectly, by state support.

In total 62 migrants were interviewed: 44 women and 18 men. Respondents were approached through non-governmental organisations and the offices of the Territorial Migration Service. The lists of migrants provided by these organisations allowed me to tailor the sample, taking into consideration not only gender, but also age and family situation (number of children and the presence of a partner). Half of my respondents lived in cities and half in rural areas. Their age ranged from 21 to 73 – only five had reached retirement age. A quarter of respondents had a university degree, 30 per cent had completed specialised secondary education and 25 per cent had finished secondary school. Fifty-nine per cent of women and 44 per cent of men with whom I spoke had children under 16 living with them. Five women were raising children alone, while all the men raising children were living with their partners or wives. This sample was not representative of the actual demographic profile of the forced migrant population. Rather, its aim was to access a diversity of experiences in migrants' stories about their lives in the receiving society.

Forced migrants in Russia: the gender order and labour market experiences

Occupational differentiation and the earnings gap

Respondents' employment experiences demonstrate a clear division of occupations between women and men (see Table 9.1). It appears that each gender operates within a specific range of jobs. A look at broader national statistics shows that this is neither coincidental nor specific to migrant experiences. The economy of the Russian Federation, like the economy of the USSR, is characterised by occupational differentiation between the genders.[14] Women and men tend to be concentrated in different sectors of the economy and the earnings gap indicates that occupational segregation continues within sectors (see Table 9.2).

It is worth noting that my respondents did not question this occupational differentiation on the grounds of gender as a feature of the

Table 9.1: Forced migrants in the Novosibirsk labour market

Occupation	*Women*	*Men*
Baker	7	
Doctor, nurse	5	
Cleaner	6	
Nanny	4	
Teacher	2	
Shop assistant	5	
Pharmacist	2	
Foundry worker	2	
Driver of tower crane	2	
Accountant	1	
Employee of social services	1	
Head of firm	1	2
Worker in a boiler-house	2	1
Driver		4
Sanitary technician		1
Metalworker		4
Welder		4
Excavator operator		3
Builder		3
Watchman		1
Cattle-farm worker		2
Electrician		1
Loader		1
Unemployed at time of interview	9	1

Note: Total is greater than 62 as several respondents held more than one job.

Russian labour market. It would seem that this phenomenon was taken for granted as a result of continuities in their experiences: occupational differentiation was a feature of the gender order of the USSR, with only slight variations between Soviet republics. In post-Soviet Russia, as in the USSR, occupational differentiation is linked with a gap in earnings between genders.[15] In 2001, 62.2 per cent of employed men, but only 37 per cent of employed women, worked in sectors where salaries were higher than the national average (see Table 9.2). The earnings gap indicated within each sector shows that women tended to hold less well-paid positions even within sectors where they dominated (see Table 9.2).

The labour market of Novosibirsk region conforms to the national pattern as far as occupational differentiation between genders is concerned. In 2001, 62.3 per cent of women employed in Novosibirsk region worked in sectors where the salary was below average[16] and the earnings gap between men and women working in Novosibirsk region was 71 per cent.[17]

Table 9.2: Women in the Russian labour market in 2001

Sector	*% women*	*Earnings gap Average women's salary as % of men's average*	*Salary rate Average salary as % of national average*
All sectors	48	63	100
Industry	38	62	124
Agriculture	38	88	40
Construction	22	77	128
Transport	25	72	137
Communication	61	58	127*
Wholesale and retail trade, catering	63	62	71
Housing/communal and consumer services	47	78	86
Health service and social security	80	76	62
Education	81	78	56
Culture and art	32	65	59
Science	54	66	126
Finance	72	70	286*
Management	34	79	112

* In 2001, only 1.9 per cent and 2 per cent of all women working in the economy, worked in the communication and finance sectors respectively.
Source: Adapted from *Rossiiskii Statisticheskii Ezhegodnik* (2002), p. 188 and *Zhenshiny i Muzhchiny Rossii* (Moscow: Goskomstat 2002), pp. 89 and 102.

Interviews with my respondents revealed that they too experienced the effect of this occupational differentiation. A woman in her late thirties with specialised secondary education explained:

> *Interviewer*: Until recently you worked in a bakery, didn't you?
> *Respondent*: Yes, but now I can't because of my health. We had to do everything manually there. We carried sacks all by ourselves. I damaged my spine . . .
> *Interviewer*: The majority of employees are women, aren't they?
> *Respondent*: There is one young man and the rest are women.
> *Interviewer*: Why does the owner of the bakery hire women for such hard work?
> *Respondent*: The pay isn't high enough to hire men . . .
> (N53; 1:31–2:10)

As indicated here, badly paid jobs are commonly viewed as 'women's work'. Wider studies of gender and labour market behaviour have argued that culturally embedded beliefs about men and women underpin and maintain occupational differentiation and a male–female earnings gap.[18] Studies of the Russian labour market have pointed out that the belief that a woman is first and foremost a mother and that, as such, her prime responsibility is to bear and look after children, plays a crucial role in shaping these phenomena in the Russian context.[19] The next section explores the ways in which this and other beliefs shaped the social practices of my respondents in the labour market.

Gender and employment

A key preoccupation on arrival in Russia for the respondents involved in this study had been getting a job to support themselves and their dependants. Most had not experienced prolonged periods of unemployment since they had taken any job available. A single mother in her late thirties with specialised secondary education reported:

> When I arrived, nobody would give me a crust. I couldn't go begging either. I read the job ads. They needed cleaners, so I took this [job].
> (N25; 4: 33–6)

Nevertheless, some of my female respondents had been out of work for a long time, whilst all of my male respondents were in some form of employment except for one man who was 60 years old and had thus reached retirement age (see Table 9.1). Other studies concerned with the processes of forced migrants' integration into Russian society have noted similar differences in experience between male and female migrants.[20] The explanations provided by my respondents indicated that it was not only external factors, such as the numbers of jobs on offer, that restricted their opportunities for finding employment. Beliefs about gender also played an important role. Amongst the most powerful beliefs about gender which influence people's labour market experiences and behaviour in contemporary Russia are perceptions of men as breadwinners and women as having prime responsibility for taking care of the home and children.[21] Such beliefs are so widespread that they have become 'invisible' to people and this only adds to their power. Thus a 45-year-old mother of two took it for granted that she needed to stay at home to look after her children. She did not even consider the idea that her husband could help her care for them so that she could go to work; instead she wondered whether another woman in the family might assist her:

> In the beginning my daughter was a baby, then she went to school. How could I leave her alone? . . . I need to check her homework and other things. I need to work somewhere nearby. It's impossible to go elsewhere, because it would mean that I had to leave early in the morning and get home late at night . . . Maybe, grandma will come to live with us and I'll go to work.
>
> (N19; 5: 27–34)

The belief that a woman's primary responsibility is to look after children can result not only in unemployment, but also in women taking on badly paid work. Another 45-year-old mother of two explained:

> When I first arrived [in Russia], my children went to kindergarten and I started to work in their kindergarten to be near them. When my son went to school, I went to work in the same school . . . I worked there for next to nothing . . .
>
> (N31; 18: 29–35)

This employment strategy might be seen as an extreme way of combining paid work with the private sphere responsibilities imposed on women by the gender order in Russian society,[22] yet, research on the Russian labour market indicates that such strategies are not so rare.[23] My data show that even where money is short, women may take such a route. The same respondent went on to explain:

> I don't have enough money . . . If I had a little more money . . . I don't need, you know, palaces . . . I just need money to buy clothes . . . Clothes for the children . . .
>
> (N31; 23: 24–30)

Research into male and female employment strategies in the Russian labour market has shown that men take on secondary employment (*podrabotka*) much more often than women.[24] This tendency was also shown amongst my respondents. For example, in the case of the respondent quoted above, who could not afford to buy clothes for her children, it was her husband who took on additional work to provide for the family:

> My husband sometimes does odd jobs on the side [*kalymit*]. He installs electricity in people's homes, from time to time, if they need this . . .

> He earns some extra on the side [*Podrabatyvaet*]. When he has additional work, we have enough money, when he doesn't, things are worse . . .
>
> (N31; 24: 3–6)

Men's labour market mobility is driven by the search for a job which will provide enough money for their families. This is illustrated in the story of a migrant in his late thirties, with a university education, who spoke of his long search for an appropriate job, which would allow him to support his mother and grandmother:

> *Respondent*: I changed jobs several times in one year before I found what I wanted. I've been working where I am now for more than a year . . . I like this place . . .
> *Interviewer*: Why did you change jobs?
> *Respondent*: You see, when I first came to 'Ekran' [the plant], they promised me more than 2000 rubles, but they changed their wage scheme . . . and as a result my salary was 1500–1700 rubles . . . I left the plant and found work at a bakery. They promised me no less than 3000 rubles, but it turned out that they had supply problems and couldn't operate regularly. They were open one month, closed the next . . . I worked there for two months and got 1000 rubles . . . Then I found this job for 6000 rubles. That's where I work now.
>
> (N32; 3: 8–36)

For many men, distance is also no obstacle in their search for a relatively well-paid job. A 52-year-old father of two explained:

> I got a job. They built a brewery, I got a job there, but I didn't like the salary . . . They promised me a flat, but I never got it. I had to leave that job. Now I work in Iskitim. Iskitim is 50 kilometres from here.
>
> (N44; 2: 8–15)

Certainly, respondents should not be seen as bearing sole responsibility for their experiences in the labour market. Theirs is only one side of the story. The other side is that employers also subscribe to certain beliefs about gender, which shape their perceptions of appropriate jobs for women and men as well as influencing their decisions about whether or not to hire someone.[25] Job advertisements in Novosibirsk newspapers,[26] for example, state requirements concerning not only the qualifications of a potential employee, but also his/her sex, family status and even appearance. My respondents had experienced the impacts of this trend. A woman in her late thirties, who had graduated from a pharmaceutical college, told me her story:

> *Respondent*: I am 38 years old, everyone wants employees who are younger than 35. You see, I've got a problem with my teeth too . . .
> *Interviewer*: And how is this connected with employment?
> *Respondent*: It spoils my appearance. I can't afford to get dentures made. I had thirteen teeth taken out. It's ruined my looks. They [employers] want someone young and beautiful. I'd need to smile at customers, speak to them. So they [employers] think I don't look right . . . They say very politely 'Sorry, but you're not what we're looking for'. There are enough young, beautiful people. In particular, I know, there's a pharmaceutical college in Novosibirsk . . . Each year there are lots of graduates from there [looking for work].
>
> (N25; 3: 19–32)

Studies into employers' preferences when it comes to employing men or women and their views on why women tend to be concentrated in poorly paid jobs, have found that they subscribe to stereotypes of women as less productive and less reliable workers.[27] These stereotypes are rooted in the perception of women as individuals whose primary responsibility is to look after their home, children and other family members. It is assumed that these family responsibilities will result in various periods of absence from work and will reduce a woman's attention and devotion to her work.[28]

Age and employment

Statistical analyses of the Russian labour market show that both men's and women's experiences are differentiated according to their age.[29] For example, the process of looking for a job takes different lengths of time for different age groups (see Figure 9.1).

'Working age' in contemporary Russia begins at 16, when according to the Russian Labour Code a person gains the right to work full-time, and ends at 55 (50) for women and 60 (55) for men, when they reach retirement age.[30] Amongst both men and women of 'working age', the age groups which experience the most difficulties in finding work are those of people with about ten years left before retirement (i.e. women aged 40–45 and men aged 45–50 (see Figure 9.1)). The vulnerability of people in these age groups was reflected in the experiences of my respondents. Even those with good qualifications and extensive work experience could

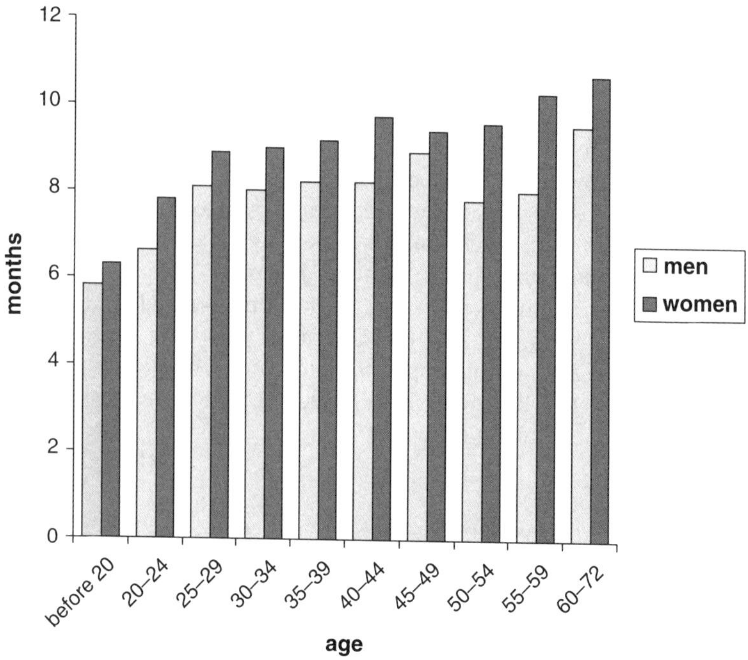

Figure 9.1: Average time needed to find a job in 2001
Source: Based on information presented in *Rossiiskii Statisticheskii Ezhegodnik* (2002), p. 150.

not secure suitable employment, because of the age limits imposed by employers. As one man with four years left before retirement explained:

> *Respondent*: It's impossible to find a job to match your qualifications at my age.
> *Interviewer*: How old are you?
> *Respondent*: I'm 56 . . . I fully understand that nobody will take me on as factory manager now. I didn't even hope that I would be a manager . . . I looked for a position as foreman. But, nobody wants me as a foreman . . . It's especially hard to live with the knowledge, that you're no use to anyone. It turns out that I worked for thirty years, gained experience, gained skills, but I'm no use to anyone now. Nobody needs my experience, knowledge . . . Who can I blame for the fact that I've lived for more than 50 years (laughs)? It's no one's fault.
>
> (N51; 28: 15–29:5)

Although my respondents did not question the gender inequalities of the Russian labour market, they found age discrimination much harder to accept. A woman in her early fifties with university education protested:

> Don't you need experience? Don't you need skills? What's age got to do with it? . . . I can run up to the ninth floor without a lift, not all young people can do that.
>
> (N12; 18: 24–9)

Such varied attitudes towards different forms of discrimination have been observed in other studies into labour-market attitudes and behaviour among former-citizens of the USSR.[31] Age discrimination may be regarded as more questionable because it signifies a discontinuity between Soviet and post-Soviet labour market experiences. While 'gender policy' in the labour market has remained more or less the same, 'age policy' has changed dramatically.[32]

Nonetheless, 'older' people should not be seen simply as victims of employers' discriminatory 'age policies'. The stories of several of my respondents tally with Marta Bruno's conclusion that:

> Belonging to a specific age group *per se* is not a meaningful category; what places people on one side or the other of the victim/survivor fence is the ability or the opportunity to decode the new economic and social environment and the mental flexibility to learn how to operate within it.[33]

My respondents were able to 'decode' the state of affairs in the Russian labour market not only as a range of constraints, but also as a range of opportunities. For example, the woman quoted above commented:

> I thought about what I could do, what skills I have and I remembered that I was good at typing. I bought a typewriter, they delivered it straight to my home. I started to put adverts in the papers, free adverts, by the way. Clients began to come round, a lot of good new acquaintances appeared!
>
> (N12; 20: 5–10)

In the face of age discrimination, my respondents continued actively to negotiate their value as potential employees with employers. The same woman continued:

> I saw an advertising agency and went in. There was a young man there. We had a chat. I told him that I'd done a course in public

> relations . . . I've learned all the methods and techniques for working in public relations . . . We spoke for a whole hour and then he says 'you know . . . we are going to open a new department, and I want you to run it'.
>
> (N12; 18: 1–6)

However, the creativity which individuals demonstrate in overcoming inequality does not eliminate inequality as such. The only means to eliminate discrimination in the Russian labour market is to develop anti-discriminatory legislation and, more importantly, to create a system which effectively enforces this legislation in employers' behaviour.[34]

Gender identities in crisis

Paid work has been shown to play an important role in the construction of gender identities.[35] Studies of the Russian labour market have also shown that employment is central to both men's and women's identities in contemporary Russia.[36] At the same time, as mentioned above, the gender order in contemporary Russian society includes a range of beliefs about men's and women's roles in the public and the private spheres, which result in significant differences between men's and women's experiences in the labour market.

The role of breadwinner is of great symbolic importance for Russian men.[37] A man's inability to perform this role can affect his position within the family and cause a crisis in relations between family members as well as a crisis of gender identity for the man in question. A gender identity crisis might be defined as a clash between a person's beliefs about how s/he should behave as a wo/man and her/his actual opportunities to live up to these expectations. A 45-year-old mother of four complained:

> My husband was a train driver there. He couldn't find a job in his line of work here and ended up as a mechanic. His wage is lower now and we can't think of him as the breadwinner anymore. If I didn't have my profession, my job, life might be much harder. He feels this fact keenly, because . . . He has always been the breadwinner, but now . . . Our relationship has changed, because my husband has lost his moral certainty . . . I try to show that he is the head of the family, but he understands everything . . .
>
> (N40; 6: 1–11)

Other studies of the Russian labour market also emphasise the significance which Russian men tend to place on their status in the public sphere and point out the negative impacts that disruption of this status can have on them.[38] My interviews with forced migrants revealed that men tended to attach more importance to their status as professionals than women. For some men the loss of this status led to a crisis of masculine identity. One of my female respondents in her early forties told me about her ex-husband:

> My husband couldn't work. He couldn't work here. The people who he worked with usually said to him: 'Don't interfere. It's none of your business. Why do you interfere?' I think that he took a job that was beneath his potential, and he had problems because of this . . . There he had a good reputation as a professional, but here he had to get any job he could. He even worked on a cattle-farm . . . Maybe he was ashamed of it . . . He couldn't be himself here.
>
> (N21; 18: 5–25)

This loss of status in the public sphere could push a man to return to the place he had left. The same woman quoted above explained:

> My husband couldn't stand it. He couldn't stand it, because nothing seemed right to him . . . He always had problems . . . He didn't work in his profession, he couldn't get a job in his profession. He worked in secondary jobs . . . He wanted to return to Tajikistan. All the time he wanted to return . . . After some time he went back.
>
> (N21; 7: 10–18)

By contrast, a woman might turn her back on an opportunity to keep her professional status, if it appeared to contradict her perception of her private sphere responsibilities. A 54-year-old woman, with university education, reported:

> In the beginning, I got an offer of work in the city airport as an environmental engineer. I thought, either I could look after my daughter or I could work. Of course I didn't choose to work there. I stayed with my daughter . . . I got fixed up as a cleaner, to be near her, to help her.
>
> (N39; 14: 18–23)

Men's and women's differing perceptions of professional status might be explained by reference to the gender order, within which they had been socialised and lived prior to migration. In the USSR both women and men had the right and an obligation to work for the state. However, gender ideology defined their rights and duties in different ways. While men were judged on their performance in the public sphere alone, women were portrayed as both workers and mothers, whose service to the state was not only in the production of goods, but also in giving birth to and bringing up children.[39] In this sense migrant experiences differed little from those of the local population.

Forced migrants and the local population in the labour market: the roots of inequality

Equal or not?

If, as illustrated above, the experience of forced migrants in the labour market is affected by the gender order in ways which closely resemble the experience of the local population, the question remains: do forced migrants enjoy equal opportunities and share the same challenges in the labour market as the local population? If 'inequality' is defined as a difference in opportunities and access to resources of the same quantity and quality by people with approximately the same levels of human capital, then forced migrants do not appear to be equal to the local population in their experiences of the Russian labour market.

Forced migrants as a group have higher levels of education than the local population with whom they are competing for jobs (see Figure 9.2). Numerous studies have also pointed out that migrants tend to be trained professionals with considerable experience of specialised employment.[40] Nonetheless, on arrival in the Russian Federation most forced migrants experience a drop in professional status.[41]

A consideration of the wider economic situation in contemporary Russia offers some explanation for this devaluation of human capital and decline in professional mobility experienced by forced migrants: the level of employment in the formal economy was falling throughout the 1990s and the local population also experienced unemployment and downward professional mobility.[42] However, research conducted amongst forced migrants has shown that they experience greater labour market vulnerability than long-term residents living in the same areas.[43]

This greater vulnerability is not the result of inequality in terms of formal rights. Forced migrants are classified as Russian citizens and as such they are not subject to those constraints which are placed on the employment of foreigners in Russian labour legislation.[44] Moreover, forced migrants are entitled to government support as part of a range of Federal programmes developed to assist their integration at the site of settlement. Nonetheless, a variety of factors have made it difficult for forced migrants to find suitable employment on arrival in the Russian Federation.

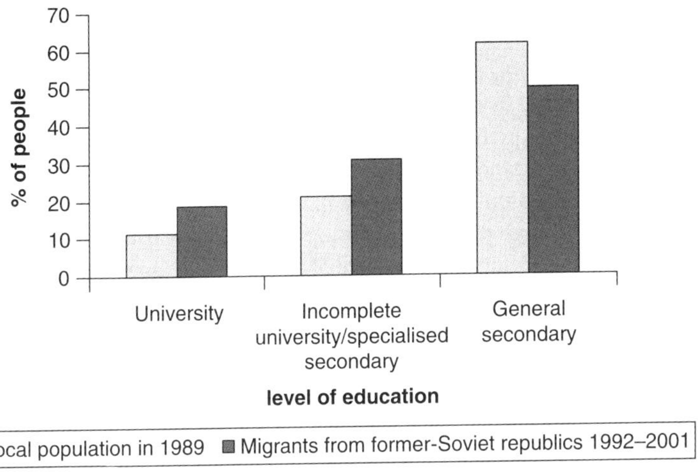

Figure 9.2: Comparison of education levels between forced migrants from the former Soviet republics and the Russian population
Sources: Created on the basis of information presented in N. Mkrtchian, 'Desiatiletie vynuzhdennoi migratsii v Rossii', *Demoscope Weekly*, 71–2, 17–30 June 2002, http://demoscope.ru/weekly/2002/071/tema05.php and *Demoscope Weekly*, http://demoscope.ru/weekly/ssp/rus_edu_89.php, accessed 18 February 2006.

Work and registration

The system of registration (*propiska*), which existed in the USSR, meant that a person had access to state resources, for example, employment, social benefits, healthcare, education for their children and so on, only in the area where they were registered. Although the 'Law on the right of citizens of the Russian Federation to freedom of movement and choice of their place of sojourn or residence within the Russian Federation', which was passed in 1993, made such restrictions illegal, the legacy of registration still exists in the minds of the people and persists in the practices of social institutions.[45] As a result, forced migrants need to register in the area where they intend to live in order to secure access to state-allocated resources and work. In Novosibirsk region, for example, temporary registration at least is required in order to get a job in the formal economy.

In order to register, an individual must have a permanent address in the area. My respondents employed a number of strategies in order to gain registration: (1) by purchasing property and registering there; (2) by finding a job which provides registration and accommodation; (3) by paying a property-owner to register them at their address; (4) by using their social networks to find somebody prepared to register them at their own address without payment. However, none of these strategies was unproblematic.

The discrepancy in property prices between Russia and the countries the respondents came from made it impossible for them to buy accommodation of the same quality. In many cases they only had enough money to buy property in economically deprived areas, mostly in villages. Prices are low in these areas but their labour markets are also characterised by low salary rates and high rates of unemployment. A 41-year-old woman, whose family had owned flats in the centre of Dushanbe (the capital of Tajikistan) complained:

> We sold two flats in the capital of Tajikistan: my husband and I had a two-room flat and my parents had a two-room flat. We couldn't even buy a one-room flat here. Here in Novosibirsk we couldn't buy a one-room flat . . . We could only afford a tiny house in Posevnaia [village].
>
> (N21; 3: 25–37)

Employers who provided accommodation and registration did not do so out of altruistic convictions, but in order to entice people to accept low-paid jobs, which were unpopular amongst the local population, who already had accommodation and registration. Once in such employment, migrants often could not leave without losing these resources. For some people this threat was enough to keep them in their poorly paid jobs. One of my female respondents reported:

> We were registered in the factory dormitory, but we lived somewhere else . . . When we were registered in the dormitory we were under constant pressure: 'If you leave the factory we will kick you out of the dormitory. If you go to work elsewhere we will kick you out of the dormitory'. It was constant pressure. They paid nothing at the factory.
>
> (N6; 4: 7–10)

One of the most common strategies used by my respondents was to pay a property-owner to register them at their address. The law exempts forced migrants from the usual restrictions which limit the number of people who can be registered at a single address. Thus, clearly, it was not a problem for forced migrants to buy temporary registration, which lasts several months. My respondents also said that it was possible to buy a permanent registration; however, buying registration required relatively large sums of money, which not all forced migrants have access to. Some of my respondents found themselves in a vicious circle – no registration without a well-paid job, no well-paid job without registration. A single mother in her early forties explained:

> It's not difficult to find out where to buy registration. I haven't got the 100 dollars [to buy registration]. There's no money. I can't . . . I can't save up to buy this registration. I work all day long. I work for 12–13 hours a day and I only earn enough to pay the rent and for food. That's all. No more.
>
> (N24; 5: 31–4)

Social networks offered a more popular strategy for acquiring registration amongst my respondents. However, forced migration could result in a situation where migrants were separated from their social networks. Even if they migrated to places where they had social contacts, it was not always certain that the people who they thought would help them, would in fact do so. The same woman cited above complained:

> I hoped that my mother-in-law would register my children, but she refused. She simply refused to do this. Maybe she was afraid that I'd try to take possession of her house . . . We had such a good relationship . . . I couldn't understand it . . .
>
> (N24; 4: 30–47)

Disruption of social networks

> It's very difficult to find a job. Nobody knows you, and you know nobody, so it's very difficult to prove that you can do something. [There] we had friends, acquaintances, relatives, everything was done with the help of others . . . Here we live in isolation . . . [it's] very difficult, very difficult . . .
>
> (N33; 7· 10–16)

These words of a 34-year-old single mother of two illustrate that the disruption of social networks which results from the process of migration is one of the main reasons for the labour market vulnerability of forced migrants. According to the nationwide New Russian Barometer survey, 50 per cent of respondents use social networks to find employment.[46] This result is supported by official statistics[47] and the results of academic studies.[48] Although forced migrants tend to migrate to areas where they have social networks,[49] inevitably a certain number of social contacts made over a long period of time are left behind. The quality and quantity of resources which they can mobilise through the remains of previous networks and new social connections are often not enough to provide them with the same standard of living which they used to have and which they expected to maintain on migration. In a situation where social networking is the main means of finding a job, the disruption of social ties results in unequal opportunities for gaining employment. A 45-year-old woman who was a qualified and experienced accountant explained:

> Here people get a job . . . on the basis of whose nephew they are, whose daughter they are, or whose son. In the factory, I was told so many times 'we don't need anyone, we don't need, we don't need'. At the same time I saw that a new girl had been taken on: somebody's niece . . . She wasn't even born when I started work as an accountant. I don't believe that she had more in her head than I do. I have experience. I've worked so many years. They're somebody's protégés and I'm not.
>
> (N19; 6: 33–41)

The questionable value of government support

At the time of fieldwork, none of my respondents had received assistance from the state in finding employment. This was despite the fact that the majority of them had been actively pursuing government support and many had already received assistance with housing. They questioned why the government appeared so disinterested in utilising their skills and knowledge more effectively. A woman in her late fifties expressed her opinion:

> They need to create jobs. This is quite possible, it's quite possible, in my opinion, if there is the will, it's quite possible, even in this Dorogino [village]. There was a pottery factory here before. They could bring it back to life, so that migrants, who settle here, would settle gladly, because there would be work there, jobs . . . At a regional level it's possible to create jobs in villages. We need so many teachers, so many drivers, so many builders and so on.
>
> (N46; 19: 27–37)

Although measures like those suggested in the citation above, as well as a range of others, may be found in the text of all Federal Migration Programmes, they have not for the most part been implemented in practice. The implementation of measures to assist migrant employment has been undermined by a lack of financial resources. The amount of money allocated to support these proposals has in reality been far less than what was originally indicated in the Federal Migration Programmes.[50] As a result, forced migrants' position in the labour market is far from enviable, since the state support to which they are entitled is rarely forthcoming.

Other measures which have been more widely implemented to support the integration of forced migrants into Russian society have had a controversial effect on migrant experiences. For example, evidence gathered during my study, through interviews with both forced migrants and officials, concurs with the findings of other studies[51] in pointing out that the assistance which migrants received in finding accommodation was often contradictory to their employment needs. Very often housing programmes placed forced migrants either in areas where the employment opportunities were entirely unsuited to their educational and professional backgrounds and skills, or in areas experiencing high rates of unemployment. The same woman quoted above complained:

> They [officials] are so out of touch with us, that, as I see it, they can't even begin to imagine who we are and what we do. All their talk is for them, not for us. They do nothing . . . to improve our life. They offered me a two-room flat in Dorogino. It's not a town, it's a village. It's a small dead village. There's no work there at all. I would have had to pay 300 rubles a month for this flat, a minimum of 300 rubles. My pension is 1500 rubles. How can I live on this money? And there is no work there. Is this a solution to our problems?
>
> (N46; 19: 16–27)

The Russian government proclaimed its programme of support for forced migrants partly as a result of a recognition of the difficulties they face on arrival in the Russian Federation. At the same time, however, this programme was designed taking account of the interests of the state, some of which may contradict the interests of those individuals who are eligible for support.

Conclusion

As a result of the gender order inherent in Russian society, forced migrants' labour market experiences are differentiated along gender lines. The occupational segregation and the earnings gap between women and men, which may be seen in a review of national statistics, were reflected in the stories of my respondents. The gender order holds in place a range of beliefs about gender and appropriate roles for women and men, which also shaped the experience of my respondents in the labour market. The perception of men as the family breadwinner and the vision of women as being primarily responsible for caring for the home and children have the most significant influence on men's and women's employment strategies.

Forced migrants' experiences in the Russian labour market were also differentiated along lines of age. The most vulnerable group were people with approximately ten years left before retirement. These people should not be viewed as passive victims, rather they were active agents, who were able to negotiate their value as employees. Nonetheless, they were very much constrained by the prejudices of employers.

While gender inequality such as occupational segregation and the earnings gap were taken for granted by my respondents, they questioned the age discrimination practised by employers. It seems that inequalities are questioned where there are discrepancies between the beliefs which an individual has internalised in the past and the practices encountered in the present social order. Discrimination in the Russian labour market is the result not only of the beliefs and practices of employers with regard to age and gender, but also of the beliefs and practices of prospective and current employees with regards to themselves as people of a certain gender and age.

Migration could create a situation where a person's beliefs about gender did not correspond to his/her (or his/her partner's) actual opportunities in the receiving society. As a result, gender relations within the family might have to be renegotiated and in some cases a crisis of gender identity was experienced. My findings suggest that men were more vulnerable to changes in their professional status than women. This would seem to be the result of their beliefs about gender stemming from the gender order of the USSR, which ascribed a single public-sphere role to men, whilst women were allocated dual roles in the public and private spheres.

Female forced migrants are doubly disadvantaged in the Russian labour market, as women and as migrants. The gender order of the Russian Federation affected the labour market experiences of forced migrants from the former-Soviet republics in much the same way as it affected the local population. Yet, it must also be taken into consideration that forced migrants were in effect starting their lives again in Russia from nothing. The loss of capital (symbolic, social and material) which occurred because of migration was verbalised in the stories of many of my respondents. These losses could constrain forced migrants in their labour market strategies and activities in the receiving society.

Table 9.3: Information about respondents cited

N	*Gender*	*Age*	*Education*	*Marital Status*	*Children under 16*
6	f	34	Incomplete university	Married	1
12	f	53	University degree	Single	0
19	f	45	Specialised secondary	Married	2
21	f	41	University degree	Single	1
24	f	43	Specialised secondary	Single	1
25	f	39	Specialised secondary	Single	1
31	f	45	University degree	Married	1
32	m	39	University degree	Single	0
33	f	34	General secondary	Single	2
39	f	54	University degree	Single	1
40	f	45	Specialised secondary	Married	4
44	m	52	Specialised secondary	Partner	2
46	f	57	Specialised secondary	Single	0
51	m	56	University degree	Married	0
53	f	38	Specialised secondary	Married	1

Although forced migrants, as Russian citizens, enjoy the same formal rights as the local population and are even entitled to additional support from the government, their experiences in the Russian labour market were complicated by a number of constraints. Problems with registration and accommodation could trap migrants in low-paid jobs. The disruption of social networks, caused by migration, undermined their competitiveness in the Russian labour market, where social contacts are amongst the most important assets for gaining employment. Imperfections in the system designed by the Russian government to support forced migrants in their integration into Russian society, as well as a lack of finance allocated to make this system work effectively, prevented the government from meeting forced migrants' interests in employment. These additional constraints were experienced by male and female forced migrants alike.

Notes

1. H. Pilkington, *Migration, Displacement and Identity in Post-Soviet Russia* (London: Routledge, 1998).
2. R. Perruchoud (ed.), *International Migration Law: Glossary on Migration* (Geneva: International Organisation for Migration, 2004), p. 25.
3. *Sobranie zakonodatel'stva Rossiiskoi Federatsii*, 52 (1995); *Sobranie zakonodatel'stva Rossiiskoi Federatsii*, 26 (1997).

4. Appendix to *Demoscope Weekly*, http://www.demoscope.ru/weekly/ssp/rus_ref.php, accessed 20 February 2006.
5. O. Komarova, 'Social'no-demograficheskaia kharakteristika i osnovnye problemy vynuzhdennoi migratsii v Rossii', in V. Tishkov (ed.), *Vynuzhdennye migranty: integratsiia i vozvrashchenie* (Moscow: Institut Etnologii i Antropologii Rossiyskoi Akademii Nauk, 1997), p. 15.
6. *Rossiiskii Statisticheskii Ezhegodnik* (Moscow: Goskomstat, 2002).
7. Zh. Zaenchkovskaya (ed.), *Migration in a Transforming Society: Annotated Bibliography of the Literature Published in the CIS States 1992–1999* (Moscow: Complex Progress, 2000).
8. M. Flynn, *Migrant Resettlement in the Russian Federation: Reconstructing Homes and Homelands* (London: Anthem Press, 2004); E. K. Kirillova, 'Problemy vynuzhdennykh pereselentsev v Rossii: glazami migrantov', *Sotsiologicheskie issledovaniia*, 11 (2004): 46–51.
9. O. Oberemko and M. Kirichenko, *Vynuzhdennye pereselentsy na Kubani: institutsional'naia perspektiva upravleniia* (Krasnodar: Izdatel'stvo Kubanskogo Universiteta, 2001).
10. G. Vitkovskaia, 'Vynuzhdennye migranty iz Novykh Nezavisimykh Gosudarstv na Rossiiskom rynke truda', in G. Vitkovskaia (ed.), *Migratsiia i rynki truda v postsovetskoi Rossii* (Moscow: Moscow Carnegie Centre, 1998).
11. N. Kosmarskaya, 'Post-Soviet Russian Migration from the New Independent States: Experience of Women Migrants', in D. Indra (ed.), *Engendering Forced Migration: Theory and Practice* (New York and Oxford: Berghahn Books, 1998a); N. Kosmarskaia, *Zhenskoe izmerenie vynuzhdennoi migratsii i migratsionnoe zakonodatel'stvo Rossii* (Moscow: Moscow Centre for Gender Studies, 1998b); L. Kosygina, *Vynuzhdennye pereselentsy i gendernyi regim upravleniia ikh obustroistvom* (Novosibirsk: Izdatel'stvo Sibirskogo Otdeleniia Rossiiskoi Akademii Nauk, 2003); H. Pilkington, 'For the Sake of the Children: Gender and Migration in the Former Soviet Union', in M. Buckley (ed.), *Post-Soviet Women: From the Baltic to Central Asia* (Cambridge: Cambridge University Press, 1997); Pilkington (1998).
12. Fellowship reference N YSF 01/1-26.
13. The gender order is described by Connell as 'an historically constructed pattern of power relations between men and women and definitions of femininity and masculinity', R. Connell, *Gender and Power: Society, the Person and Sexual Politics* (Cambridge and Oxford: Polity Press, 1987), p. 99.
14. J. Chapman, 'Equal Pay for Equal Work?', in D. Atkinson, A. Dallin and G. W. Lapidus (eds), *Women in Russia* (Hemel Hempstead: Harvester Press, 1978); T. N. Dodge, 'Women in the Professions', in Atkinson et al. (1978); G. Lapidus, *Women in Soviet Society: Equality, Development, and Social Change* (Berkeley, Los Angeles and London: University of California Press, 1978).
15. Chapman (1978); Lapidus (1978).
16. *Rynok truda Novosibirskoi oblasti* (Novosibirsk: Goskomstat, 2002), p. 27; *Novosibirskaia oblast' v tsifrakh* (Novosibirsk: Goskomstat, 2002), p. 33.
17. *Zhenshiny i Muzhchiny Rossii* (2002), p. 108.
18. B. Reskin, and H. Hartmann, *Women's Work, Men's Work: Sex Segregation on the Job* (Washington, D.C.: National Academy Press, 1986).
19. I. Kozina and E. Zhidkova, 'Sex Segregation and Discrimination in the New Russian Labour Market', in S. Ashwin (ed.), *Adapting to Russia's New Labour*

Market: Gender and Employment Behaviour (London and New York: Routledge, 2006).

20. Pilkington (1997); Kosmarskaia (1998b).
21. R. Kay, *Men in Contemporary Russia: the Fallen Heroes of Post-Soviet Change?* (London: Ashgate, 2006); S. Ashwin, 'The Post-Soviet Gender Order: Imperatives and Implications', in Ashwin (ed.) (2006).
22. S. Ashwin, 'Introduction: Gender, State and Society in Soviet and post-Soviet Russia', in S. Ashwin (ed.), *Gender, State and Society in Soviet and Post-Soviet Russia* (London and New York: Routledge, 2000).
23. S. Ashwin, I. Kozina, I. Popova and E. Zhidkova, 'Work Orientations and Employment Behaviour', in Ashwin (ed.) (2006), pp. 126-7.
24. S. Yaroshenko, E. Omel'chenko, N. Goncharova and O. Issoupova, 'Gender Differences in Employment Behaviour in Russia's New Labour Market', in Ashwin (ed.) (2006).
25. Kozina and Zhidkova (2006), p. 68.
26. I analysed two Novosibirsk news papers: *Rabota dlia vas* and *Navigator*. My analysis covered the issues published in summer 2001.
27. A. Moskovskaia, 'Stereotipy ili konkurentsiia? Analiz nekotorykh gendernykh predstavlenii rabotodatelei', *Sotsiologicheskie issledovaniia*, 3 (2002): 59.
28. M. Baskakova, *Ravnye vozmozhnosti i gendernye stereotipy na rynke truda* (Moscow: Moscow Centre for Gender Studies, 1998).
29. See also, S. Bridger and R. Kay, 'Gender and Generation in the New Russian Labour Market', in H. Pilkington (ed.), *Gender, Generation and Identity in Contemporary Russia* (London and New York: Routledge, 1996); M. Bruno, 'Employment Strategies and the Formation of New Identities in the Service Sector in Moscow', in Pilkington (ed.) (1996); T. Jyrkinen-Pakkasvirta, 'Women's Work and the Threat of Unemployment in St. Petersburg', in E. Haavio-Mannila and A. Rotkirch (eds), *Women's Voices in Russia Today* (Aldershot: Dartmouth, 1996).
30. Russian labour legislation lists a number of jobs, positions and working conditions which give people the right to receive their pension five years earlier than the standard ages of 55 and 60 for women and men respectively.
31. Kozina and Zhidkova (2002), p. 74.
32. Ashwin (2006).
33. Bruno (1996), p. 46.
34. Article 63 of the Labour Code of the Russian Federation prohibits discrimination on the basis of sex and age; however, discriminative social practices continue and enforcement of such laws has been notoriously ineffectual.
35. D. Collinson and J. Hearn, 'Men and Masculinities in Work, Organizations, and Management', in S. M. Kimmel, J. Hearn and R. W. Connell (eds), *Handbook of Studies on Men and Masculinities* (Thousand Oaks, London and New Delhi: Sage Publications, 2005).
36. E. Zdravomyslova, 'Problems of Becoming a Housewife', in Haavio-Mannila and Rotkirch (eds) (1996).
37. S. Ashwin and T. Lytkina, 'Men in Crisis in Russia: the Role of Domestic Marginalization', *Gender and Society*, 18, 2 (2004): 189–206; Kay (2006).
38. Yaroshenko et al. (2006); I. Tartakovskaya and S. Ashwin, 'Who Benefits from Networks?', in Ashwin (ed.) (2006).
39. Ashwin (2000).

40. Pilkington (1998); Vitkovskaia (1998).
41. Pilkington (1997); Vitkovskaia (1998); Flynn (2004).
42. T. Gerber, 'Structural Change and Post-Socialist Stratification: Labour Market Transitions in Contemporary Russia', *American Sociological Review*, 67 (2002): 629–59; K. Sabirianova, 'The Great Human Capital Relocation: Study of Occupational Mobility in Transitional Russia', *Journal of Comparative Economics*, 30 (2002): 191–217.
43. E. Filippova, 'The Migration of Russian Germans to Saratov Region: the Problems of Socioeconomic adaptation', http://fmo.qeh.ox.ac.uk/Repository/getPdf.asp?Path=Oxford/1609/10/12&PageNo=1; Pilkington (1998).
44. Russian legislation indicates a range of jobs and positions which are unavailable for foreigners. Foreigners who do not have a permanent residence permit are not allowed to move freely from region to region in search for a job. Those with neither permanent nor temporary residence permits must acquire a work permit before taking on paid employment.
45. E. Filippova, 'Vynuzhdennye Migranty i Gosudarstvo', in V. Tishkov (ed.), *Vynuzhdennye Migranty i Gosudarstvo* (Moscow: Institute of Ethnology and Anthropology of the Russian Academy of Sciences, 1998); V. Tishkov, 'Sotsial'naia Priroda Instituta Propiski', in Tishkov (ed.) (1998).
46. R. Rose, 'Getting Things Done in an Antimodern Society: Social Capital Networks in Russia', in P. Dasgupta and I. Serageldin (eds), *Social Capital: a Multifaced Perpective* (Washington, D.C.: World Bank, 2000).
47. *Kniga truda (*Moscow: Goskomstat, 2002), p. 149.
48. S. Clarke, *The Formation of a Labour Market in Russia* (Cheltenham: Edward Elgar, 1999); V. Yakubovich, and I. Kozina, 'The Changing Significance of Ties: an Exploration of the Hiring Channels in the Russian Transitional Labour Market', *International Sociology*, 1 (2002): 479–500.
49. Flynn (2004).
50. O. Vorob'eva, *Migratsionnaia Politika* (Moscow: Ministry of Federal Affairs, National and Migration Policy, 2001).
51. See, for example, Pilkington (1998).

10
Press Images of Human Trafficking from Russia: Myths and Interpretations[1]

Mary Buckley

In recent years a spate of publications by academics in the west and inside Russia has exposed the global stretch, dimensions, estimated size and significance of human trafficking whose thousands of victims are girls, women, boys and men. Research by Donna M. Hughes, Louise Shelley, Sally Stoecker, Natal'ia Khodyreva, Elena Tiuriukanova, L. D. Erokhina, M. Iu. Buriaks and others has neatly illustrated how the collapse of the Soviet state and the more permeable borders that resulted from it gave rise to new migration flows.[2] At a time of economic difficulties, unemployment and rising costs, citizens were looking for more lucrative jobs elsewhere. Criminal gangs, however, exploited those who aspired to a better life, duping them through newspaper advertisements for false jobs, through crooked employment agencies and marriage bureaux. Willing to pay the job seekers' fares to other states, traffickers enforced situations of debt-bondage. When girls and women arrived in states as far flung as the United Arab Emirates, Germany, Israel, China, Japan, Australia and the USA, expecting to become nannies, dancers, cleaners or nurses, they had their passports confiscated and were forced into prostitution. They thus found themselves enslaved and frequently subject to physical and psychological abuse.

Although the Russian government was extremely slow to recognise the existence of this problem, persistent pressure from the US State Department, NGOs and women's groups inside Russia finally made an impact. The Duma failed to adopt draft laws on trafficking tabled in 2002 and 2003, but in December 2003, President Vladimir Putin finally called for amendment of the Criminal Code, making human trafficking punishable. What had been a 'non-issue' was gradually transformed into a recognised 'problem' and 'issue', finding a place on political agendas.[3]

Thus, to date, research has discussed the problem of human trafficking in some depth and Russian researchers in particular have interviewed the trafficked once they have returned and also surveyed, before they leave, those aspiring to work outside Russia.[4] Although samples are rarely representative since they are self-selecting due to the sensitive nature of the problem, numerous pictures of how trafficking occurs, the demands made of the trafficked and its dire results on physical and mental heath have been documented. Similarly, US State Department's annual Trafficking in Persons (TIP) reports specify what anti-trafficking measures have been taken by governments in the last year and what remains to be done. High on the State Department's list of priorities for Russia in 2005 were witness protection legislation specifically for trafficking, serious provision for protection and rehabilitation of the trafficked (particularly the establishment of a network of shelters), more co-operation between government and NGOs, implementation of the law and prosecution of the traffickers. Measures to tackle corruption in the police and among politicians were also deemed vital.[5]

What has not yet been discussed in any depth concerning human trafficking from Russia is how its press deals with the topic and packages its meanings. So far, scholars have not looked at what sorts of stories newspapers tell, with which emphases and slants and with what significance. This chapter sets out to explore the nature of press coverage in Russia, how it constructs and delivers messages about trafficking and what judgements it makes. Since educating the public is vital if women are to be deterred from activities which leave them vulnerable to being trafficked, these messages are most important, even if not all listen or act upon them. Some preliminary remarks, however, are necessary about key concepts, particularly 'power'.

'Power' and other concepts

The concept of 'power' has been central to political philosophy throughout its history and at the core of most analyses in political science since that discipline became established. As with concepts in all fields, however, its meaning, contours and dimensions have been vigorously debated. For instance, there is a useful distinction between power 'over' individuals, groups and states and power 'to' achieve something or to cause harm. There is also a difference between 'power' and 'influence', with the latter defined as the ability of A to get B to do what B would not otherwise have done. Some, however, prefer to subsume this definition of 'influence' under power too, giving it wider boundaries, whereas other analysts insist that influence is distinct.[6] Then again there is a distinction between 'power' and 'authority'. Someone may be 'in' power, such as Mikhail Gorbachev as executive president of the USSR after 1990, but his *de jure* power was stronger than his waning *de facto* power. In short, his authority was weak.

Power, influence and authority have traditionally been key concepts in political analysis concerning the international political arena and in discussions of the relationships between states. They have also been applied to categorisations of the *polis* and in the twentieth century to explorations of stasis and change in domestic and regional politics, the functioning of governments, organisations and pressure groups and to the nature of relations between citizens and leaders. Most political scientists have not, however, applied these terms to gender relations.

Kate Millet's contention that 'the personal is political' challenged 'malestream' political science to reset its conceptual state-centred boundaries.[7] Those who remained firmly wedded to a rigid distinction between the 'public' sphere where 'politics' took place and the 'private' sphere where it did not, could not make this conceptual shift. Feminists, however, and more critically minded social scientists could see that dimensions of 'power' were prominent in the 'private' sphere where concepts of influence, authority, dominance, subordination, threat and violence could just as easily be applied as they could to the international political arena. By the 1990s, even the heavily male-dominated field of international relations was affected by feminist scholarship with the highly traditional state-centred concept of 'security' being redefined to incorporate dimensions of individual security.[8] For some theorists, security had to take on board not just a freedom from physical violence but also the environmental health of the planet.[9] Likewise, the call went out for less militarised models of citizenship to facilitate a genuine security for all individuals.

The past twenty years have not brought guarantees of individual security on the ground in Russia. Neither have the consequences of socio-economic transition in the states of Central and Eastern Europe after the collapse of the Soviet empire in 1989 and of the Soviet state itself in 1991 included a steady advance towards gender awareness and equity. Here we see personal security under serious threat, with differential unemployment patterns for men and women, a feminisation of poverty in some areas, the spread of pornography and with it a sexualisation of society which includes a sexualisation of hiring and firing processes in the workplace and patterns of criminality and organised crime which result in serious forms of violence against women and girls through their trafficking into prostitution and domestic labour. Patterns of deception, force and sexual exploitation are integral to human trafficking. Patriarchal attitudes of disrespect towards women reinforce the notion that they can be used, abused and degraded for profit at a time of economic opportunities brought about by more open borders, declining numbers of jobs at home, possibilities for migration and a buoyant demand for the services of prostitutes, both at home and abroad.

In the growing literature on human trafficking from and within East-Central Europe and the former Soviet Union, key concepts include 'migration', 'transition', 'globalisation', 'deception', 'force', 'debt-bondage', 'victim', 'vulnerability', 'powerlessness', 'security' and 'human rights'. Approaches to its study have been shaped by the discipline and broader interests of authors, although arguably its full dimensions can only be grasped through interdisciplinary research. Researchers investigating human trafficking come from backgrounds in the social sciences, most notably sociology, political science, international relations, economics and psychology and also area studies, women's studies, criminology, migration studies (particularly the Organisation for Migration [IOM] in Geneva), government departments (especially the US State Department), law and non-governmental organisations.

Chris Corrin has pointed out that each starting point of investigation can carry negative consequences. Citing the conclusions of Marjan Wijers, she notes that those who come from moral perspectives and who view trafficking as evil run the risk of stigmatising the trafficked.[10] Those concerned first and foremost with criminality risk dubbing women 'guilty'. Scholars of migration may stress the importance of border controls and reflect no more than state interests. Those preoccupied with human rights may be too narrow in their definition of what needs to be addressed. Those who discuss health issues may be limited to proposing control by medical examination. Economists may dwell on the need for state benefits. Moreover, further complications in analyses may arise between those who insist that prostitution means sexual slavery and those prostitutes who wish to be seen as legitimate sex-workers.

However, it does not necessarily follow that those who experience moral outrage at human trafficking and who do view the practice of trafficking as 'evil', see the trafficked themselves as evil for engaging in prostitution. Far from it. Those concerned with criminal dimensions may be much more interested in tackling the criminal gangs and in fostering a 'legal state' devoid of bribery than in dubbing the trafficked as 'guilty'. Rather, some in this field argue that trafficked women need to be helped, not locked up for prostitution. Those who trace migration are not just interested in border controls, although they are one part of the wider picture. In short, one should not assume that possible limitations of some perspectives automatically result in a form of tunnel vision. Moreover, interdisciplinary and multidisciplinary research are good ways of militating against narrowness.[11] Furthermore, the wide scope of the dimensions of the problem of human trafficking does demand both breadth and collaboration.

Media images

The Soviet and Russian press has always treated issues differentially. Quite how varied the coverage of a particular topic may be has been shaped by factors of political context, the degree of permitted political debate, the daring of journalists and the preferences of editors. For much of the history of the Soviet state, many 'problems' were not openly named, officially declared to be a blight on capitalist states but not on the USSR. From 1986 to 1991, however, in its treatment of socio-economic issues and political problems, journalism delivered exposés, sensationalism and varying degrees of critical reporting ranging from the superficially banal or distorted to hard-hitting analysis. *Perestroika* and *glasnost* under Gorbachev permitted an 'opening' of many social problems, a lifting of the lid of silence. Across newspapers, however, throughout the Gorbachev era and since, there have been variations in content, slant, emphasis, style, tone and silences.[12] These were linked to the type of paper, the confidence of its editors and the given year and month.[13] Whereas, in the 1980s, *Ogonek* and *Moskovskie novosti*, for instance, produced good investigative journalism, *Komsomol'skaia Pravda* and *Moskovskii Komsomolets* dwelt on more sensational angles.[14]

In post-Soviet Russia, political pressures on journalists have fluctuated. Despite accusations of 'creeping authoritarianism' under Putin, papers nonetheless do discuss social problems – human trafficking among them. Moreover, although newspapers may impart similar statistics on the number trafficked and tell like tales of debt-bondage and abuse, their concepts, interpretations, emphases, conclusions and recommendations vary. In this process, the constructed image of the trafficked woman also varies.

My methodology is simple and not exhaustive. In 2004 and 2005, I selected eight national Russian newspapers, namely, *Izvestiia*, *Rossiiskaia gazeta*, *Nezavisimaia gazeta*, *Kommersant*, *Pravda*, *Argumenty i Fakty*, *Komsomol'skaia Pravda* and *Moskovskii Komsomolets* as loosely representative of different readerships (serious, popular, pro-reform, anti-reform, youth) and then conducted web-based searches for articles using the terms *torgovlia liud'mi*, *treffik*, *seks-rabstvo*, *prostitutsiia*, and so on. Thus what I have read is linked to the nature of the newspapers' own categorisations and selections of articles. Most of those which appeared were written after 2000, although one can find occasional articles published in the 1990s and I did begin a manual library trawl dating back to 1988, finding mainly silences. After examining the respective contents of articles, mainly those from 2001 to 2005, I concluded that three clear sorts of messages about trafficking could be inductively reached. In all cases, they reflected the newspaper's general style and standard of reporting and it is worth noting that one would most likely see similar sorts of comparative patterns when analysing different topics.

For analysis here, I have focused on these three different types of prominent messages: first, stories which dwell on 'who is to blame', which can be distorting and miss out key points; second, crisp informative and constructive reporting which avoids myths, plays down sensationalism and attempts a reasonably objective analysis; and third, sensational and titillating coverage with attention-grabbing headlines. These three styles of reporting stand out as useful and representative categories.

Who is to blame? The fault of the West, world economy and sex mania

As the problem of human trafficking was slowly gaining recognition in Russia, one response was outrage and to deny that Russia itself could in any way be to blame. *Pravda,* in particular, dwelt upon anger at the west and innocence in the east, constructing a dualistic 'bad/good' dichotomy, much reminiscent of Soviet times.

The main target of criticism of *Pravda*'s early analysis of the problem in 2003 and 2004 (which came later than exposés in some other papers) was the way of life in big cities in other countries, particularly 'sex-mania' in western Europe, which it named as partly to blame, itself linked to the global economy. Whilst indeed there is a sexualisation of life and an international economy around that, it is instructive that *Pravda* blamed a way of life elsewhere, not mafia gangs from the former Soviet Union. Nor does *Pravda* admit to a similar problem of 'sex mania' in Moscow or in other Russian cities, where practices presumably find a parallel with lifestyles in western cities.

Unlike many papers, *Pravda* is particularly quick to blame European countries with legalised prostitution, highlighting Holland and Germany as dangerous magnets. The interpretation here is that these are the 'most popular countries for selling women' and that the legalisation of prostitution 'leads to a rise in the sex-trade'.[15] In drawing this conclusion, *Pravda* is actually at one with some western and east European feminists and researchers who stress that legalised prostitution fuels trafficking and provides a ready market for its victims, one which is insufficiently scrutinised by the police.[16] *Pravda*'s position here also coincides with that of the Swedish legislation which in 2000 made prostitution illegal, criminalised the client and has since claimed that as a consequence prostitution has decreased.[17] This is ironic since one may not necessarily have expected *Pravda* to agree with the conclusions of some western feminists but nonetheless underscores the fact that these views on trafficking are being voiced by those coming from quite different socio-political analytical perspectives, showing a wide appeal.

The Russian press is not clamouring for the criminalisation of the client in Russia or worldwide as a solution to the problem of trafficking. Rather there is an acceptance that the need for prostitution 'has always existed and always will'. Debate pivots more around the question of whether prostitution should be legalised in Russia, as some advocate, versus the status quo. The loudest advocates of criminalising the client are currently some international NGOs in Russia.

Pravda has also been rather keen to stress Slavic innocence. In 2003, *Pravda* argued that 'No Russian women willingly become sexual slaves', although aware that some do 'willingly go abroad as prostitutes'.[18] Although, indeed, research has established that the majority of trafficked women do not wish to become prostitutes, and certainly not to become enslaved, a tiny number nonetheless have entered into trafficking a second time around, naïvely hoping that this time it will be better, often because they can see no other options open to them.[19] In another article, *Pravda* highlights what it classifies as a rich/poor divide across states (in which it constructs a duality of 'rich' foreign states versus 'poor' Russia) and blames trafficking on the demand by 'rich foreigners' for prostitutes.[20] But whilst many a western client may be rich, many may not be. Moreover, there are rich Russian clients both in the west and inside the Russian Federation. The underpinning suggestion is that western men are guilty and all Russian men are blameless.

Pravda goes on to argue that 'world economic development requires more and more workers and international labour is cheaper'.[21] Whilst this is indeed true, *Pravda* does not address the mechanisms through which human trafficking in this wider context occurs. These arguments overlap with those of western academics who talk about globalisation and the 'commodification of persons' and a growing 'international political economy of sex'.[22] But again, *Pravda* puts the blame on the world economy just as it operates in western cities, not the role of those Russians who participate in it to traffic and exploit others. The loudest silence is on the issue of criminal gangs from Russia, Albania and elsewhere in eastern

Europe; another is on the extent of corruption inside Russia and what Louise Shelley dubs the 'political-criminal nexus'.[23]

Pravda has also engaged in a differential treatment of nationality within the geographic space of the former Soviet Union. In some articles, individual men are criticised for corrupting a woman, such as a citizen's 'brother' or 'friend of a friend'. In these instances, however, their nationality is not stressed or even mentioned. If, however, non-Russian men are involved, then nationality is noted, such as 'the man in the marketplace from the Caucasus suggested that Svetlana find three more girls and become the boss for them'.[24] Whilst the man may indeed have been from the Caucasus, it is significant that this is indicated, with the implication that Russian men would not do this.

Pravda's reports rarely use social scientific concepts or cite much academic work. Rather, articles tend to refer to *rabstvo* (slavery), *rabskii trud* (slave labour), *seks-rabstvo* (sex slavery), *seks-torgovlia liud'mi* (sex trade in people), *seksomania* (sex mania), *torgovlia zhivym tovarom* (trade in living wares), *kabal'nyi trud* (bondage labour), *dolgovaia kabala* (debt servitude), *nochnye babochki* (night butterflies), *ekzoticheskii tovar* (exotic ware) and the standard *torgovlia liud'mi* (trade in people) and *treffik zhenshchin* (traffic in women).[25] Description far outweighs serious analysis, although there are some articles which give statistics, present the findings of conferences on trafficking and talk about legislation and views on the legalisation of prostitution.[26] In mid-2005 in *Pravda*, the more analytic concepts *prinuditel'naia seksual'naia ekspluatatsiia* (forced sexual exploitation) and *seksual'naia ekspluatatsiia* (sexual exploitation) began to appear.

Another example of 'blame reporting' is found in *Moskovskii Komsomolets*. Under the eye-grabbing headline of 'The Anatomy of Life of Love Slaves', is the quotation 'Five girls bought – and you're a millionaire'.[27] The quotation comes from Elena Mizulina, a people's deputy in the previous Duma who tried to push through anti-trafficking legislation in 2002 and 2003. On one half of the page, the paper quotes those conversant with the topic such as academic researcher Elena Tiuriukanova, Boris Gavrilov in his capacity as deputy director of a Research Committee under the Ministry of Internal Affairs, and Mizulina, who all impart useful information. The other side of the page tells three painful stories of the trafficking victims Zhanna, Masha and Sveta.

The blame in this article falls on the profitability of the business, noted as more lucrative than drug trafficking. The message is clear: 'so long as the difference in living standards in different countries is preserved, then firms will flourish, promising illegal journeys, work and blood abroad.'[28] Here the finger of blame is not pointed directly at the international economy itself, although that is implicated indirectly as offering huge financial opportunities, but squarely at the flow of people looking for a better life precisely because of the perceived gaps in opportunities between rich and poor states. The message is that 'not one' militia or special service in the world can stem this flow. Thus the article was written specifically for the eyes of those aspiring to migrate. Poverty is faulted here as the cause and magnet that attracts inhabitants of poorer states to travel to richer ones rather than the traffickers themselves, although the three vivid tales show how cruel the traffickers and final owners of their victims were in places as diverse as Uzbekistan, the USA and Japan. Here Zhanna was forced into domestic labour and then fieldwork on a tomato plantation and Masha and Sveta ended up in prostitution. Sveta commented that it was a 'nightmare', although in her nightclub women were given back their passports after 3 to 6 months and allowed to go home because the clients were calling for 'new girls'. The message here was that clients kept the business going and affected the turnover of prostitutes, but the role of clients was not challenged or linked to an exploration of how the trafficked could be freed or whether the client should be punished by the state.

Informative reporting

In contrast to *Pravda*, as in the years of *glasnost* under Gorbachev, reporting in *Izvestiia* has been fuller and more informative. Moreover, *Izvestiia*'s analyses have generally been more biting than those of stories found in *Moskovskii Komsomolets*. For example, in a dispassionate factual vein, quoting Maria Mokhovo, Director of the Moscow hotline *Sestry*, *Izvestiia* in 2002 imparted that precise statistics on the number of women illegally leaving was unknown, but it was evident that in 2001 '60 000 illegal women disappeared without a trace in the USA, the majority of whom were Russians and Ukrainians.'[29] *Izvestiia* also quoted the head of the MVD press centre to the effect that in 1989, 3000 women departed from the USSR but by 1996, 124 000 had already left Russia and the CIS, with the numbers increasing.[30] Thus the contrast with *Pravda*'s more emotive reporting is huge. Although *Izvestiia* does describe horror stories, such as the sad case of Tamara from Petrozavodsk who married a Finn, unaware at the outset of his violent tendencies after they had become acquainted through a marriage bureau, but was later found dead in Finland, *Izvestiya* is nonetheless crisper in its coverage, not dwelling on moral conclusions or offering distorting explanations or myths such as the dualistic 'bad' west and 'innocent Russia'.[31] A similar bland and informative style applies to other articles which discuss attempts by foreigners to trick orphans into paedophilia or which report on the passage and intended passage of related legislation such as the UN convention against transnational organised crime in April 2004 and general witness protection.[32]

Izvestiia is also far more likely than *Pravda* to impart the results of academic research into trafficking. In April 2004, for instance, Anastasiia Naryshkina and Ilona Vinogradova reported on the findings of interviews conducted by Russian sociologists with returning sex slaves, funded by the UN. Elena Tiuriukanova, Elena Mikhailova and Maiia Rusakova surveyed thirteen returnees, aged between 16 and 28 years old. They found that their parents tended to have average or low social status and that many of them were alcoholics. The returnees had secondary-level education and had trained as a cook, seamstress, salesgirl, cashier or teacher. Some had worked in these areas, others had sold on the markets and a few had been prostitutes. All were single or divorced, some with children. What stood out was that without exception, they were poor and suffering from hunger and destitution, which had been the push factors behind their migration for work. Moreover, it had not been difficult to deceive them about life elsewhere. Those who had suspected that prostitution might be required had not imagined the sort of exploitation that it would entail. *Izvestiia* described these findings much as an academic report might.[33]

In its treatment of trafficking, *Izvestiia* does not dwell on the issue of blame, instead using the more analytic concept of 'sexual exploitation'. Naryshkina and Vinogradova see human trafficking as such and report that its size worldwide is refected in the statistic of 700 000 to 2 million women and girls taken every year from their own country and subjected to sexual exploitation. They note that on average each 'girl' brings her owner around $200 000 a year, illustrating how lucrative sexual exploitation can be.[34]

The use of concepts varies across the press. Those adopted in *Rossiiskaia gazeta*, for example, are less academic than those in *Izvestiia*. Popular terms such as *zhivoi tovar* (live wares), *rabyni liubvi* (love slaves) and *zhritzy liubvi* (priestesses of love) are interspersed in its articles. A story by their Budapest correspondent, Fedor Luk'ianov on why Budapest has become the capital for auctioning trafficked 'priestesses of love' is punctuated with such phrases. He does not once talk of 'sexual exploitation' although that underpins everything he examines.[35]

Like *Izvestiia*, however, *Rossiiskaia gazeta* imparts much useful information. For instance, Luk'ianov's article revealed that according to UN reports, out of 500 000 prostitutes working in Western Europe, one in three comes from eastern Europe, in particular from Ukraine, Moldova, Russia, Hungary or Romania. In addition, Germany has the most prostitutes from the former Soviet bloc – around 15 000 – who make up 60–80 per cent of the German 'sexual market'.[36]

Papers like *Izvestiia, Rossiiskaia gazeta* and also *Nezavisimaia gazeta* offer the most serious analyses of a problem which in 1999 and 2000, they were reluctant to name, describe or debate. Now they all support legislation, want to deter potential victims through exposés and warnings and refrain from sensationalism and cheap reporting. There has been a slow transformation in the nature of their coverage in a context of wider socio-economic and migratory transformations.

Sensational reporting

Considerably more sensational has been coverage in papers such as *Komsomol'skaia Pravda, Argumenty i fakty* and *Moskovskii Komsomolets*. In these, articles are often accompanied by photographs which show either sexually alluring women or women in compromising situations. For example, one article was illustrated by a half-dressed woman in a car, another by girls who are minimally dressed, all covering their faces to avoid the camera.[37] The images entice, titillate, surprise or shock and are effective at capturing attention.

Accompanied by similarly vivid images, one sensational and surprising serialised story, entitled 'I am a sex-slave', was printed in *Komsomol'skaia Pravda* in September and November 2003. It told how a journalist, Tankova, 'risking her life, took the path of Russian girls who were promised "high paid work abroad" '.[38] Tankova responded to an advertisement asking for dancers to work in Israel and allowed herself to be trafficked as a participant observer.

The result of Tankova's diary, however, was not just sensational reporting but a useful passing on of information to Russians. In her first story, she described the sorts of advertisements girls might see and told how a seemingly normal office operating out of the Moscow hotel 'Stolichnaia' on Tverskaia worked as a fake agent. When Tan'kova went there and asked if the work entailed prostitution, she was told 'Whatever next. What prostitution!' She was then shown 'thank-you' letters written from women and girls sent from all over Russia as a way of convincing her of the organisation's legitimacy. She reported how the 'kind' woman 'poured me tea, talked about her two sons'. The atmosphere was convincing and confidential, 'the setting office-like'.[39] Thereafter, writing in short crisp sentences, Tankova told in diary form 'Early morning. Road to Egypt. I go into slavery.'[40] The only guarantee of her safety was the fact that friends knew she was doing this. The story is highly original reporting and a gripping read.

Across editions, Tankova describes her tiring journey alongside three Moldovan girls and two from Khabarovsk. Accompanying each story were various sexy pictures of a semi-clad woman in a veil, a woman reclining on a couch in a low-cut thin gown, a naked woman balancing oranges on her head in auction and a smoking women in bra and pants on a sofa waiting for clients. Papers like *Izvestiia, Nezavisimaia gazeta* and *Rossiiskaia gazeta* do not carry such hard-hitting visual images. *Komsomol'skaia Pravda*'s articles serve to grab readers' attention and also to convey a message about the fate of trafficked women. They thus serve a dual purpose. They sell the paper through sensationalism, titillate through images, but also educate and inform the public about a topic insufficiently debated at that time in public arenas. This sort of sensational reporting, however, did not analyse in terms of social scientific concepts such as 'sexual exploitation', 'discrimination', 'male dominance', 'hegemony' or 'patriarchy'. Rather, reporting describes what happens, focusing on reactions and emotions.

In later reporting in November, Tankova explained how 'up to 2003 official Russian circles thought that Russia did not have a problem of human trafficking'.[41] She explained the significance of the forthcoming amendment to the Criminal Code and printed a commentary from Miramed's Dr Juliette Engel about her concern that some in the government wanted to legalise prostitution as 'business'. Were prostitution legalised, then the state would get revenue through taxation. She also described the work of the Angel Coalition.[42]

By November, the newspaper had prompted 3000 readers to discuss the issue online. Two hundred e-mails had been received and 100 letters through the mail. 'Several tens' of women who were planning to work abroad had rung the author in order to ask her questions. As a result, most changed their minds about leaving. Also thanks to this article, trafficking was subsequently discussed on five programmes across four Russian television channels (RTR, TVS, TVTs, NTV) and four foreign ones (on German and Israeli television) and Russian and Canadian film producers were planning a documentary.[43] Thus sensational reporting should not necessarily be dismissed out of hand as of little value to society if simultaneously it informs and advises. The risk is that it might simultaneously attract some into becoming traffickers for the advertised financial gains resulting from it and its success at evading detection and prosecution. This may indeed also apply as a consequence of more factual reporting, although perhaps wrongly one finds oneself stereotypically assuming that an avid reader of sensational stories might be more likely to seek such rewards. This is an open empirical question and awaits comparative research into how traffickers get started in business and what influenced them at the outset.

In similar style of reporting, under the headline of 'Beautiful Slaves', *Argumenty i fakty* tells the story of Lisa. Her father was buried in a mine and her mother took an overdose of sleeping pills from which doctors could not save her. Lisa's grandparents attempted to keep her on a tiny pension. A neighbour, however, told 14-year-old Lisa about the opportunities of work abroad. Lisa was then sold to a brothel in Tel Aviv for $8000 where she was raped, beaten, barely fed and only permitted 3–4 hours' sleep a night. Five years later Lisa 'went out of her mind'. Her last owner bought her a ticket home to Russia and put her on the plane to Moscow. She was lucky to be met by a member of the Angel Coalition who helped her back to Saratov oblast. There, every time she saw a man, she became hysterical and ended up in a psychiatric hospital.[44]

Stories such as this often focus on the human dimension such as sad childhood, tragic developments in the family and a consequent struggle for survival. These factors are part of many stories and may help to combat prejudice against the trafficked who are often victims of extremely dire and unfortunate circumstances. There is a tendency for some families and communities to shun trafficked women if they return home, on the grounds that they bring shame, are now only good for prostitution anyway since they have 'lowered themselves' and also brought this fate upon themselves by agreeing to leave in the first place. One myth holds that girls and women must have known that prostitution would be expected of them and therefore they do not deserve help and rehabilitation now. Stigma and discrimination thus await their return, whether to Russia, Ukraine or any of the states of the former Soviet Union.[45] If 'sad circumstances' stories can combat these prejudices, then they serve a useful function. Research, however, needs to be done to discover the impact of different types of story and the extent to which they may alter social attitudes.

One technique adopted in this type of reporting on 'sad circumstances' is to begin with kind words, such as a father saying to his 15-year-old daughter: 'I hope you don't like it there and will quickly return.' The story then unfolds to reveal quite how prophetic these words were. Iana is taken to the Czech Republic, hidden in a van and told not to make a sound at the border. She was not fed, then sold to Marek who forced her to work as a prostitute with clients from Western Europe. Violence from one client meant that Iana lived 'in permanent fear' until she managed to escape, reach the border and reveal what had happened to her. In this case, her initial couriers were apprehended.[46]

Like reporting in *Pravda*, this article in *Argumenty i fakty* targets Westerners for their poor treatment of Russian women. As clients they are described as demanding, selfish and sadistic, treating women solely as sexual objects for their own gratification. When the situation does not please them, they turn against the woman. There is no sophisticated analysis here of what it means for society and interpersonal relations for women to be viewed entirely as sex objects. Notions of 'power', 'denigration', 'mechanisms of disrespect' and 'patriarchy' are wanting, but could be usefully employed. Despite the huge controversies about pornography, prostitution and sex work, these issues would benefit from being in the public domain with a greater degree of sophistication.

Conclusion

One expects such variations in reporting across newspapers worldwide. What, however, is its significance? One can argue that all sorts of articles, whether crisply informative in *Izvestiia* or sensational in *Komsomol'skaia Pravda* and *Argumenty i fakty*, ultimately do pass on necessary information of some of the dimensions of the traffickers' power 'over' the trafficked and their power 'to' abuse them. Given that trafficking is increasing in scale, the more exposés the better. One cannot always assume, however, that this automatically deters unsuspecting victims who are conned into believing that the authority of false employment agencies is genuine and legitimate. The trafficked thus find themselves influenced to do what they normally would not have chosen to do, i.e. become trafficked into a job which they did not knowingly choose. The influence of the traffickers results in their power over the trafficked and brings with it an illegitimate, non-state-centred, use of force and coercion. The individual's security is denied.

Reporting on human trafficking also carries its own possibilities for exploitation of the trafficked. Sexy and titillating images immediately suggest that woman is, above all, a sex object and there for the taking. She is for pleasure, as defined not by her but by the client who requests the services he requires, or forces them upon her. Woman's personality, goals and non-sexual achievements are absent. This silence dehumanises, degrades, distorts and undervalues. Thus, it undermines and exploits. Moreover, sensationalism can reinforce the notion that women are also to blame for the situation in which they find themselves. Do they not lure men through their sexuality, runs the suggestion, and invite them by their very existence?

Discourses are several here. Some arguments blame women. Others blame poverty, the west, marketisation and criminal gangs. Governments face tough choices in attempting to solve such huge problems. Poverty cannot be eradicated overnight. The western demand for prostitutes is not abating. Russia is now committed to a market economy, like all states in the post-Soviet space. Criminal gangs are tough and not easy to catch and punish. Thus woman's victimhood is hard to prevent in the face of these overwhelming policy challenges, suggesting a powerlessness of the

Russian system, compounded by the mistaken choices of many women. Thus woman is victim.

Woman, however, need not always be victim, even if the constellation of socio-economic, criminal and political contexts may appear in some circumstances to weigh against her. Indeed, they also weigh against trafficked men once trapped. It must be stressed alongside this point that just as thousands of women are trafficked into prostitution, millions are not. Although the indeed tragic case of any trafficked person illustrates that they have come under the 'power' and 'influence' of their traffickers, pimps and clients, many evade this before they have been conned, particularly if informed and wary. Moreover, the 'authority' of these power holders over the trafficked is successfully denied or challenged by some of the trafficked, even if at times to their cost. Returning women, if lucky and able, manage to regain their sense of self and identity through the minuscule number of counselling services available. Others, for longer or shorter periods, suffer serious mental breakdown, depression and anxiety. They are the genuine victims of abuse at the hands of those who wield illegitimate violence against them, their offspring or their relatives. Moreover, their reaction is 'normal' in the circumstances in which they have been duped, enslaved and abused.

What is needed is an end to these illegitimate mechanisms of influence and power. Along with education campaigns to make women and girls more 'savvy', increased numbers of jobs are required in Russia to stem this flow and above all clamp-downs on the traffickers along with altered perceptions and expectations about the supposedly massive salaries waiting to be earned in the West. Furthermore, without effective witness protection, a reduction of corruption in the militia and in higher echelons of the MVD and a snapping of the 'political-criminal nexus', rigorous clamp-downs are unlikely, despite heavy pressure from the USA.

It must also be borne in mind, however, that the intended effects of education campaigns and the media generally are not always achieved and unanticipated results may be found. For example, in the Gorbachev era the film *Interdevochka* (Hard Currency Prostitute) was expected to deter women from prostitution and from emigrating. When Tania married one of her clients and moved to Sweden she was bitterly unhappy in a foreign land. The film's intended message backfired since many audiences blamed Tania herself for finding her life in Sweden difficult and for not making a go of it. Audiences did not condemn finding a foreign husband through prostitution but instead criticised Tania's failure to reap full advantage of this and for her pining to return to Russia. Coverage of trafficking could also have the undesired result of producing more traffickers who read of its financial rewards and set out to profit from those prepared to migrate. Evidence suggests that some individuals, not necessarily members of criminal gangs at the outset, have decided that this ready market for huge financial gain at relatively low risk (lower than trafficking drugs or guns) is one that they will exploit.[47] They thus set out to find their own unsuspecting targets. Wider publicising of instances in which traffickers are caught and successfully brought to justice might to some extent deter, but hitherto such cases have been few due to difficulties in catching the culprits, corruption, inability to prove guilt, fears of the trafficked to come forward and testify and a sluggish legal system.[48]

Finally, it is worth underscoring that whatever the scale of the challenge on the ground to policy-makers, key concepts of the disciplines of both political science and gender studies can profitably be applied in analyses of different dimensions of the issue of human trafficking. What is certain, moreover, is that the security and human rights of global citizens are denied and flouted by the bestial, degrading and morally repugnant practice of human trafficking. Whatever the blend of motivations that drive the traffickers (financial gain, greed, easy opportunities) and whatever their individual psychological make-up (insecure personality, sadist, inability to empathise, abused background), they behave without any sense of obligation to the state, duty to fellow citizens or any motion of the importance of a 'social contract'.

Notes

1. Thanks are due to the Centre for Research in the Arts, Social Sciences and Humanities (CRASSH) of the University of Cambridge where I enjoyed a Visiting Fellowship in the Easter term of 2004 under their 'Migration' theme. The British Academy and Russian Academy of Sciences supported fieldwork in Moscow and Petersburg in September 2004 and the Elisabeth Barker Fund of the British Academy provided research expenses in 2004–5. Gratitude is also due to those who asked questions and offered comments in the subsequent debate that took place at the panel on 'Politics, Transformation Processes and Gender' at the ICCEES VII World Congress in Berlin and to Rebecca Kay for sound editorial advice.
2. See D. M. Hughes, 'The "Natasha" Trade: the Transnational Shadow Market of Trafficking in Women', *Journal of International Affairs*, 53, 2 (2000): 455–81; D. M. Hughes, 'The "Natasha" Trade: Transnational Sex Trafficking', *National Institute of Justice Journal*, 246 (2001): 8–15; D. Hughes, 'Trafficking for Sexual Exploitation: the Case of the Russian Federation', *International Organisation for Migration (IOM)*, Migration Research Series, 7, June (2002) at http://www.uri.edu/artsci/wms/Hughes/Russia. pdf; D. Hughes, 'Sex Tours via the Internet', available at http://www.feminista.com/archives/v1n7hughes.html; D. M. Hughes, '*Nyet* to Trafficking', *Feminista! The Online Journal of Feminist Construction*, 1, 7 (1997) at http://www.nationalreview.com/comment/

comment-hughes061803.asp; E. Tiuriukanova, V. Anishina, D. Poletaev and S. Shamkov, *Prinuditel'nyi trud v sovremennoi Rossii* (Moscow: Mezhdunarodnaia Organizatsiia Truda, 2004); E. Tiuriukanova and L. Erokhina (eds), *Torgovliia liud'mi* (Moscow: Izdatel'stvo Academia, 2002); Z. Lukovtseva (ed.), *Protivodeistvie torgovle liud'mi: trenerskii portfel'* (Moscow: 2004); L. Erokhina and M. Buriak, *Torgovlia zhenshchinami i det'mi v tseliakh seksual'noi ekspluatatsii v sotsial'noi i kriminologicheskoi perspektive* (Moscow: Profobrazovanie, 2003); L. Shelley, 'The Changing Position of Women: Trafficking, Crime, and Corruption', in D. Lane (ed.), *The Legacy of State Socialism and the Future of Transformation* (Lanham: Rowan and Littlefield, 2002); S. Stoecker and L. Shelley (eds), *Human Traffic and Transnational Crime* (Lanham: Rowan and Littlefield, 2005); N. Khodyreva and M. Tsvetkova, 'Rossiianki i iavlenie treffika', *Sotsiologicheskie issledovanniia*, 11 (2000); and N. Khodyreva, 'Sexuality For Whom? Paid Sex and Patriarchy in Russia', in A. Stulhoger and T. Sandfort (eds), *Sexuality and Gender in Postcommunist Eastern Europe and Russia* (New York: Haworth Press, 2004).

3. M. Buckley 'Trafficking in People', *The World Today*, 60, 8/9 (2004): 30–2; and M. Buckley, 'Menschenhandel als Politikum: Gesetzgebung und Problembewusstsein in Russland', *Osteuropa*, 56, Heft 6, June (2006): 195–212.
4. See, for example, Khodyreva and Tsvetkova (2000).
5. Ibid. See also, the TIP reports on the webite of the US State Department; for instance, at http://www.state.gov/g/tip/rls/tiprpt/2004/33192.htm.
6. See, for example, T. Parsons, 'On the Concept of Political Power', in T. Parsons, *Politics and Social Structure* (New York: Free Press, 1969); S. Benn and R. Peters, *Social Principles and the Democratic State* (London: George Allen & Unwin, 1958); and D. Raphael, *Problems of Political Philosophy* (London: Macmillan, 1976).
7. Kate Millet, *Sexual Politics* (New York: Doubleday, 1970).
8. J. Tickner, 'Re-visioning Security', in K. Booth and S. Smith (eds), *International Relations Theory Today* (Cambridge: Polity Press, 2004), pp. 175–97.
9. T. Terriff, S. Croft, L. James and P. Morgan, *Security Studies Today* (Cambridge: Polity Press, 2003).
10. C. Corrin, 'Transitional Road for Traffic: Analysing Trafficking in Women from and through Central and Eastern Europe', *Europe-Asia Studies*, 57, 4 (2005): 543–60.
11. See, for example, Hughes (2001).
12. M. Buckley, *Redefining Russian Society and Polity* (Boulder, CO: Westview, 1993).
13. For instance, political agendas in 1985 did not permit discussion of bullying in the army. As *glasnost* became wider, by 1989 the topic was no longer taboo, but was less explored than the issue of prostitution which, as less politically subversive, was considered as early as 1986 and 1987. Months mattered in discussions since key events (such as the 27th Party Congress, the 19th Party Conference or the absence of Gorbachev from Russia) could affect what was published.
14. Buckley (1993), pp. 44–139. See also M. Buckley, 'Glasnost and the Woman Question', in L. Edmondson (ed.), *Women and Society in Russia and the Soviet Union* (Cambridge: Cambridge University Press, 1992), pp. 202–26.
15. No named author, 'Ni odna Rossiianka ne prodala sebia v rabstvo dobrovol'no', *Pravda*, 11 December 2003, at http://www.news.pravda.ru/abroad/2003/11/12/57115.html.
16. See the work of Donna M. Hughes cited above as well as D. Hughes and T. A. Denisova, 'The Transnational Political Criminal Nexus of Trafficking in

Women from Ukraine', *Trends in Organised Crime*, 6, 3–4, Spring-Summer (2001) at http://www.uri.edu/artsci/wms/hughes/tpcnexus.

17. See http://www.prostitutionresearch.com/swedish.html. At this point one cannot definitely know the extent to which legislative changes had an impact on trafficking or on prostitution amongst trafficked women.
18. No named author, 'Ni odna Rossiianka', *Pravda*, 11 December 2003, at http://www.news.pravda.ru/abroad/2003/11/12/57115.html.
19. Khodyreva and Tsvetkova (2000) illustrate how just a minuscule percentage expects that prostitution will be required.
20. No named author, 'Lolity ponevole, ili kto torguet russkimi devushkami', *Pravda*, 16 October 2003, at http://www.society.pravda.ru/printed.html?news_id=14220.
21. 'Ni odna Rossiianka' (2003).
22. S. Stoecker, 'The Rise of Human Trafficking and the Role of Organized Crime', *Demokratizatsiia*, 8, 1 (2000): 129–44; and J. Pettman, *Worlding Women: a Feminist International Politics* (London: Routledge, 1996), pp. 185–207.
23. Shelley (2002).
24. No named author, 'Two terrible months of sex slavery for 16-year-old Svetlana', *Pravda*, 10 March 2004, at http://www.english.pravda.ru/accidents/21/96/383/12243_.html.
25. 'Ni odna Rossiianka' (2003); also http://www.Society.pravda.ru/printed.html?news_id=14220.
26. See no named author, 'Seksual'noe rabstvo – bich XXI Veka', *Pravda*, 6 August 2004, at http://www.news.pravda.ru/main/2004/06/08/63874_.html; Anastasiia Zagoruiko, 'Militsiia – za legalizatsiiu prostitutsii', *Pravda*, 28 May 2003, at http://www.society.pravda.ru/printed.html?news_id=10789; 'Lolity ponevole, ili kto torguet russkimi devushkami' (2003).
27. No named author, 'Anatomiia zhizni rabyniliubui', *Moskovskii Komsomolets*, 24 April 2004, p. 5.
28. Ibid.
29. Irina Podlesova, 'Naidena al'ternativa prostitutsii', *Izvestiia*, 23 January 2002, at http://www.main.izvestia.ru/russia/article13245/index.html. Leaving is itself not illegal, but false documentation and fake identities are.
30. Ibid.
31. Ibid.
32. Aleksandr Latkin, 'V internete torguiut kradenym s pomoshch'iu rossiiskikh sirot', *Izvestiia*, 16 March 2004, at http://www.izvestia.ru/tech/article45328; and Anzhelika Salik, 'Ratifitsirovana konventsiia protiv torgovli liud'mi', *Izvestiia*, 15 April 2004, at http://www.izvestia.ru/press/article635116.
33. Anastasiia Naryshkina and Ilona Vinogradova, 'Kazhdaia Rossiiskaia "devochka" prinosit khoziaevam pritonov po $200', *Izvestiia*, 16 April 2004, at http://www.izvestia.ru/community/article68338.
34. Ibid.
35. Fedor Luk'ia, ' "Zhivoi Tovar" – potok s Vostoka', *Rossiiskaia gazeta*, 3 November 2000, at http://www.rg.ru/prilog/es/031100/1.htm.
36. Ibid.
37. Iaroslava Tankova, 'Ia – seks-rabynia', *Komsomol'skaia Pravda*, 2 September 2003, at http://www.kp.ru/daily/23106/23031; Mikhail Lamtsov, 'Seks-rabyni v Karlovykh Varakh', *Argumenty i Fakty*, 14 August 2001, at http://www.aif.ru/

online/sv/146/13_01?; Ekaterina Karacheva, 'Krasavitsy-rabyni', *Argumenty i Fakty*, 5 January 2004, at http://www.aif.ru/onlineair/1210/ll_02.

38. Tankova, 'Ia – seks-rabynia', *Komsomol'skaia Pravda*, 2 September 2003.
39. Tankova, 'Ia – seks-rabynia', *Komsomol'skaia Pravda*, 1 September 2003, at http://www.kp.ru/daily/23105/22999.
40. Tankova, 2 September 2003.
41. Tankova, 'Ia – seks-rabynia', *Komsomol'skaia Pravda*, 18 November 2003, at http://www.kp.ru/daily/23159/24734.
42. The Angel Coalition was set up in 1999 as an anti-trafficking umbrella of 43 non-governmental organisations and groups. It was spearheaded by Dr Juliette Engel whose offices are in Moscow. One of her aims is to bring together Russian groups and to co-ordinate their activities. Some collaborated willingly, others not. See Buckley (2006).
43. Tankova, 18 November 2003.
44. Karacheva (2004).
45. For discussion of the shame and stigma suffered by returnees see D. Hughes, 'The Corruption of Civil Society: Maintaining the Flow of Women to the Sex Industries', paper presented at the Andalusian Women's Institute, Malaga, Spain, 23 September 2002; and also Hughes (2000).
46. Lamtsov (2001).
47. The general view in the OSCE and in the US State Department is that the 'risk/reward equation' needs to be rebalanced. Rewards are deemed high by traffickers due to the amount of money that can be earned. Risks are relatively low since convictions are still few, sentences tend to be short and corruption helps the traffickers. Deterrents are thus few. See 'United States Mission to the OSCE Statement on Trafficking in Human Beings', at http://www.humantrafficking.org/updates/282. For discussion of global reactions to human trafficking and the policies of states, regions and international organisations, see Mary Buckley, 'Human Trafficking in the Twenty-first Century: Implications for Russia, Europe and the World', in K. O'Sullivan See and L. Racioppi (eds), *Gender and Transition in Post Communist Eurasia* (East Lansing: Michigan State Press, forthcoming).
48. For discussion of reported cases refer to Vadim Reshetniak, 'Intim iz-pod palki', *Zolotoi Rog v Khabarovske*, 22 (2005) at http://www.zrpress.ru/khv/2005/22/10; Dmitrii Borodin, 'Seks-rabstvo po-primorski', *Zolotoi Rog*, 7 (2005) at http://www.zrpress.ru/zr/2005/7/22; Andrei Kozenko, 'Voennyi inzhener pogorel', *Kommersant'* (Nizhnee Polzh'e), 44, 15 March 2005; Iuliia Sukhonina, 'Rabotorgovliu poboriut zakonodatel'no', *Kommersant'* (Nizhnii Novgorod), 61, 7 April 2005; and http://www.regnum.ru/news/419748.html; I am grateful to Alexei Trochev for bringing these articles to my attention.

Index

NB: Page numbers in bold refer to figures and tables